CompTIA

SECURITY+ STUDY GUIDE SY0-701

Hopperfield
EDUCATION

TABLE OF CONTENTS

Introduction

If you are picking up this book, there is a good chance you are somewhere along the early stages of an IT career path. You may already be working in a help desk role, or you might be studying for CompTIA A+ or Network+ while planning your next move. Security+ sits right at that transition point where general IT support skills begin to turn into focused security skills. This chapter is about orienting you before we touch a single technical control. You will see what the Security+ SY0-701 exam actually looks like, how CompTIA thinks when it designs questions, and how to use this guide in a way that builds both exam readiness and the professional mindset expected in entry-level security roles.

Why Security+ Matters - Especially After A+

CompTIA designed Security+ as a vendor-neutral, foundational security certification. That phrase "vendor-neutral" is important. It means the exam is not about memorizing the menus in a particular firewall brand or the exact command syntax of one Linux distribution. Instead, you are expected to understand the concepts, processes, and reasoning that apply no matter what tools a particular organization has chosen. This is the same philosophy you may have already seen in A+. There, you learned how to troubleshoot a boot problem in general, not only how to click through one BIOS vendor's interface. Security+ keeps that broad, conceptual focus, but with security as the center of gravity.

If you already have A+ knowledge, you have more of a security foundation than you might realize. When you reset a user's password, you are participating in **identity and access management**, even if the goal in that moment was simply to get someone back into their email. When you configure a wireless access point with WPA3-Personal instead of leaving it open, you have just made an **encryption** decision. A+ tends to frame these actions as "get the system working properly." Security+ asks you to think one level deeper: why is that setting there, what risk does it reduce, and what are the trade-offs if you tighten or loosen it?

This shift in thinking mirrors what happens in many career paths. A support technician who is good with users and comfortable with systems often becomes the person others naturally go to when a "weird" or suspicious issue comes up. A machine is behaving strangely, a user reports odd pop-ups, a web application feels "off." At first you approach it as another troubleshooting ticket. Over time, you realize you are essentially doing the early stages of incident response, even if no one has called it that. Security+ formalizes and validates that transition. It is widely recognized by employers and, in many government and Department of Defense roles, explicitly required for certain entry-level security positions. Understanding how the exam works is not just about earning a line on your résumé; it is about aligning your study efforts with the expectations of real jobs.

A High-Level View of the SY0-701 Exam

The Security+ SY0-701 exam is delivered as a computer-based, proctored test through Pearson VUE testing centers or their online proctoring platform. It is closed-book; you cannot bring notes, books, or access to external sites. You will have up to 90 minutes to answer a maximum of 90 questions. That timing alone shapes how you must prepare. On average, you have about one minute per question, but in reality some questions will take only a few seconds, while others—especially performance-based ones—demand more thought.

Not all questions look the same. The most familiar ones are **multiple-choice** items, with either a single correct answer or multiple correct responses that you must select. These questions often test your ability to distinguish between similar concepts, recognize definitions in context, and choose the best option among several that might all seem somewhat reasonable. Alongside these are **performance-based questions**, often abbreviated as PBQs. Rather than asking you to click a radio button, these present a small simulated environment or a more interactive task. You might need to drag and drop items to match them to categories, arrange steps into the proper sequence, configure a simplified firewall rule set, or interpret a log snippet and take the appropriate action.

Behind the scenes, CompTIA scores the exam on a scale from 100 to 900, with 750 as the passing score. You will not see a percentage, and you will not know how much each question is worth. Some questions may be experimental or "beta" items that CompTIA is evaluating for future exams; those do not count toward your score, but they are indistinguishable from scored questions when you are taking the test. The practical consequence is that you must treat every question as if it matters and manage your time across the entire set. There is no benefit to obsessing over which questions "feel" important. Consistency and pacing outweigh perfection on individual items.

This structure should feel familiar if you have studied for other CompTIA exams. The environment is controlled, the timing is tight but fair, and the focus is on applied understanding rather than rote regurgitation. That does not mean you can ignore terminology—far from it—but it does mean that knowing a definition is only the entry ticket. The exam will then ask you to deploy that knowledge in a realistic situation.

How CompTIA Questions Really Work

A recurring theme throughout this book will be that Security+ is as much a reasoning exam as it is a knowledge exam. If you have seen A+ style scenario questions—"A user reports X. What is your next best step?"—you already have a sense of this. Security+ takes the same approach but frames the scenarios around risk, policy, and protection. Instead of "the printer is not responding," you might see "a user in accounting clicked a link in an email and now their system is behaving unusually." The surface details change, but the mental habits you use to approach the question are the same.

Almost every well-written CompTIA question has a core goal hidden in its wording. It might be to "prevent unauthorized access," "limit the impact of a potential breach," "improve availability of a critical service," or "ensure that actions can be attributed to a specific user." Your first task is to extract that goal from the text. Around that goal, the question will often provide contextual clues about the environment: the size of the organization, whether it is a regulated industry, the user's role, budget constraints, or whether the system is cloud-hosted or on-premises. Many wrong answers are wrong not because they are technically impossible, but because they ignore these constraints. For example, installing a multi-million-dollar security information and event management (SIEM) solution might be a great idea for a large enterprise, but it is not a practical next step for a three-person startup described in the question.

This is where Security+ demands more than vocabulary. CompTIA likes to give you two answers that are clearly wrong and two that are plausible. You earn points by choosing the one that is "best," "most effective," "most appropriate," or "most likely," based on the goal and environment. This is directly analogous to troubleshooting in a support role. When a workstation cannot reach a web application, you might have several potential fixes. Replacing the network card could work. Rebooting the router could sometimes help. But the best first step is probably to verify the network configuration or check whether others are affected. The process matters. Security+ questions reward that same disciplined prioritization.

Throughout this book we will refer back to a simple framework you can apply to each question: **READ**—Read, Extract, Analyze, Decide. You start by reading the entire question stem slowly once, without glancing at the answers. Then you extract the core goal: what outcome is desired—prevention, detection, response, or something else. You analyze the environment and constraints mentioned explicitly or implied. Only then do you decide on the best option by eliminating choices that do not meet the goal or that ignore the constraints. This small discipline will prevent many of the common mistakes students make under time pressure, such as latching onto the first familiar term they see.

Multiple-Choice vs Performance-Based: Two Different Mindsets

Although all questions contribute to your overall score, the way you mentally approach multiple-choice items and PBQs should differ slightly. Multiple-choice questions tend to be shorter and more focused on conceptual distinctions. You might need to distinguish between two similar attack types, compare security controls, or identify which policy best addresses a scenario. Paying attention to qualifiers in the wording is critical. A question that asks for the "least expensive" control expects a different answer than one asking for the "most robust." A question that says "primarily addresses confidentiality" is nudging you to think in terms of the core security objectives, not just any benefit a control might provide.

A useful technique is to pause for a moment after reading the stem and, before looking at the options, form a rough idea of what you expect the answer to look like. If the question describes a need to detect unauthorized file changes, your mind should drift toward monitoring, file integrity tools, or logging, even before you see any choices. When you then read the options, you can immediately discard those that have nothing to do with that general direction. This habit cuts through ambiguity and reduces the chance that you are seduced by a familiar term that does not actually fit the problem.

Performance-based questions, by contrast, are more like mini-labs or condensed work scenarios. In many exams, they appear at the beginning, but you are typically allowed to skip ahead, flag them, and return later. PBQs might show you a simplified firewall interface and ask you to implement rules to satisfy a written security policy. They might present a list of security incident descriptions and ask you to drag each into the correct incident response phase. They could display log entries with timestamps, IP addresses, and event codes, and ask which host you would isolate first. These questions reward not only factual knowledge but familiarity with workflows and sequences.

Because PBQs can be time-consuming, your pacing strategy matters. At the start of the exam, if you encounter a PBQ, scan it briefly and ask yourself whether you can complete it in a few minutes. If the answer is no, it is often smarter to flag it and move on to quicker multiple-choice items, returning later with whatever time remains. Many candidates sabotage themselves by spending 15 minutes wrestling with a single, complex PBQ, leaving too little time for dozens of easier questions they were fully capable of answering correctly. We will come back to a simple timing model later in the book, but for now remember that you control the order in which you invest your mental energy.

Using This Study Guide as a Training Ground

The rest of this book is not meant to be something you skim passively the week before your test. If you treat it that way, you are likely to emerge with lots of half-remembered terminology but little of the judgment Security+ actually tests. Instead, think of each chapter as a training ground for both your knowledge and your thinking process.

Chapters will explore core topics—threats, technologies and tools, architecture and design, risk management, and incident response—through explanations, examples, and exam-style questions. Along the way, you will occasionally see call-outs that highlight an "exam tip" or a "real-world" angle. These are not decorations; they are bridges between vocabulary and practice. When you read about, say, a particular authentication method, you should immediately ask yourself what problem it solves, when you would recommend it, and what its limitations are. That habit directly counters one of the biggest pitfalls in Security+ prep: treating the subject as a giant list of terms to memorize.

To get the most from the material, you should study actively. After a section, pause and try to explain the core ideas in your own words, as if you were clarifying it for a non-technical user on a help desk call. If the chapter references a network diagram, sketch a simplified version. When a new type of control is introduced, think of a concrete example from your own experience or from a previous job, even if it was not formally labeled as such. This act of connecting abstract concepts to something tangible cements understanding and makes scenario questions feel much more intuitive.

Hands-on practice amplifies this effect. Many learners preparing for A+ already experiment in virtual machines; you can extend that habit here. Set up a small lab with a couple of VMs and explore OS security settings, user and group management, local firewall rules, and basic logging. Even simple tasks—like creating a standard user versus an administrator, or enabling a host-based firewall—will make future performance-based questions feel far less intimidating. When an exam scenario describes restricting a user's permissions to reduce risk, you will be able to visualize exactly what that looks like in a system you have touched.

A practical routine can be to read a section, pause to identify how the key terms relate to one another, and then attempt a set of practice questions without looking back for the answers. When you review the explanations, do it even for questions you got right. Often, the reasoning CompTIA expects goes one or two steps beyond the obvious, and understanding that nuance now pays off on exam day.

Growing a Security Mindset from an A+ Foundation

If you have been immersed in A+ or support work, your instinct when you hear about a problem is usually "how do I get this working again?" That instinct is valuable; organizations need systems to be available. Security+ does not discard that mindset but adds a second, equally important question: "how do I get this working again without making things less secure—and ideally, while improving security?" It is a dual-check that eventually becomes automatic.

Consider a user who cannot access a shared folder. An A+-style thought process might lead you to check network connectivity, verify the share path, and perhaps reset the user's credentials if nothing obvious stands out. A security-infused mindset asks additional questions. Has the user's role changed recently? Were the permissions deliberately adjusted as part of a least privilege initiative? Are there any alerts or logs indicating suspicious access attempts from this account? The ultimate resolution might still be to correct a misconfigured permission, but you will document it, verify policy compliance, and remain alert to the possibility of intentional misuse rather than assuming every problem is purely accidental.

Later chapters will explore frameworks you will see repeatedly, such as the classic trio of **confidentiality, integrity, and availability**. At this point, you do not need to memorize formal definitions, but it is helpful to start hearing those words in the back of your mind as you think about scenarios. When a question asks how to prevent unauthorized disclosure of data, you are in the realm of confidentiality. When it asks how to detect unauthorized changes, integrity is at stake. When it describes keeping a service online during an outage, it is testing availability. Seeing how each control aligns with one or more of these goals builds the sort of structured thinking that the exam, and real employers, look for.

In a similar way, you will learn that many decisions involve trade-offs. A control that greatly improves security might also make users' lives harder, and sometimes that is not acceptable for a particular environment. An answer choice that completely locks down a system but makes it unusable for its intended purpose is likely not the "best" answer, even if it seems very secure in the abstract. CompTIA's questions often sit right in this tension between usability and protection. Your task is to choose options that let the business function while reasonably managing risk.

Building Confidence and Managing the Exam Experience

Many candidates approach Security+ with some anxiety, especially if it feels like a step up from A+. The good news is that the same methodical habits that helped you troubleshoot stubborn hardware issues or parse A+ scenario questions will serve you well here. Reading carefully, resisting the urge to skim, ruling out obviously wrong options before choosing among the remaining ones, and thinking in clear steps all reduce the cognitive load on exam day.

You will benefit from exposing yourself to exam-style questions early in your study journey rather than saving them for the end. The goal is not to chase a high score on every practice set, but to get used to the structure, wording, and "traps" CompTIA tends to use. When a question feels tricky, analyze not just why the correct answer is right, but why the others are wrong in that specific scenario. Over time, you will start to recognize patterns: answers that overengineer a solution for a tiny environment, options that make sense if you ignore the user's role, or controls that address a different problem than the one actually described.

As you work through the book, we will occasionally refer back to timing considerations. A simple way to keep yourself on track in practice sessions is to set a timer and aim for an average of about a minute per question, occasionally pausing to mimic what it feels like to flag and move on from a hard item. By the time you sit for the real exam, the mechanics of reading, analyzing, and deciding should feel routine, leaving your brain free to focus on the substance of each question rather than the stress of the environment.

With that foundation in place—an understanding of the exam's structure, the way CompTIA thinks, and how this guide will support your preparation—we can turn to the first major piece of content: the security controls themselves and the categories they fall into.

CHAPTER 1

General Security Concepts

1.1 Security Controls & Control Categories

When people first think about "computer security," they usually picture firewalls, antivirus software, maybe a locked server room. Those are important, but they are only part of a much larger picture. Organizations do not stay secure just because someone installed a good firewall once. They stay secure because they deliberately put **controls** in place and keep using them, day after day, in consistent ways. As an entry-level IT professional, you will live in this world of controls. You will configure them, enforce them, sometimes annoy users with them, and just as often protect those same users from very real problems because of them.

Imagine a small office with twenty employees, a few laptops, a shared network printer, a file server, and an internet connection. Users are checking email, accessing cloud apps, saving files on the server, and maybe connecting their phones to the Wi-Fi. Now think about what can go wrong. Someone might lose a laptop in a taxi. A user might click on a malicious attachment. A visitor could wander into the server room if the door is left open. An employee might accidentally delete an important folder. None of these risks can be eliminated completely, but they can be reduced and managed. Every measure the organization takes to reduce these risks is a **security control**—a safeguard or countermeasure put in place to bring risk down to a level the business can live with.

It is important to notice how broad that definition is. A control can be as technical as an encryption setting deep inside an operating system, or as simple as a written rule that says, "Visitors must be escorted at all times." It can be a metal lock on a laptop, a training class about phishing emails, or a configuration that locks a screen after ten minutes of inactivity. All of these serve the same basic function: they change how likely a bad event is to happen, how quickly we notice it, or how much damage it does if it occurs. When you begin to see "security" as the collection of these controls working together, exam questions and real-world decisions both become much easier to reason about.

Two ways of looking at controls

There are two helpful lenses you will use over and over to classify controls: **how** the control is implemented, and **what** the control is trying to accomplish. These lenses overlap, and most real controls can be described both ways at once.

The first lens is about implementation. Some controls are built into technology—hardware, software, or firmware—and operate automatically once configured. These are **technical controls**. Others are written down as rules, documented procedures, or management decisions and rely on people following them. Those are **administrative controls**. A third category deals with the tangible, physical world—doors, locks, cameras, fences. Those are **physical controls**. Even without memorizing the terms, you probably already separate these in your mind: "something the system does," "something the policy says," and "something in the building."

The second lens is about purpose and timing. Some controls are designed to stop incidents from happening in the first place. These are **preventive controls**. Others are designed to notice that something is happening, or has already happened. These are **detective controls**. A third group is designed to fix or limit the damage after something goes wrong. Those are **corrective controls**. If you think about a security incident as a timeline, preventive controls act before the incident, detective controls recognize it during or after, and corrective controls act afterwards to repair the situation and reduce the chance of a repeat.

Once you have both lenses, you can describe any control along two dimensions at once. A firewall rule that blocks inbound traffic from the internet is a technical preventive control: it is implemented in technology and its primary purpose is to prevent unwanted connections. A log file that records failed login attempts is a technical detective control: again implemented in technology, but this time its main role is to help you notice suspicious activity. A written security awareness policy that requires annual training is an administrative preventive control. The rest of this chapter will keep circling back to this simple matrix, because being able to classify a control quickly is exactly what many Security+ questions are really testing.

Technical controls: where you spend much of your day

For most people starting in IT support, **technical controls** are the most familiar, because they are the ones you touch all the time. These are the protections that are enforced by hardware, software, or firmware and do not depend on someone remembering to act in a certain way every time. Once you configure a password policy in an operating system, that rule is enforced consistently for every user, regardless of whether they think it is convenient.

Consider a typical day on a help desk. You might be asked to set up a new user account in Active Directory or in a cloud identity platform. When you assign that user a password that must meet certain length and complexity requirements, you are applying a technical control. When you configure the account so that it locks after five failed login attempts, that is another technical control. The computer enforces those rules automatically, without you having to watch every login attempt yourself.

Host-based firewalls offer another clear example. Enabling the built-in firewall on a workstation and configuring it to block unsolicited inbound traffic is a technical preventive control; you are reducing the chance that an attacker can connect to that machine directly. If you also enable firewall logging, you are adding a technical detective control, because those logs can later be reviewed to spot unusual patterns of traffic. Similarly, when you deploy antivirus or endpoint protection software that scans files and blocks known malware, the real-time protection component is preventive, while the alerting and logs provide detective capabilities.

It is also useful to connect technical controls with familiar identity concepts. When a user logs in with a username and password, the system is performing **authentication**—verifying that the user is who they claim to be. Once they are authenticated, the system uses **authorization** controls to determine what that identity is allowed to do. Can this user access the payroll database? Can they install software? Are they allowed to connect via remote desktop? Those authorization rules are themselves technical controls, usually enforcing the security principle of least privilege. They restrict what users and processes can do, which greatly reduces the chance of accidental or intentional damage.

Not every configuration change you make is a security control, though. Changing a screen's resolution or a printer's default tray is configuration, but it does not change the risk profile of the system in a meaningful security sense. On the other hand, enabling a screen lock that kicks in after ten minutes of inactivity is clearly a control, because it prevents an unauthorized person from walking up to an unattended machine and using the active session. Over time, you will build an instinct for which settings are part of "just making it work" and which ones are actually changing the organization's security posture.

Administrative controls: rules, processes, and people

While technical controls get most of the attention, **administrative controls** are just as important. These are the policies, standards, guidelines, and procedures that shape how people and systems are supposed to behave. They do not directly flip bits in memory or move packets on a network, but they guide the decisions of everyone who does.

If your organization has an Acceptable Use Policy that explains what users may and may not do with company systems, that is an administrative control. It might say that employees cannot install unapproved software, must not share their passwords, and must report suspected phishing emails to the help desk. Security awareness training builds on this by teaching people how to recognize phishing, social engineering, and other common threats. The training itself is a preventive control, because its goal is to stop users from making risky choices in the first place.

Administrative controls apply to IT staff as well as end users. Onboarding and offboarding processes describe exactly how new accounts should be created and how quickly old accounts must be disabled when someone leaves. Change management procedures might specify that any modification to a production server requires documented approval and testing before deployment. Incident response plans spell out what you must do when you suspect a security incident: who to notify, how to preserve evidence, and what actions you are authorized to take on your own.

As an entry-level technician, you may not be the person writing these policies, but you absolutely enforce and follow them. When a user calls and asks you to share their manager's files because "she said it's okay," the correct response is grounded in administrative controls: you follow the documented access request process rather than taking someone's word over the phone. When you document the work you do in a ticketing system, you are complying with change management. When you escalate a suspicious issue to the security team rather than ignoring it, you are following the incident response procedure. Many exam scenarios test whether you recognize that the best answer is not just what is technically possible, but what aligns with the organization's policies and procedures.

Sometimes students make the mistake of thinking administrative controls are "soft" or less real than technical controls, but in practice, weak or ignored policies can completely undermine strong technical measures. A perfect access control system does little good if administrators share their accounts or routinely bypass approval processes. On the exam, when a question emphasizes words like "policy," "procedure," "approval," "training," or "management decision," it is usually pointing you toward an administrative control.

Physical controls: the tangible layer of security

The third major type, **physical controls**, lives in the real, tangible world. These are the measures that protect buildings, equipment, and the people who use them. While they may seem outside the core of IT at first glance, you will see physical issues constantly in everyday support work.

Think about a server room in a small office. A solid door with a lock or keycard reader is a physical preventive control, restricting who can physically enter the room. A locked rack or cabinet adds another layer, making it harder for an unauthorized person to directly touch switches, routers, or servers. Security cameras pointed at the entrance serve as physical detective controls: they record who came and went and can be reviewed after an incident. If the server room door lock is damaged during a break-in and then repaired or replaced, that repair is a corrective physical control—it restores the protective barrier that was compromised.

You will also encounter physical controls in more ordinary settings. Laptops in public-facing areas might be secured with cable locks to prevent casual theft. Public kiosks or reception desks might use privacy filters on monitors to prevent shoulder surfing, protecting sensitive information from people walking by. Visitor sign-in logs and escort requirements help ensure that strangers cannot wander unobserved through office space or near sensitive equipment.

Your role in physical security is often about awareness and diligence. You might not install the building's access control system, but you are expected to notice when a secure door is propped open, to challenge tailgating politely when someone tries to follow you through a badge-controlled entrance, or to report a lost keycard. When you check that a replacement laptop includes a cable lock or that a new server is installed in a locking rack, you are actively participating in the organization's physical control environment. The exam frequently embeds clues about physical context—shared workspaces, unlocked closets, lost devices—and expects you to recognize that the right answer involves a physical control, not another piece of software.

Preventive, detective, and corrective: what controls are trying to do

So far, the focus has been on how controls are implemented—technically, administratively, or physically. The second classification focuses instead on what the control is trying to accomplish in relation to an incident. This is where timing and intent come into play, and it is very helpful to think in terms of a before–during–after timeline.

Preventive controls are those designed to stop an incident from occurring in the first place. Account lockout policies that block repeated failed login attempts are preventive, because they make brute-force password guessing much harder. Least privilege access is preventive, because limiting a user to only the resources they truly need reduces the chance they can accidentally delete critical data. Enforcing screen lock timeouts prevents someone from walking up to an unattended workstation and misusing it. Security training that teaches users to spot phishing emails is preventive as well—its whole purpose is to prevent the click on the malicious link. Physical measures like cable locks or locked doors also fall into this category when their main goal is to stop theft or unauthorized entry.

Detective controls do not necessarily stop an incident, but they help you notice that something is happening or has already happened. System logs that record login attempts, file access, or administrative actions are classic detective controls. If your endpoint protection software generates an alert when it sees suspicious behavior, that is detection at work. A network intrusion detection system, log monitoring tools, or even simple notification emails from cloud services about new device logins all fit into this space. In the physical world, security cameras, motion sensors, and visitor logs are detective controls because they create a record and provide visibility into events you could not otherwise see.

After something goes wrong, **corrective controls** step in. Their goal is to restore systems, data, and processes to a normal, secure state and to reduce the likelihood of the same problem recurring. Restoring from a backup after a ransomware infection or an accidental deletion is a corrective control; it repairs the damage that has already occurred. Reimaging an infected workstation from a clean, known-good image is another example. Applying a patch that closes a vulnerability exploited in an attack has both corrective and preventive aspects, but in the immediate aftermath of an incident, it is often classified as corrective because it is part of the response to a problem that has already surfaced. Updating a written procedure or adding extra training after a security incident can also be corrective, because you are correcting weaknesses that were revealed by the event.

A common mistake on exams is to misclassify controls based purely on when you happen to apply them rather than their purpose. For instance, you might schedule additional training after a phishing incident, but the training itself is still designed to prevent future incidents, so its primary classification is preventive. When in doubt, ask yourself a simple question: is this control mainly trying to stop, spot, or fix? If the answer is "stop," you are in preventive territory. If it's "spot," that is detective. If it's "fix," you are dealing with a corrective control.

Putting the pieces together in everyday work

The real power of this model appears when you start combining the two dimensions—type and purpose—in practical situations. Suppose your organization issues laptops to sales staff who travel frequently. To protect those devices, you might enable full disk encryption. That is a technical preventive control, because it uses technology to prevent data disclosure if a laptop is lost or stolen. You might also require that laptops be secured with cable locks when used in shared hotel conference rooms, which is a physical preventive control. On the administrative side, the company may have a policy requiring employees to report lost devices immediately, which is an administrative preventive measure aimed at triggering a quick response that limits damage.

Now imagine that one of those laptops goes missing anyway. You use logging from your mobile device management (MDM) platform to check when it last checked in and what data it accessed. Those logs are technical detective controls. You may then remotely wipe the device or revoke its access tokens—technical corrective controls that reduce ongoing risk and restore security. The facilities team might review security camera footage from the office parking lot to see when the laptop left the building, another physical detective control. If the organization later revises its procedures to require devices be stored in a locked cabinet when not in use, that new rule is an administrative corrective control that will operate as a preventive control going forward.

The same thinking applies to something as routine as malware on a workstation. When your antivirus software signals that it blocked a malicious file, its real-time scanning engine was a technical preventive control that stopped execution, while the alert itself is part of a technical detective control that draws your attention to the attempt. If the malware did run and the system is compromised, reimaging it and restoring user data from backup are technical corrective controls. Afterward, you might work with your team to roll out more frequent patching or restrict the user's ability to install software, strengthening preventive controls. You might also update training materials to remind users not to open unexpected attachments, using an administrative control to modify behavior.

On the exam and on the job, thinking in this structured way helps you select appropriate actions instead of reacting randomly. If a scenario describes a problem that keeps happening—multiple users repeatedly click phishing links, or devices are regularly stolen from a shared lab—adding another corrective step, like "reinstall the OS," misses the point. The better answer usually involves strengthening preventive controls, perhaps through improved training, policy changes, or physical measures like locks and secure storage. If, on the other hand, a scenario clearly takes place after an incident has already occurred, you should expect to choose corrective and detective steps first: gather information using logs, contain the damage, restore normal operations, and then think about improving prevention.

As you progress into later chapters, nearly every new tool, setting, or process you encounter will fit naturally into this framework. Firewall rules, encryption, access controls, backup strategies, and even change management processes are all specific examples of technical, administrative, or physical controls that serve preventive, detective, or corrective purposes. Keeping this simple mental matrix in mind will help you not only remember the details, but also understand why you are configuring a setting a certain way and how it supports the organization's overall security posture.

Knowledge Check

Question 1: A security analyst enables full disk encryption on all company laptops to protect data if devices are lost or stolen. How is this control BEST classified?

A. Physical detective control
B. Technical preventive control
C. Administrative corrective control
D. Technical detective control

Question 2: An organization requires all employees to complete annual security awareness training focused on spotting phishing emails. Which type of control does this requirement represent?

A. Technical detective control
B. Administrative preventive control
C. Administrative corrective control
D. Physical preventive control

Question 3: A help desk technician reviews firewall logs to investigate unusual inbound traffic to a web server. How should the firewall logging feature be classified?

A. Technical preventive control
B. Administrative detective control
C. Physical detective control
D. Technical detective control

Question 4: A company installs a keycard reader on the server room door to restrict access to authorized staff only. What type of control is this MOST accurately?

A. Physical preventive control
B. Physical detective control
C. Technical preventive control
D. Administrative preventive control

Question 5: After a ransomware incident, the IT team restores affected file servers from known-good backups. How is this action BEST categorized?

- **A.** Technical preventive control
- **B.** Administrative preventive control
- **C.** Technical corrective control
- **D.** Technical detective control

Question 6: A security engineer configures an account lockout policy so that user accounts are locked after five failed login attempts within 10 minutes. How should this control be described?

- **A.** Administrative detective control
- **B.** Technical detective control
- **C.** Technical preventive control
- **D.** Physical preventive control

Question 7: A new policy states that any changes to production servers must be approved through a documented change management process before implementation. What type of control does this MOST clearly represent?

- **A.** Administrative preventive control
- **B.** Technical preventive control
- **C.** Administrative corrective control
- **D.** Technical detective control

Question 8: A company installs CCTV cameras monitoring the entrance to the data center and retains the footage for later review if an incident occurs. How are these cameras BEST classified?

- **A.** Physical preventive control
- **B.** Technical corrective control
- **C.** Administrative detective control
- **D.** Physical detective control

ANSWERS

1: Correct Answer: B
Rationale: Full disk encryption is a technology-based safeguard that prevents unauthorized access to data on lost or stolen devices, so it is a technical preventive control.

2: Correct Answer: B
Rationale: Security awareness training is an administrative (policy and people) measure intended to stop unsafe behavior before it occurs, making it an administrative preventive control.

3: Correct Answer: D
Rationale: Firewall logging is a technical feature that records activity so abnormal or malicious events can be identified, classifying it as a technical detective control.

4: Correct Answer: A
Rationale: A keycard reader on a door is a physical mechanism that blocks unauthorized entry, so it is a physical preventive control.

6: Correct Answer: C
Rationale: An account lockout policy is enforced by the system and stops further login attempts after several failures, helping to block brute-force attacks, so it is a technical preventive control.

7: Correct Answer: A
Rationale: A documented change management requirement is an administrative policy designed to stop unapproved or risky changes before they occur, so it is an administrative preventive control.

8: Correct Answer: D
Rationale: CCTV cameras are physical devices that record and allow review of events to identify incidents, so they function as physical detective controls.

1.2 Core Security Principles

If you work in IT support for more than a day or two, you discover that most "simple" requests are not actually simple. A manager wants "access to everything so I don't have to keep asking." A user insists their password policy is "ridiculous" and begs you to "turn it off just this once." The organization has just experienced a data leak, and overnight every ticket suddenly has the word "urgent" and "security" in it. You are stuck in the middle, trying to keep people productive without putting the company at risk. This is where core security principles matter. They give you a way to think about these decisions, to explain them, and to make consistent choices instead of improvising under pressure.

These principles are not tied to any one vendor or platform. Whether you are working with Windows domain accounts, macOS laptops, Linux servers, cloud applications, or mobile devices, the same ideas appear in slightly different clothing. Later chapters will walk through specific tools and configurations; here, you are building the mental model underneath those tools. When an exam question asks what you should do next in a scenario, the right answer almost always aligns with one or more of these principles. The more naturally you can see which principle is in play, the easier it becomes to reason your way to an answer rather than trying to memorize every possible situation.

The CIA Triad: What Security Is Trying to Protect

The starting point for almost all information security thinking is the **CIA triad**: confidentiality, integrity, and availability. You can think of these as three main "goals" that any security control should support. Every time you choose a setting, implement a policy, or respond to a ticket, you are affecting at least one of these.

Confidentiality is about keeping data and resources hidden from people who are not authorized to see them. The word "authorized" is critical here; confidentiality does not mean "nobody can access this," it means "only the right people can access this." In a typical office, this shows up in obvious ways, such as an HR share that only HR staff can open, or an accounting application that only the finance team can log into. It also shows up in more everyday habits. Locking your screen when you walk away from your desk, enforcing password policies so someone cannot guess a coworker's credentials, or encrypting the hard drive of a company laptop so that a thief cannot read its files—all of those are fundamentally about confidentiality. On the flip side, when users share passwords so "we can all just log in as 'admin'," or email salary spreadsheets to a personal email address to "work at home," they are breaking confidentiality, even if they do not mean any harm.

Integrity focuses on whether data is accurate, complete, and trustworthy. It is not about hiding information, but about making sure that what you see is what was intended. Imagine an order database in an online store: if malware or a buggy update silently alters order quantities, changes shipping addresses, or corrupts records, the integrity of that data is broken. The same concern applies to system files. If critical operating system files are modified by malware, the system may no longer behave as expected. Even backups are an integrity story: when you restore from backup, you expect to get back exactly what was there at the time, not a half-complete or corrupted version. Later, when you study hashing and digital signatures, you will see technical tools designed specifically to verify integrity. At an entry level, though, you help protect integrity when you confirm backups are actually completing, monitor for disk errors, or use change logs to track what was modified and when.

Availability rounds out the triad by asking whether systems and data are accessible to authorized users when they need them. Availability is sometimes neglected in casual discussions of security, but from a business perspective it is often the most visible. If the file server is down and no one can access project documents, or the ticketing system is unavailable during business hours, security has failed just as surely as if an attacker stole data. Routine admin tasks directly impact availability: scheduling reboots outside of peak hours, ensuring critical servers are patched without taking them offline for days, setting up UPS devices to ride through short power glitches, and validating that backups can be restored after a disaster. Even denial-of-service attacks, which you will study later, are fundamentally attacks on availability rather than on secrecy.

What makes the CIA triad interesting—and sometimes tricky—is that these goals can conflict. Tightening confidentiality by locking down access too aggressively can hurt availability if users constantly hit permissions errors trying to do their jobs. Sloppy, hurried changes made in the name of "getting the system back online quickly" can damage integrity if they introduce misconfigurations or data corruption. You will see these tensions in both real life and exam questions. For example, imagine a policy requiring extremely long, complex passwords that must be changed every 15 days. On paper it might look like a win for confidentiality, but in practice users start writing passwords on sticky notes under keyboards or reusing predictable patterns. The result is actually worse confidentiality. As you work through scenarios, it helps to pause and ask yourself which part of the triad is the primary concern. Is this mostly a secrecy problem, a correctness problem, or an uptime problem?

AAA: Controlling and Tracking Access

If CIA describes what you are trying to protect, **AAA**—authentication, authorization, and accounting—describes how you control and record who does what in your environment. You encounter these ideas constantly in user account management, yet many people blend them together. Keeping them separate in your mind gives you much clearer thinking.

Authentication answers the question, "Who are you?" This is the process of proving identity when you log on to a system or an application. A username alone is not enough; anyone can type "jsmith." The system must verify that the person at the keyboard is truly that user, typically through something they know (a password or PIN), something they have (a smart card, token, or phone with an authentication app), or something they are (a fingerprint or facial recognition). Multi-factor authentication, which combines more than one of these, is simply stronger authentication. From a support perspective, password resets, helping a user enroll in MFA, or verifying someone's identity before you make changes to their account are all part of the authentication story.

Once a user has proven who they are, **authorization** decides, "What are you allowed to do?" This is all about permissions. One user may be able to read files in a shared folder but not modify or delete them. Another may be able to create new accounts in an application but not approve financial transactions. An administrator may have broad control over system settings, whereas a standard user cannot install software. You implement authorization by assigning users to groups, defining roles in applications, and setting permissions on resources. A common mistake, both on the job and on the exam, is to assume that if someone authenticated successfully they must be allowed to access whatever they are trying to reach. In reality, logging in just gets you in the front door; authorization decides which rooms you can enter and what you can do inside them.

The third element, **accounting** (often called auditing), asks, "What did you do, and when did you do it?" This is about logging and tracking activity. System logs that show who logged into a server and from where, audit records of group membership changes, and application logs recording who edited a customer record are all examples of accounting. When you are troubleshooting, you may use these logs to check whether a user attempted to log in and what error they received, or to confirm that a certain change occurred at a specific time. In a security investigation, accounting is essential for reconstructing events and understanding the scope of an incident.

AAA ties directly back to the CIA triad. Strong authentication and well-designed authorization help protect confidentiality by limiting access to sensitive data. They also protect integrity; if only certain roles can modify critical records, you reduce the chance of accidental or malicious changes. Accounting supports integrity by providing a trail of who changed what, and it can indirectly support availability, since detailed logs often help you restore normal operations faster after an incident.

Non-Repudiation: Proving Actions and Enforcing Accountability

From AAA, it is a short step to **non-repudiation**, a formal way of saying, "You cannot credibly deny that you performed this action." In business, there are many situations where it must be possible to prove that a particular user approved a purchase, signed a contract electronically, or changed a critical configuration. Non-repudiation requires a few ingredients working together: reliable identification of the user, strong authentication so others cannot easily impersonate them, and accurate, tamper-resistant records of what they did.

Later in the book you will examine cryptographic mechanisms such as digital signatures and signed logs that provide very strong non-repudiation. At the support level, you see the concept in more everyday forms. When approvals in a change management system are tied to specific login accounts instead of generic email replies, the organization can point to an audit trail that says, "This change was approved by this manager at this time." When your ticketing system logs which technician performed a password reset and at what time, it provides accountability for support actions. Even something as basic as requiring users to log in individually, rather than sharing a generic "frontdesk" account, supports non-repudiation by tying actions to specific people.

Least Privilege: "Just Enough" Access

Among all the core principles, **least privilege** is probably the one you will grapple with most often day to day. Least privilege states that users, and even applications and services, should have the minimum level of access they need to perform their job functions, and no more. The goal is not to punish people or make their jobs harder; the goal is to limit the damage that can be caused by mistakes, malware, or intentional misuse.

In practice, least privilege shows up every time you decide what rights an account should have. Instead of making every employee a local administrator "because it's easier," you create standard user accounts and reserve administrative rights for IT staff or specific roles that genuinely require them. When a new hire in the sales department starts, you add them to the sales group that has access to the relevant folders and systems, rather than simply giving them full control over the entire shared drive "in case they need it later." If they must occasionally perform a task requiring elevated rights, you might use a "run as administrator" option or a temporary elevation tool instead of making them a permanent admin.

Least privilege is deeply connected to authorization in the AAA model. When a question describes a proposed permission change, you can often test it against this principle by asking, "Does this give the user more access than is strictly necessary for their role?" If the answer is yes, you should be cautious. Over-privileged accounts are a gift to attackers; if malware runs under an account that has broad rights, it can do far more harm than if that account were tightly scoped. Keeping privileges limited also makes it easier to understand and investigate incidents, because fewer people have the ability to make critical changes.

Defense in Depth: Layering Protections

Another recurring theme in modern security is **defense in depth**, the idea that no single control is perfect, so you design multiple, overlapping layers of protection. If one layer fails, others are still in place to reduce the impact or stop the attack entirely. Think of it as not relying on one lock to secure your entire house. You might have a lock on the front door, an alarm system, motion lights outside, and perhaps a safe for particularly valuable items inside. Any one of those might be defeated, but getting through all of them is much harder.

In IT environments, defense in depth plays out across devices, networks, accounts, and data. A phishing email might slip past the organization's email filtering and land in a user's inbox. That is one layer failing. If the user clicks the link, endpoint protection on the laptop may still detect and block the malicious file. If malware manages to execute, least privilege may prevent it from installing system-wide or accessing sensitive network shares. If it still manages to encrypt some files, reliable backups provide another safety net by allowing recovery. At each stage, a different type of control is at work, and together they create a more robust defense than any single control alone could provide.

This does not mean that "more is always better" in some random sense. Effective defense in depth is thoughtful and complementary, not just a pile of tools. You do not, for example, need three different antivirus products fighting with each other on the same workstation. But you do want host-based protections on endpoints, network-based controls like firewalls and secure Wi-Fi, strong access control and authentication policies, and solid backup and recovery processes. When exam scenarios describe multiple types of controls being used together—access policies plus network segmentation plus encryption—there is a good chance the underlying idea is defense in depth.

Zero Trust: "Never Trust, Always Verify"

Traditional network security was often built on a castle-and-moat mindset: keep attackers out of the network perimeter, and largely trust what is inside. That model has not aged well in a world of remote work, cloud applications, mobile devices, and sophisticated attackers. **Zero trust** is a modern philosophy that turns this thinking on its head. Its basic message is "never trust, always verify." Being on the corporate network, or having authenticated once this morning, is not enough to be trusted indefinitely. Every access request should be evaluated based on who is asking, what device they are using, where they are connecting from, and what they are trying to do.

You will see zero trust in practical ways even as a junior technician. Internal applications that once accepted a simple username and password might now demand multi-factor authentication, even from users sitting in the office. Access to a sensitive HR portal from a corporate laptop on the internal LAN may still require a VPN connection or a device compliance check to ensure the system is patched and running approved security software. Users may be asked to reauthenticate to critical systems every few hours, rather than staying logged in for days at a time. These can feel like annoyances from the user's perspective, but from a zero trust point of view they are ways to limit how far an attacker can get if they manage to steal a password, a device, or a session token.

Zero trust does not replace the other principles; it builds on them. It relies on strong authentication, carefully designed authorization, and continuous accounting. It supports confidentiality by making it harder for an attacker who gets "inside" in one way to roam freely to everything else. It supports integrity and availability by limiting the spread and impact of incidents. In exam questions, when you see references to not automatically trusting internal users or devices, or to making access decisions based on context and continuous verification, you are almost certainly looking at a zero trust concept in action.

As you keep reading and start working through more detailed topics—encryption, identity management, network security, incident response—these principles will keep showing up in different forms. When you are stuck on a scenario, stepping back to ask which of these ideas is really at stake often reveals what the best course of action should be.

Knowledge Check

Question 1: A help desk technician reminds users to lock their screens when leaving their desks and enables full-disk encryption on all laptops. Which primary security goal is the technician supporting with these actions?

A. Confidentiality
B. Availability
C. Non-repudiation
D. Accounting

Question 2: A financial application allows users to log in with MFA, but a junior accountant cannot approve large payments even after successfully authenticating. Which concept best explains why the user is blocked from this action?

A. Non-repudiation
B. Integrity
C. Defense in depth
D. Authorization

Question 3: A security analyst reviews system logs to determine which administrator changed a firewall rule at 2:00 p.m. yesterday. Which AAA component is the analyst primarily relying on?

A. Authentication
B. Authorization
C. Accounting
D. Non-repudiation

Question 4: A manager requests domain administrator rights "just in case" they ever need to install software or change settings on their laptop. Which security principle best supports denying this request?

A. Least privilege
B. Availability
C. Zero trust
D. Defense in depth

Question 5: An organization implements email filtering, endpoint anti-malware, strict user permissions, and regular offline backups to limit the impact of phishing attacks that may lead to ransomware infections. Which principle do these combined controls best represent?

A. Zero trust
B. Non-repudiation
C. Defense in depth
D. Accounting

Question 6: A company moves to a model where internal web apps require MFA, device compliance checks, and periodic reauthentication, even for users on the corporate LAN. Which principle is this approach MOST closely associated with?

A. Availability
B. Least privilege
C. Integrity
D. Zero trust

Question 7: A PKI-based system uses digitally signed change approvals that are tied to individual user accounts, preventing users from credibly denying they approved a specific configuration change. Which concept does this best illustrate?

A. Availability
B. Defense in depth
C. Non-repudiation
D. Authorization

Question 8: A database admin verifies that backup restore tests consistently produce complete and uncorrupted copies of production data. Which element of the CIA triad is the admin MOST directly validating?

A. Confidentiality
B. Integrity
C. Availability
D. Non-repudiation

ANSWERS

1: Correct Answer: A
Rationale: Screen locking and disk encryption prevent unauthorized access to data, directly supporting confidentiality.

2: Correct Answer: D
Rationale: After authentication, authorization controls which actions a user can perform, such as approving high-value payments.

3: Correct Answer: C
Rationale: Accounting (auditing) uses logs to track who performed which actions and when, enabling activity reconstruction.

4: Correct Answer: A
Rationale: Least privilege requires users to have only the minimum rights needed for their role, so "just in case" admin access is denied.

5: Correct Answer: C
Rationale: Using multiple, overlapping controls to mitigate the same threat exemplifies the defense-in-depth principle.

6: Correct Answer: D
Rationale: Zero trust assumes no implicit trust, requiring continuous verification of users and devices, even on internal networks.

7: Correct Answer: C
Rationale: Non-repudiation ensures actions can be definitively linked to individuals, here via digitally signed, identity-bound approvals.

8: Correct Answer: B
Rationale: Verifying that restored backups are complete and unaltered confirms the integrity of the data.

1.3 Change Management & Security Impact

In a lot of entry-level IT jobs, the day feels like a constant race to "just get things working." A user can't print, a laptop won't boot, an application keeps crashing, and everyone wants an instant fix. It is very tempting to make quick changes wherever you can: tweak a group policy, disable a security control "just for a minute," or install a patch because an article says it's critical. In a home lab or a small personal setup, you might get away with that. In an enterprise environment, that same behavior can quietly turn into a security incident, an outage, or both. The difference is not just the size of the environment; it is the presence of **formal change management** as a safety system around what you do.

Change management is simply the idea that any meaningful modification to systems, configurations, or access is planned, reviewed, documented, and executed in a controlled way. That concept might sound like bureaucracy at first, but from a security perspective, it is a powerful control. Almost every serious problem in IT can be traced back to something that changed: a misconfigured firewall rule, a rushed patch, a new permission that exposed data, a hardware swap that broke redundancy. When those changes are made without a record, without testing, and without proper approval, you lose visibility and control over your environment. As you study for Security+ and prepare for real work, it helps to reframe "following the process" as part of defending confidentiality, integrity, and availability—not just filling out forms.

Think first about how broadly the word "change" applies in IT. When an operating system update is installed, when a router is replaced, when a Wi-Fi configuration is modified, when a user is added to a group, when logging is turned off "temporarily," every one of those actions adjusts how the system behaves. Any one of them can impact security. A minor-looking adjustment to file share permissions can accidentally grant a whole department access to HR records. A firmware upgrade to a switch pushed during the workday can drop network connectivity for hundreds of users. Even physically moving servers in a rack without updating documentation can slow down incident response because nobody is sure which device is which. Change management exists to catch those potential issues before they turn into real damage.

From a Security+ perspective, it helps to connect change management to the core principles you already know. **Confidentiality** can be broken when permission changes are made casually, without verifying who really needs access or how those permissions are meant to be assigned. **Integrity** suffers when you have undocumented configuration edits—someone tweaks a registry key or service setting to "get something working" and no one records it, so the system drifts away from its baseline configuration and future patches behave unpredictably. **Availability** is directly threatened when someone applies a driver update, changes a DNS setting, or reboots a critical server in the middle of the workday without coordinating and scheduling. Good change control is the practical mechanism organizations use to protect those three principles in day-to-day operations.

In most environments, your interaction with change management starts with a **change request** or **change ticket**. This is the formal record of what is about to be done, on which systems, and why. You usually submit or update these through a ticketing system or service desk portal. For a junior technician, that might be as simple as filling out a web form that asks you to describe the change ("apply the March Windows security updates to finance department laptops"), the systems affected, the expected impact, and the timing. It is easy to think of this as extra work, but this ticket becomes the backbone of accountability: it shows who requested the change, who approved it, who carried it out, and what the outcome was. Auditors, security teams, and incident responders rely on that history later.

Organizations commonly distinguish between different classes of changes. Routine, predictable modifications that have been tested many times before—like a monthly patch cycle or a standard new-user onboarding workflow—might be handled as **standard changes**. These follow the same steps each time and may have pre-approved procedures. On the other end, **emergency changes** are those you carry out under pressure, often to fix a critical outage or address a serious security vulnerability. For example, a zero-day exploit is being actively used against your VPN gateway, and the vendor has just released a hotfix. You may not have time for the full review cycle, but you still document the change, get whatever rapid approval is available, and conduct a post-implementation review afterward. Both standard and emergency changes are part of the same philosophy: nothing substantial happens without a trace.

Different kinds of work you handle fall under change management in different ways. Software and firmware updates are a good place to start. Security training constantly talks about patching as a way to close vulnerabilities, and that is absolutely correct. But patches are still changes. An operating system update might fix one security issue and simultaneously break compatibility with a business-critical application. A firmware update on a network switch might introduce a new bug. Formal change management wraps discipline around patching by requiring testing before broad deployment, scheduling during maintenance windows, and having a rollback plan if something goes wrong. You will often see this on the exam in questions where the technically "secure" step—immediately applying a patch to all systems—is not the best answer because it ignores process and risk assessment.

Configuration changes are similar. Something as simple as adjusting a **group policy** that controls password lockout thresholds or changing a default port used by an internal web application can have wide-reaching effects. If a firewall rule is modified to allow new traffic from the internet to an internal server, that may open a service to external attackers. If DNS entries are edited incorrectly, users may suddenly be unable to resolve hostnames, disrupting many services at once. Change management asks you to stop and consider the scope and risk of such actions before you edit configurations on production systems. Even when you know exactly which command to run, the process might require a peer review or approval from a team lead or a change advisory board before you proceed.

Access and permission changes are where the security impact is often most obvious. When you add a user to a group, grant them rights to a file share, or modify a role in an application, you are directly influencing who can see and modify which data. These changes almost always require explicit approval from a manager or data owner because they are tied to policy and sometimes legal compliance. It is not unusual to see exam scenarios where a user asks you to "just give me the same access as my coworker." Technically, you could copy the permissions in seconds, but change management—and good security practice—pushes you to check whether access is meant to be granted through standardized security groups, whether an approval is recorded, and whether the role actually requires that level of access. The secure answer often involves opening or updating a ticket, obtaining the appropriate authorization, and then implementing the change in a way that is consistent with organizational standards.

Even hardware changes connect to change management. Swapping out a firewall, adding a new switch, replacing storage in a RAID array, or moving servers to a new rack alters your infrastructure. If you replace a firewall and forget to migrate the rule set correctly, services might become unavailable or, worse, default-allow rules might expose internal services to the internet. If you change a network topology without updating diagrams and asset records, troubleshooting and incident response become more difficult. Hardware maintenance often requires coordination with multiple teams, planned downtime, and verification testing after the work is complete—all of which are controlled through a formal change process.

Underneath all these categories is a basic **change lifecycle** that you will see again and again, even if each organization labels its steps slightly differently. It usually begins when someone identifies a need for change: a vulnerability scan reports missing patches, users complain about application performance, a manager requests access for a new employee, or a switch starts failing intermittently. Your first job is to define the scope clearly. Vague tickets like "fix the network" are not helpful; precise descriptions such as "replace the failing access switch S3 in closet 2B with model X, using the existing configuration backup dated this week" set the stage for safe execution.

Once the change is clearly described, there is a period of basic risk and impact assessment. At the Security+ level, you are not expected to run a full formal risk analysis, but you should be able to recognize which changes have high potential impact. Updating a single user's printer driver is not the same as pushing a browser upgrade to every workstation. Asking yourself simple questions—How many users will this affect? Does it touch critical systems? Does it involve security settings or external connectivity?—helps you decide whether you can proceed within your own authority or need to escalate for formal review.

Approval and authorization come next. In many organizations, small, low-risk changes may be approved at the team level by a supervisor, while anything that affects production systems broadly, or anything with security implications, must go to a **change advisory board (CAB)** or equivalent group. From a security perspective, unapproved changes are a serious issue even if they "work." They break accountability and can violate policies, regulatory requirements, or contracts with customers. On the exam, when you see an answer choice that involves obtaining approval or following organizational policy, it is often the better path compared to options that prioritize speed or individual initiative.

Planning, especially around scheduling, testing, and rollback, is where change management clearly supports both availability and integrity. Most real-world environments designate **maintenance windows**—time periods, often outside normal business hours, when disruptive changes can be made with minimal impact. Before you touch production systems, you should ideally test the change in a lab or on a limited group of pilot users. For example, you might first deploy a new antivirus version to a handful of machines in the IT department to confirm there are no unexpected side effects. At the same time, you prepare a rollback plan: a way to return the system to its previous state if the change causes problems. That might be as simple as creating a restore point on a Windows machine, taking a virtual machine snapshot, or ensuring you have current configuration backups before altering a router.

Implementation then becomes the execution of the plan, not improvisation. As a technician, your responsibility is to follow the approved steps as written, including prerequisites like checking backups, verifying you are connected to the correct device, and confirming maintenance-window timing. If you discover something unexpected mid-change, you do not silently adjust on the fly; instead, you pause, evaluate whether the deviation needs additional approval or documentation, and, if necessary, postpone or roll back. That discipline is part of why organizations trust their change processes.

After you implement the change, verification and monitoring are essential. You do not simply reboot a server, see that the service starts, and walk away. You validate that the intended effect occurred and that related services still function. That might involve having users test an application, checking that logging is still working, briefly reviewing CPU and memory usage, or scanning for new errors in system logs. In security-focused environments, you may also confirm that security controls, such as antivirus or intrusion prevention systems, are still active and correctly configured after the change.

Finally, you return to the ticketing system or documentation repository and record what actually happened. Good documentation includes the final state of the system, any deviations from the original plan, issues encountered, and how they were resolved. Network diagrams, asset inventories, and configuration baselines get updated if they are affected. Only then is the change considered complete and the ticket closed. The often-repeated phrase "if it's not documented, it didn't happen" reflects how critical this is for audits and incident response. When something goes wrong days or weeks later, investigators will ask: what changed recently? Without accurate records, that question becomes much harder to answer.

All of this process depends heavily on communication. Before a change, users and stakeholders should know when it will occur, what is likely to be affected, how long any downtime may last, and where to go for help if something is not working afterward. Sending a well-timed notice that "email will be unavailable from 10:00 p.m. to midnight for maintenance" prevents a flood of tickets and builds trust that IT is organized and considerate of business needs. After the change, you may need to distribute new instructions, such as telling users to restart their machines, log off and back on to pick up group policy changes, or use a new URL for a migrated application. The Security+ exam frequently rewards answers that combine sound technical steps with clear communication.

There will also be times when the luxury of extended planning is not available. A zero-day attack may be targeting your environment, or a critical server may have crashed in the middle of the workday. In these emergency scenarios, organizations still expect you to follow as much of the process as possible. That might mean getting verbal approval from an on-call manager, documenting actions as you take them, and then conducting a formal review afterward to understand what was changed and whether further remediation is needed. What you do not do, even under pressure, is make undocumented, ad hoc modifications that no one can later reconstruct.

When change management is ignored or treated as needless bureaucracy, the security consequences are very real. A technician disables endpoint protection to troubleshoot performance issues and then gets pulled into another task, forgetting to re-enable it; days later, a malware outbreak spreads far more easily because one control point was quietly removed. A firewall rule is hastily added to "get the vendor remote access working," but no one restricts it to the vendor's IP range or logs the exception; months later, that open path is exploited. A domain administrator changes an account policy on the fly to help a manager who keeps getting locked out, lowering password complexity for the entire domain instead of for a single service. In each of these cases, a straightforward adherence to change procedures—approval, documentation, testing, rollback planning—would have forced a pause and likely prevented the misstep.

As you move through more advanced topics like patch management, identity and access management, backup and recovery, and incident response, you will see the same theme repeating: technical controls only work well in an environment where changes to those controls are themselves controlled. Your role, even as a junior technician, is not just to know how to type the right command or click the right checkbox, but to make sure those actions happen within a process that keeps the organization secure and stable.

Knowledge Check

Question 1: A junior technician wants to immediately deploy a newly released critical security patch to all production servers to "fix the vulnerability as fast as possible." From a change management and Security+ perspective, what is the most appropriate next step?

A. Apply the patch immediately to all systems during business hours to minimize exposure time
B. Submit a change request, test the patch on a limited group, and schedule deployment during a maintenance window
C. Delay any action until the next annual security review to avoid unplanned work
D. Allow each system owner to decide independently whether and when to apply the patch

Question 2: Which scenario best illustrates an **emergency change** within a proper change management process?

A. Performing a routine monthly OS patch deployment after full CAB approval
B. Replacing a printer driver on a single user's workstation during lunch
C. Updating office Wi-Fi passwords during a pre-planned weekend maintenance
D. Rapidly applying a hotfix to an actively exploited VPN zero-day, with expedited approval and post-change review

Question 3: A technician disables endpoint protection "just for a minute" to troubleshoot performance issues and forgets to re-enable it. Which change management weakness most directly allowed this security gap?

A. Failure to obtain updated network diagrams
B. Lack of user communication about the change
C. Overuse of standard changes instead of emergency changes
D. Making an undocumented, unapproved change without a rollback or verification plan

Question 4: A manager emails the help desk asking: "Give our new hire the same access as Alice; she does the same job." What is the most appropriate response according to good change management and security practice?

A. Copy Alice's permissions immediately so the new hire can start working
B. Grant the new hire temporary domain administrator rights until proper access can be determined
C. Open or update a change ticket, obtain formal approval from the data owner/manager, and grant access using the organization's standard security groups
D. Deny the request because new hires should never receive access similar to existing staff

Question 5: Which action best demonstrates how change management protects **availability**?

A. Editing a DNS zone file in production immediately after discovering a typo
B. Scheduling a network switch firmware upgrade during a maintenance window with a tested rollback plan
C. Allowing technicians to reboot critical servers whenever they notice high CPU usage
D. Applying new group policy settings to all domain controllers at noon to ensure quick propagation

Question 6: A team plans to replace a failing access switch in a wiring closet. Which step should occur **first** in a formal change lifecycle?

A. Clearly define and document the scope of the change, including which switch, configuration, and affected users
B. Power off the old switch and connect the new one to minimize downtime
C. Notify users that the network will be down "until further notice"
D. Update all asset inventories and diagrams after the change is completed

Question 7: An organization's process states that potentially disruptive changes to production systems must be reviewed by a Change Advisory Board (CAB). From a security standpoint, why is bypassing CAB approval a significant concern?

A. It breaks accountability and may violate policies or regulatory requirements, even if the change appears to work
B. It prevents technicians from fixing issues quickly enough
C. It guarantees that the change will fail and cause an outage
D. It eliminates the need for documenting the change outcome

Question 8: After implementing a planned change to a production web application, which of the following best completes the change management process?

A. Assuming everything is fine if there are no immediate user complaints
B. Waiting a week before documenting anything to see if issues appear
C. Closing the ticket as soon as the service restarts successfully
D. Verify functionality and security controls, communicate any needed user actions, and update the ticket and documentation with the final state and issues encountered

ANSWERS

1: Correct Answer: B
Rationale: Security+ stresses controlled, documented changes: submit a request, test on a subset, and deploy in a maintenance window with rollback and validation, even for critical patches.

2: Correct Answer: D
Rationale: An emergency change addresses an immediate, high-risk issue (active zero-day) using expedited approval and implementation, followed by proper documentation and review.

3: Correct Answer: D
Rationale: The technician made an unapproved, undocumented change without verification or rollback, leaving protection disabled and creating an avoidable security exposure.

4: Correct Answer: C
Rationale: Access changes should follow a formal request, approval by the data owner/manager, and use of standard roles or groups to enforce least privilege and consistency.

5: Correct Answer: B
Rationale: Planning disruptive work for a maintenance window and having a tested rollback plan reduces downtime risk and helps maintain system and service availability.

6: Correct Answer: A
Rationale: The lifecycle starts by defining and documenting the change scope so impact, risk, and required approvals can be assessed before any technical work begins.

7: Correct Answer: A
Rationale: CAB review enforces governance, risk assessment, and accountability; bypassing it can violate policy or regulations, even if the change appears successful.

8: Correct Answer: D
Rationale: A change is complete only after confirming functionality and security, informing users as needed, and fully updating tickets and documentation with results and issues.

1.4 Cryptographic Concepts & Use Cases

If you strip away the math and the intimidating terminology, cryptography is really just about controlling who can see what, and how you can tell if something has been tampered with. Think about a few situations you see all the time in IT support. An executive checks webmail from an airport lounge. A sales rep's laptop goes missing from a rental car. A user calls because their browser is warning, "This site is not secure," when they try to log in to an internal tool. In each of these cases, the underlying question is the same: can we trust the confidentiality and integrity of the data involved? Cryptography is one of the main toolsets we rely on to answer "yes" to that question.

From the security principles you saw earlier—confidentiality, integrity, and availability—cryptography focuses primarily on the first two. It hides data from eavesdroppers and proves when data has stayed the same or when it has changed. For an entry-level cybersecurity or IT professional, that means you do not need to design encryption algorithms, but you absolutely need to recognize when encryption should be used, whether it is configured correctly, and what the consequences are if keys or passwords are lost. That might sound abstract, but it becomes much more concrete when you realize it's behind things like the padlock icon in your browser, the WPA2 setting on a home router, and the BitLocker prompt on a company laptop.

Plain Text, Ciphertext, and the Big Three Operations

To understand how all of this fits together, start with the simplest distinction: plain text versus ciphertext. Plain text is information in its original, readable form—a password you type, a message in an email, or a file saved on disk. Ciphertext is the scrambled version of that information after an encryption process. If you look at ciphertext without the right key, it should appear as random, meaningless data. Turning plain text into ciphertext and then back again is what we usually mean by encryption, but cryptography actually includes a few different operations with different purposes.

First is encryption itself. Encryption is a reversible process: if you know the right secret, called a key, you can convert ciphertext back into the original plain text. We use encryption when we want confidentiality, in other words when we need to hide the contents of something but still be able to read it later. When you connect to your bank's website over HTTPS, the traffic between your browser and the bank's servers is encrypted. When a laptop uses full-disk encryption, the files on the drive are encrypted. Later, when the right key is provided, the system decrypts the data, returning it to a readable state.

Next is hashing, which looks similar on the surface but has a very different goal. A cryptographic hash function takes an input—any data at all—and produces a fixed-length output, often called a hash or digest. The key point is that this process is designed to be one-way. You can easily compute the hash of a piece of data, but you cannot feasibly take a hash and reverse it to get the original input. Hashing is mostly about integrity. If you hash the same file twice, you should get the same hash value both times. If even a single bit of the file changes, the hash will be completely different. That makes hashing ideal for checking whether data has been altered, whether intentionally or accidentally.

A common place you see hashing in action is password storage. Secure systems do not store your actual password; instead, they store a hash of your password. When you log in, the system hashes the password you type and compares that result to the stored hash. If they match, you are authenticated. That design explains a behavior that confuses many users: when they forget a password, the system cannot "look it up," because the original password was never stored—only its hash. The only safe option is to reset the password and store a new hash.

There is also encoding, which is frequently mixed up with encryption but is not a security control at all. Encoding transforms data into a different format for compatibility or transport—Base64, for example, or how characters are represented as bytes—but it is not meant to provide confidentiality. Anyone who knows the encoding scheme can reverse it easily. If an exam question describes something like Base64 and asks whether it protects the confidentiality of data, you should recognize that this is not encryption and provides no real protection against an attacker.

At this point, a lot of people feel like they understand the three operations, but exam questions rarely stop at "define encryption" or "define hashing." CompTIA usually gives you a scenario and asks what you should do next, what control best fits the goal, or what is missing from a solution. That is where the most common mistake happens: choosing encryption when the problem is really integrity, or choosing hashing when the goal is confidentiality.

A useful rule is to separate two different questions: "Can someone read this?" and "Has this changed?" Encryption answers the first question. Hashing answers the second. Encoding answers neither—it is about formatting, not protection.

This matters because encryption and hashing solve different problems, and using the wrong tool can leave a gap even if it sounds "secure." Encryption alone does not prove integrity. If you encrypt a file and send it to someone, you have protected confidentiality, but you have not automatically proven the file was not changed in transit. Depending on the system, an attacker might still be able to tamper with encrypted data in ways that cause meaningful damage, or the receiver might have no reliable way to confirm they received the exact original content. In real systems, we usually pair encryption with an integrity mechanism—such as a message authentication code (MAC), an authenticated encryption mode, or a digital signature—so the receiver can detect tampering. The exam-level takeaway is simple: if a question is about proving data is unchanged, encryption by itself is not the best answer.

The reverse mistake is just as common: hashing alone does not provide confidentiality. If you "hash" a sensitive document, you haven't protected its contents—you've created a fingerprint of it. Anyone who gets the original document can compute the same hash, and anyone who gets only the hash cannot read the document, but they also cannot reconstruct it. That means hashing is not a way to "hide" data you still need to access later. It's a way to verify data, not store it securely for future reading.

An exam-style scenario makes this clearer. Imagine your team downloads an installer for a security agent that will be deployed to all company laptops. You do not need to hide the installer file from anyone; you just need to confirm the file you downloaded is exactly the one the vendor published. In that situation, encryption would be the wrong choice. If you encrypt the installer, you create extra work (key management) and you still have not addressed the real risk, which is tampering. What you actually want is an integrity check: compute the file's hash (for example, SHA-256) and compare it to the hash published by the vendor. If they match, you have strong confidence the file has not changed. If they differ, you stop and investigate. That is a classic "hashing is correct, encryption is tempting" question.

Now flip the goal. Suppose an employee needs to store a spreadsheet containing salary information on a laptop that sometimes travels. Here, integrity matters, but the first problem is confidentiality: you do not want unauthorized people to read that spreadsheet if the device is lost. A hash would be useless for that purpose because it does not protect the contents. Encryption is the correct tool because it keeps the data unreadable without the key. In many real deployments, you get both: full-disk encryption to protect confidentiality and additional controls (permissions, logging, backups, and sometimes signatures) to help with integrity and accountability. But if CompTIA forces you to pick the single best control for protecting sensitive data from being read, encryption is usually the right answer.

Encoding sits in its own category. It is commonly described in scenarios involving Base64 strings, "obfuscated" data, or data that was transformed so it could be transmitted through systems that only accept certain characters. Encoding is useful, but it is not security. If someone can view the encoded data, they can reverse it. CompTIA likes to test whether you recognize that "looks scrambled" does not automatically mean "encrypted."

So, when you are deciding between the three operations under pressure, anchor yourself in the goal statement. If the question is really asking, "How do I keep this secret?" choose encryption. If the question is really asking, "How do I prove this hasn't changed?" choose hashing (or a signature/MAC, depending on the wording). If the question is really asking, "How do I make this data fit a system or travel safely through a format limitation?" encoding is the clue—but it should never be treated as protection on its own.

Symmetric and Asymmetric Encryption in Practice

When we say "encryption," there are actually two main styles you need to understand from a practical perspective: **symmetric encryption** and **asymmetric encryption**. The difference comes down to how keys are used, but for Security+ the bigger point is this: these two styles are rarely "either/or" in real systems. Most modern secure communications use them together, each one doing the part it is best at.

In **symmetric encryption**, the same secret key is used to encrypt and decrypt. You can picture this like a locked box: everyone who needs to put something in or take something out uses the same key. Because the math and operations stay compact, symmetric encryption is fast and efficient. That speed is the reason it becomes the workhorse whenever you need to protect a lot of data. Technologies such as full-disk encryption (like BitLocker or FileVault), Wi-Fi protection under WPA2 or WPA3, and the bulk encryption inside most VPN tunnels rely on symmetric algorithms such as **AES (Advanced Encryption Standard)**. When you hear "encrypt the drive," "encrypt the tunnel," or "encrypt the traffic," you should instinctively think: the data volume is large, so the encryption doing the heavy lifting is almost always symmetric.

The practical challenge with symmetric encryption is not that it is weak. The challenge is **key distribution**. A symmetric system is only as secure as the process used to get the key to the right people and keep it away from everyone else. If two parties on opposite sides of the internet need to share the same symmetric key, you immediately run into an uncomfortable question: how do you deliver that key securely before you have a secure channel? If you send it in plain text, you defeat the entire purpose. If you "hide" it with something like Base64, you are not securing it at all. This is where many real-world systems lean on asymmetric cryptography to solve the "first contact" problem.

With **asymmetric encryption**, also called **public key cryptography**, each participant has a key pair: a **public key** that can be shared and a **private key** that must be protected. The keys are mathematically linked so that something done with one key can only be undone with the other. From a practical support and exam perspective, there are two key ideas to keep straight. The first is that asymmetric cryptography helps establish trust and exchange secrets without already sharing a secret. The second is that asymmetric cryptography is not just about encryption; it is also the foundation for **digital signatures**, which is how systems prove identity and integrity in a way that scales.

Asymmetric encryption can be used for confidentiality, but it is slower and more resource-intensive than symmetric encryption, which is why it is rarely used for high-volume data streams. Instead, it is commonly used to protect small but crucial pieces of information, like the "starter" secrets that allow two parties to safely switch into a fast symmetric mode. This is exactly what happens in **TLS (Transport Layer Security)**, the technology underneath **HTTPS** and many other secure communications. For Security+, you want a mental model that explains not only that TLS uses both encryption styles, but also which problem each one is solving.

Think of a TLS connection as a short sequence of checks and agreements that happens quickly behind the scenes before any real data is exchanged. First, the server presents a **certificate**. That certificate is not just a random file; it is an identity statement that binds the server's identity (often a domain name) to a public key, and it is signed by a trusted authority. At this stage, the goal is not to encrypt all traffic yet. The goal is to answer a trust question: "Am I actually talking to the real server I intended to reach?" In other words, TLS begins with identity.

Next, the client verifies that identity. This is where most "why did I get a browser warning?" scenarios live. The browser checks whether the certificate is valid and appropriate for the site. It checks whether the certificate is expired, whether the domain name in the certificate matches the name the user typed, and whether the certificate chains back to a trusted **Certificate Authority (CA)**. If any of those checks fail, the browser cannot reliably establish trust, which is why it interrupts the user with warnings like "Your connection is not private." In exam terms, the certificate is not there to "turn on encryption" by itself. Its real job is to enable the client to verify the server's identity so the client does not accidentally set up an encrypted session with an impostor.

Once identity is verified, the session has a green light to negotiate a shared secret for bulk encryption. This is the moment where TLS uses asymmetric cryptography as a bridge. The client and server perform a key agreement process to arrive at a **session key** (or session keys) that both sides know but that an eavesdropper cannot derive. The details of the handshake vary depending on the exact TLS version and configuration, but the exam-relevant point is consistent: asymmetric methods are used to securely establish or protect the exchange of the symmetric key material. That negotiated session key is temporary and specific to that session, which is why it is commonly described as a session key rather than a long-term key.

After the session key has been negotiated and both sides agree they are talking securely, the connection switches into high-speed mode. This is where the line you already wrote becomes the anchor: once that key has been securely exchanged, the actual web traffic is encrypted using a fast symmetric algorithm like **AES**. At this point, the client and server have a shared secret, and symmetric encryption can handle the ongoing conversation efficiently. If you keep that flow in mind—certificate presented, identity verified, session key negotiated, symmetric encryption begins—you can answer the kinds of questions Security+ likes to ask, especially PBQs that test your ability to spot where the chain broke.

That step-by-step model also helps you distinguish between two very different failures that students often blend together. If the certificate step fails, the encryption might still be technically possible, but trust is not established, which is why the browser warns you. If the session key negotiation fails, you might see handshake errors or connection failures even if the certificate looks fine. And if symmetric encryption begins but you still have a security problem, the problem is often not "the encryption is weak," but something around configuration, downgrade risks, or endpoint compromise—issues that happen outside the math itself.

It also helps to keep one more practical distinction clear, because CompTIA frequently tests it indirectly: the **private key** is what the server must protect at all costs. The public key can be shared widely because it is meant to be shared. In an HTTPS scenario, the server's certificate contains the server's public key, but the server's **private key** stays on the server. If that private key is stolen, attackers can do far more than "read one message." Depending on the situation, they can impersonate the server, decrypt captured traffic in certain configurations, or sign things in the server's name. That is why private keys are treated like crown jewels and often stored in hardened systems or protected by hardware modules, and why certificate management is a real operational security responsibility rather than paperwork.

When you step back, the practical exam-ready summary becomes intuitive. Symmetric encryption is fast, so it protects the bulk data. Asymmetric encryption solves the key-sharing and identity problems that appear when you do not already have a shared secret. TLS is the classic example of them working together: the certificate establishes trust by proving who the server is, asymmetric cryptography helps negotiate the secure session secrets, and then symmetric encryption takes over for everything that follows. If you can track that sequence in your head, you can handle the "what failed?" questions, the "why is the certificate needed?" questions, and the PBQs that ask you to choose the best fix when a secure connection is not behaving as expected.

Hashing and Integrity in Real Systems

Because hashing is a **one-way** operation, it is an ideal building block for **integrity checks**. When you apply a cryptographic hash function to data, you are not trying to hide that data or make it unreadable later. Instead, you are creating a fixed-length digital fingerprint that represents the exact contents of the original input at a specific moment in time. If the input changes in any way, even by a single bit, the resulting hash changes dramatically. This property is what allows hashing to answer a very specific security question: "Has this data stayed the same?"

A common real-world example is downloading software from a vendor's website. To help users verify the integrity of a file, vendors often publish a hash value alongside the download, typically using a modern algorithm from the **SHA-2 family**, such as **SHA-256**. After downloading the file, you can compute the hash locally and compare it to the published value. If the two hashes match, you have strong assurance that the file you received is exactly the file the vendor intended to distribute. If the hashes differ, something is wrong. The file may have been corrupted during transfer, or in a more serious scenario, it may have been modified by an attacker. The key point for the exam is that hashing does not tell you who created the file or whether it is safe to run, but it does tell you whether the file has been altered since the hash was generated.

Hashing also plays a central role in **password storage**, which is an area CompTIA returns to frequently because it combines security principles with everyday system behavior. Secure systems do not store users' passwords in plain text. Instead, when a user creates a password, the system runs that password through a hash function and stores the resulting hash. When the user later attempts to log in, the system hashes the password they type and compares that result to the stored hash. If the values match, the system assumes the correct password was provided. This design explains why systems cannot simply "show you your password" when you forget it. The original password was never stored, only its hash, and the hashing process cannot be reversed.

While hashing greatly improves security compared to plain-text password storage, it is not a complete solution by itself. Attackers who obtain a database of hashed passwords cannot immediately read the passwords, but they can still attempt **password-guessing attacks**. They do this by hashing large numbers of guessed passwords and comparing the results to the stolen hashes. If a guess produces the same hash, the attacker has effectively recovered the password. This is why password strength still matters even when hashing is used, and why short, common, or reused passwords remain dangerous.

To make this kind of attack harder, modern systems almost always use **salting** in addition to hashing. A **salt** is a random value that is generated for each user and combined with the password before it is hashed. The salt itself is not secret and is typically stored alongside the hash in the password database. Its purpose is not to hide the password, but to change the hashing outcome in a predictable way that defeats large-scale attacks. When salting is used correctly, two users who choose the same password will still have different hash values stored in the database, because their salts are different. This is a crucial exam concept. If you see a question describing identical hash values for multiple users who supposedly have different accounts, that should raise a red flag that salting is missing or improperly implemented.

Salting also protects against **precomputed attacks**, such as rainbow table attacks, where attackers rely on massive lists of pre-hashed common passwords. Without salting, an attacker could compare stolen hashes directly to these tables and instantly identify weak passwords. With salting, those precomputed tables become useless, because the attacker would need a separate table for every possible salt value. In exam terms, salting does not make weak passwords strong, but it significantly increases the time and resources required to attack hashed password databases.

Another area where hashing and integrity intersect is in detecting **collisions**, which occur when two different inputs produce the same hash output. For a cryptographic hash function to be considered secure, collisions should be extremely difficult to find. Older algorithms such as **MD5** and **SHA-1** were once widely used, but researchers have demonstrated practical collision attacks against them. This means attackers can intentionally craft different inputs that result in the same hash, undermining integrity checks and digital signatures. Because of this, MD5 and SHA-1 are no longer considered appropriate for security-critical purposes, even though they may still appear in legacy systems or on the exam.

Modern systems have largely moved to stronger algorithms like **SHA-256** and other members of the SHA-2 family, which are designed to resist known collision and preimage attacks. For Security+, you are not expected to understand the mathematical details of these attacks, but you are expected to recognize which algorithms are considered outdated and why. If an exam question asks which hashing algorithm should be used to protect passwords or verify file integrity today, MD5 and SHA-1 should immediately be ruled out, even if they still appear as answer choices.

Web Security, TLS, and the "Not Secure" Warning

One of the most visible and frequently tested applications of cryptography is web browsing. When you access a website over plain **HTTP**, your requests and the site's responses travel across the network in **clear text**. Anyone in a position to observe that traffic—another user on the same open Wi-Fi network, a compromised router, or a system somewhere along the path across the internet—can potentially read the data or even modify it in transit. This is why HTTP by itself is considered insecure for anything involving logins, personal information, or sensitive business data. To address these risks, modern web traffic relies on **HTTPS**, which is simply HTTP running inside a **TLS (Transport Layer Security)** session.

TLS performs several critical security functions at the same time, and understanding those roles helps you interpret both real-world issues and exam questions. First, TLS establishes an **encrypted channel**, which protects the **confidentiality** of data in transit so that eavesdroppers cannot read it. Second, TLS uses **digital certificates** and **public key cryptography** to help the browser verify the identity of the server it is communicating with. When you visit a site like "mail.company.com," TLS is meant to give your browser confidence that it is actually talking to that server and not to an attacker impersonating it. Third, TLS provides protection against **undetected modification**, helping ensure that the data you send and receive has not been quietly altered along the way. Most of this process is invisible to the user; what you typically notice is a padlock icon in the address bar and a URL that begins with "https://" instead of "http://".

Because TLS combines encryption and trust, it is important to understand that these two ideas are related but not identical. It is possible for a connection to be encrypted while still being untrusted, and this distinction is at the heart of many Security+ questions. When everything works as intended, the browser validates the site's certificate, establishes trust, and then proceeds with encrypted communication. When something goes wrong in that validation step, the browser interrupts the process and warns the user before sensitive data is exchanged.

This is where messages like "Your connection is not private" or "This site is not secure" appear. These warnings do not usually mean that encryption is completely absent. Instead, they mean that the browser cannot establish trust in the identity of the site it is connecting to. In most cases, the underlying TLS encryption mechanisms are still available, but the browser is deliberately refusing to rely on them because it cannot confirm who is on the other end of the connection.

Several common certificate-related problems trigger these warnings, and CompTIA expects you to recognize what each one implies. An **expired certificate** is often an availability or maintenance issue rather than an active attack. Certificates have a defined validity period, and if they are not renewed in time, browsers will no longer trust them. From a security perspective, this does not automatically mean the site is malicious, but it does mean the organization has failed to maintain a critical security control. On the exam, an expired certificate points toward poor certificate management rather than broken encryption algorithms.

A certificate issued to the **wrong domain name** is more serious. If the certificate presented by the server does not match the domain name in the address bar, the browser cannot be confident that it is talking to the intended site. This could be a simple misconfiguration, such as a service being moved to a new hostname without updating the certificate, but it could also indicate **impersonation**. From an exam perspective, this type of error raises the possibility of a **man-in-the-middle attack**, where an attacker is presenting a certificate that does not legitimately belong to the site the user intended to reach.

Another common cause of warnings is a certificate signed by an **untrusted Certificate Authority**. Browsers and operating systems come with a built-in list of trusted CAs. If a certificate is signed by an authority that is not on that list, the browser has no reliable way to verify the site's identity. In some corporate environments, this can be expected behavior. Organizations often use an **internal PKI** to issue certificates for internal websites, VPN gateways, or inspection devices, and those internal CAs must be explicitly trusted by company-managed systems. In other contexts, however, an untrusted CA can indicate interception, such as a rogue access point or a device attempting to decrypt and re-encrypt traffic without proper trust configuration.

These distinctions matter because they explain a behavior that confuses many users: seeing a warning even though the URL shows "https://". HTTPS tells you that encryption is intended, but the browser warning tells you that **trust has failed**. The encryption may still exist, but without validated identity, that encryption does not provide the assurance it is supposed to. This is why security guidance consistently says users should not ignore certificate warnings, especially on public networks or when accessing sites that handle credentials or sensitive data.

From a support and exam standpoint, your response to these warnings depends on context. On a public-facing website, certificate errors should be treated as serious issues and escalated, because users cannot safely authenticate or transmit sensitive data until trust is restored. On an internal site, the correct action might involve checking certificate expiration dates, confirming that the correct domain name is being used, or ensuring that internal CAs are properly trusted on managed devices. What should never be done is training users to blindly click through warnings, because that undermines the entire trust model TLS is built on.

Wi-Fi Protection: Open vs. WPA2 and WPA3

Wireless networks are another area where cryptography directly shapes configuration options you will handle. When a Wi-Fi network is configured as **open**, meaning there is no password to join, the wireless traffic between devices and the access point is not encrypted at all. Anyone within radio range with the right tools can capture and read that traffic. This is why using open Wi-Fi for sensitive activities, especially without a VPN or HTTPS, carries real risk.

To address this, modern Wi-Fi security standards like **WPA2** and **WPA3** use encryption—specifically AES-based algorithms—to protect the wireless communication. In a typical home or small office deployment, you will see **WPA2-Personal** or WPA3-Personal, where all users share a pre-shared key, essentially a shared passphrase. That key is used to derive the encryption keys that protect each device's traffic. Older standards like **WEP** are now considered fundamentally broken; an attacker can often recover the WEP key in minutes. For any real-world deployment or exam scenario, WEP should be viewed as insecure and unacceptable.

When you are setting up or advising on a small office or home router, the best practice is to enable WPA2 or, where hardware supports it, WPA3, and to choose a strong, non-obvious passphrase. Choosing "Open" just because it is convenient effectively means choosing no cryptographic protection at all. In an exam question that asks which wireless configuration best secures a small office, you should expect the correct choice to be WPA2 or WPA3 with a strong key, not WEP and certainly not an open network.

Protecting Data at Rest: Disk and File Encryption

So far, the focus has been on data in transit: traffic moving across networks. Cryptography is equally important for data at rest, such as files stored on a laptop or smartphone. If someone steals an unencrypted laptop that is powered off, they may be able to remove the drive, connect it to another system, and read everything on it. To mitigate this, organizations increasingly require **full-disk encryption** on portable devices.

On Windows systems, this is commonly implemented with **BitLocker**; on macOS, with **FileVault**; on many smartphones, storage encryption is enabled by default. Full-disk encryption uses symmetric encryption to protect the entire contents of the drive. When the device is powered off, all data is stored as ciphertext. At boot, the user provides some form of key material—a PIN, password, or, in some designs, a cryptographic key stored in a hardware **TPM** (Trusted Platform Module) chip—to unlock the drive. Once unlocked, the operating system can read and write data as usual, and the user typically does not notice the encryption in day-to-day use.

The crucial operational point is that without the correct key, the data is simply not recoverable. This is not a matter of "administrator override"; strong encryption is designed to prevent anyone, including attackers and administrators, from accessing data without the key. That is why many enterprises maintain a system of **recovery keys**, which are securely stored in a directory service, mobile device management platform, or key management system. If a user forgets a BitLocker PIN, for example, support staff can verify the user's identity, retrieve the recovery key, and unlock the drive.

If no recovery key exists or it cannot be accessed, the situation changes dramatically. In that case, the only realistic option may be to wipe and reimage the device, with all existing data lost. For you as a support professional, this means two things. First, when configuring or deploying devices, you must follow organizational processes to ensure encryption keys are backed up appropriately. Second, when users ask about encryption passwords and what happens if they forget them, you need to be clear that in many designs, forgetting both the password and losing the recovery key means permanent data loss.

Sometimes organizations choose **file-level encryption** rather than or in addition to full-disk encryption. Here, specific files or folders are encrypted, rather than the whole drive. This can be more flexible and, in some cases, easier to share securely, as users can encrypt a single document before sending it as an email attachment or storing it in the cloud. The trade-off is that data outside those encrypted areas may remain exposed. In exam scenarios, if the goal is to protect a portable device against theft, full-disk encryption usually aligns better with that requirement. If the goal is to protect a particular document in transit, encrypting the file itself is often the right choice.

Certificates, Digital Signatures, and PKI

You have already seen certificates in the context of HTTPS warnings, but it helps to step back and describe what a certificate really is. A **digital certificate** is like an electronic ID card that binds a public key to some identity information, such as a website's domain name or an organization's name. This certificate is itself digitally signed by a **Certificate Authority (CA)**, an entity that your operating system or browser is configured to trust. When your browser sees a certificate for "www.example.com" that is signed by a trusted CA, and that certificate has not expired or been revoked, it can be reasonably confident it is really talking to that site.

Together, CAs, intermediate authorities, certificate servers, policies, and clients that trust them form what is known as a **Public Key Infrastructure (PKI)**. You do not need to design PKI, but you will interact with its results whenever a browser accepts or rejects a certificate, when Windows warns about installing an unsigned driver, or when an application refuses to connect to a server with an invalid certificate. Many enterprise tools rely on internal PKI to issue certificates for VPN concentrators, internal websites, and other services.

Digital signatures build on both hashing and asymmetric encryption to provide authentication and integrity. When a software vendor signs an installer, they compute a hash of the file and then use their private key to create a signature over that hash. When you download and run the installer, your system uses the vendor's public key (distributed via a certificate) to verify that signature. If the signature is valid and the certificate chains back to a trusted authority, your system can be confident the software really came from that vendor and has not been altered. That is why some operating systems warn you before installing unsigned drivers or software: without a signature, there is no strong cryptographic proof of origin or integrity.

Keys, Passwords, and Everyday Key Management

Underlying all of these technologies is the notion of a **key**. In cryptography, a key is just a piece of information that controls the encryption and decryption process. The algorithms themselves are usually public and standardized; what keeps your data secure is the secrecy and strength of the keys. If someone learns the key for your encrypted drive, they do not have to "break" AES—they just decrypt the data using the key, the same way your system does.

From a support perspective, keys often show up as passwords, PINs, recovery keys, or passphrases that protect encrypted data. The strength of those passwords matters enormously. A weak, easily guessed password can make even strong encryption vulnerable, because attackers will attack the password, not the encryption algorithm. This is why organizations push for complex, unique passwords and often add additional protections like multi-factor authentication. It is also why password reuse is dangerous: if encryption on one system is protected by a password that is already known from another breach, an attacker meets much less resistance.

Key backup and recovery is equally important. If your organization encrypts laptops with BitLocker but does not store recovery keys anywhere, a single forgotten PIN could mean the loss of important business data. If on the other hand recovery keys are stored casually in unprotected spreadsheets or text files, an attacker who gains access to those locations can quietly bypass your encryption. Good practice, and common exam logic, involves storing recovery keys in controlled systems, restricting who can access them, and requiring proper identity verification before using them.

In day-to-day work, you will help users reset passwords, unlock encrypted devices, and respond to warnings about certificates and secure connections. Each of those tasks benefits from a clear mental model of what cryptography is doing behind the scenes: whether you are trying to protect confidentiality with encryption, verify integrity with hashing, or establish trust through certificates and public keys. When you can recognize which tool fits which goal, you are not just memorizing exam facts—you are making sound, defensible decisions in real IT environments.

Knowledge Check

Question 1: A security analyst wants to verify that a large installer downloaded from a vendor's website has not been altered. Which cryptographic function is MOST appropriate for this task?

- **A.** Symmetric encryption with AES
- **B.** Base64 encoding of the file
- **C.** Asymmetric encryption with RSA
- **D.** Hashing with a secure algorithm such as SHA-256

Question 2: A help desk technician explains to a user that the company's authentication system cannot "look up" their forgotten password, only reset it. Which cryptographic property BEST explains this behavior?

- **A.** The password is symmetrically encrypted and can be decrypted only by admins
- **B.** The password is stored as a one-way hash, so the original value cannot be recovered
- **C.** The password is obfuscated with Base64 and must be re-encoded
- **D.** The password is stored in clear text but not displayed for security reasons

Question 3: A developer needs to convert binary data into a format that can safely be sent in an email body without worrying about character set issues. Confidentiality is not a concern. Which approach is MOST appropriate?

- **A.** Encrypt the data with AES-256
- **B.** Hash the data with SHA-256
- **C.** Encode the data using Base64
- **D.** Protect the data with a digital signature

Question 4: A network engineer is configuring a new HTTPS-enabled web server. During the TLS handshake, which type of cryptography is PRIMARILY used to establish the initial secure session and authenticate the server's identity?

- **A.** Symmetric encryption with a pre-shared key
- **B.** Asymmetric encryption using public and private keys with a certificate
- **C.** Hashing only, using SHA-256 digests
- **D.** Encoding using Base64 for the certificate contents

Question 5: A laptop protected with BitLocker is stolen while powered off. The organization has correctly implemented key management and did not lose the recovery key. Which statement BEST describes how BitLocker is protecting this data?

- **A.** It uses public key encryption so anyone with the public key can read the drive
- **B.** It uses hashing to conceal the data until the user logs in
- **C.** It relies on Base64 encoding of all files to prevent access
- **D.** It uses symmetric full-disk encryption, requiring the correct key or recovery key to decrypt

Question 6: A user reports a browser warning stating, "Your connection is not private," when accessing an internal web portal over HTTPS. Which is the MOST likely underlying cause?

- **A.** There is a problem with the site's TLS certificate, such as being expired or not trusted
- **B.** The site is using AES for encryption instead of RSA
- **C.** The page content was hashed with MD5 instead of SHA-256
- **D.** The portal is using WPA2-Enterprise on the wired network

Question 7: A small office asks how to configure their Wi-Fi router to best protect wireless traffic from being read by nearby attackers. Which configuration is the MOST appropriate recommendation?

A. Enable WPA2 or WPA3 with a strong pre-shared key
B. Use WEP with a complex passphrase
C. Configure an open network and rely on HTTPS only
D. Disable all encryption and use MAC filtering

Question 8: A security engineer is asked to ensure users can verify that a downloaded software installer truly came from the vendor and has not been modified. Which technology BEST meets this requirement?

A. Full-disk encryption on the user's workstation
B. Base64 encoding of the installer before distribution
C. A digital signature created with the vendor's private key and verified with its public key
D. Encrypting the installer with a symmetric key shared with all customers

ANSWERS

1: Correct Answer: D
Rationale: Hashing with a secure algorithm (e.g., SHA-256) provides integrity; matching hashes indicate the file was not altered.

2: Correct Answer: B
Rationale: Passwords stored as one-way hashes cannot be reversed; the system can only compare hashes or reset the password.

3: Correct Answer: C
Rationale: Base64 is an encoding scheme that safely represents binary data as text for transport, without providing confidentiality.

4: Correct Answer: B
Rationale: The TLS handshake primarily uses asymmetric cryptography and certificates to authenticate the server and establish session keys.

5: Correct Answer: D
Rationale: BitLocker uses symmetric full-disk encryption; data is unreadable without the correct decryption key or recovery key.

6: Correct Answer: A
Rationale: "Connection is not private" warnings typically indicate TLS certificate issues such as expiration, mismatch, or untrusted CA.

7: Correct Answer: A
Rationale: WPA2/WPA3 with a strong pre-shared key uses robust encryption (e.g., AES) to protect Wi-Fi traffic from eavesdropping.

8: Correct Answer: C
Rationale: A digital signature created with the vendor's private key and verified with its public key provides authenticity and integrity.

CHAPTER 2

Threats, Vulnerabilities, and Mitigations

2.1 Threat Actors & Motivations

When you first start working with computers and networks, it is easy to think of "security" as a set of checklists and tools: install antivirus, apply patches, require strong passwords, lock the server room. Underneath all of that, though, security is really about people. Every security control you implement is ultimately a response to someone who might want to misuse systems or data. In security language, that "someone" is called a **threat actor**—any person or group that intentionally causes, or attempts to cause, harm to systems, data, or users.

Seeing security through this human lens is especially important for an entry-level IT support role. You are often the first person to see odd error messages, user complaints, strange network behavior, or unusual account activity. If you treat everything as "just a glitch," you can easily miss early signs that a real attacker is involved. On the other hand, you are not expected to be a detective or a digital forensics expert. What you are expected to do—both on the job and on the exam—is recognize patterns, understand when something looks like deliberate malicious activity, and know when and how to escalate the issue using your organization's procedures.

A useful way to think about threat actors is to ask three simple questions: why are they doing this, how capable are they, and where are they in relation to your organization. The **motivation** question is about why: are they after money, political impact, sensitive secrets, bragging rights, or revenge. The **capability** question is about how strong or sophisticated they are: are they using simple tools anyone can download, or are they building custom malware and planning long-term attacks. The **opportunity or access** question asks whether they are outside your organization, trying to break in, or already inside with legitimate accounts and physical access. Most exam scenarios will give you enough hints along these lines to infer what type of actor you are dealing with, even if the question never uses the phrase "threat actor" explicitly.

A memorable way to organize the main motives is to think of the word **FIRE-IP**. The F stands for financial gain, the classic motive of organized criminals. I represents ideological motives, the driving force behind hacktivists. R reminds you of revenge or personal grievance, which often shows up in malicious insiders. E points to espionage and national interest, typical for nation-state actors. The second I is immaturity or curiosity—"I'm bored, let's see what I can break"—which you see with low-skill attackers often called script kiddies. Finally, P reminds you of policy violations and negligence, the non-malicious insider activity that still creates serious risk. When you look at a scenario, you can usually start by asking which of these motives fits best and then match the description to a threat actor type.

Script Kiddies: Low Skill, High Noise

At one end of the spectrum are **script kiddies**. Despite the insulting nickname, you will see this term on exams and in the field to describe individuals with limited technical skills who use tools, scripts, and attack kits they did not create and do not fully understand. Their main motivations are usually curiosity, boredom, or the desire to impress friends. They are not building complex campaigns or doing months of research; they are downloading a scanning tool, pointing it at random IP ranges, and seeing what responds.

Because their capability is low, script kiddies depend heavily on automation and on obvious, well-known vulnerabilities. A typical pattern might be running a mass port scan to find systems with an old, unpatched service, then launching a prepackaged exploit that anyone can grab from a public site. They are opportunistic: they are not out to "get your company" in particular, they just want to find anyone who is vulnerable. In practice, that means organizations that have neglected patching and basic security hygiene end up being the easiest targets.

From an IT support perspective, script kiddie activity often shows up as noisy, generic behavior. You might see a surge of failed login attempts from random IP addresses against your VPN or remote desktop gateway. You might notice log entries showing repeated attempts to exploit a very old web server vulnerability that your company already patched years ago. You might not even be specifically targeted—if your network block happens to be in a list the attacker is scanning, your systems get swept up along with thousands of others. The impact can still be real if they happen to find an unpatched system, but the clues rarely indicate careful planning or a deep understanding of your environment.

On the exam, a scenario that mentions low skill, downloaded tools, broad untargeted scanning, or someone "just trying out" an exploit kit is pointing you toward a script kiddie rather than a professional criminal or a nation-state team. Recognizing that tells you something about both the capability and the likely persistence of the attacker: they may be persistent in the sense of "keep pressing the button," but they are unlikely to adapt if their first tactic fails.

Organized Criminals: Professional and Profit-Driven

As soon as you add money to the equation, the picture changes. **Organized cybercriminals**—whether individual fraudsters or larger criminal groups—are primarily motivated by financial gain. They want to steal money directly, obtain data they can sell, extort payment from victims, or otherwise turn access to systems into profit. That motivation drives their behavior: they prefer targets that hold payment data, personal information, intellectual property, or any asset that can be monetized.

Their capability is generally moderate to high. They may not always be inventing brand-new attack techniques, but they are willing to invest in phishing campaigns, rent botnets, buy stolen credentials, and even purchase zero-day exploits if the return justifies the cost. Ransomware is a classic expression of this motive. You might see multiple systems suddenly displaying a ransom note claiming that files have been encrypted and offering to restore access in exchange for cryptocurrency. There is no political message, no ideological slogan, just payment instructions and a countdown timer. The entire attack chain—from phishing email to file encryption to ransom demand—is designed around that one financial outcome.

For an IT support technician, criminals are one of the most relevant external threat actors. The "suspicious mass email" scenario illustrates how this can play out: multiple users report that their point-of-sale application will not start, and when you investigate, you find a ransom note on the desktop demanding Bitcoin. As you put the pieces together—multiple business PCs affected, clear ransom demand, no political or social messaging—the picture lines up with financially motivated cybercrime. Your role is not to negotiate with criminals, but to recognize that this is now a security incident, not just a software glitch. At that point, you follow your incident response procedures: isolate affected machines from the network as directed, preserve logs, and escalate to your security or management team promptly.

Criminals can also show up in less dramatic ways. You may see a stream of realistic-looking phishing emails that mimic your company's bank or a major cloud provider, urging users to "verify their account" and capturing credentials. You might be asked to investigate unexplained transactions or complaints that customer information seems to have been exposed. In all of these cases, if you recognize that the goal is to extract money or valuable data, you can better appreciate why your organization insists on training users about phishing, enforcing strong password policies, or requiring multi-factor authentication.

Hacktivists: Attacks for a Cause

Not all attackers care about money. **Hacktivists** are individuals or groups who use hacking techniques to promote a political, social, or ideological cause. Their motivation is ideological: they may want to protest an organization's actions, expose what they see as wrongdoing, or draw attention to a controversial issue. That motive shapes the kinds of targets they choose and the effects they want to create. Public-facing websites, social media accounts, and systems that store embarrassing internal documents are especially attractive, because they can be used to send a message.

Hacktivist capability ranges widely. Some participants may have skills similar to script kiddies, joining in distributed denial-of-service (DDoS) attacks using tools provided by more experienced organizers. Others may be very capable attackers, able to break into web applications, exfiltrate internal communications, and publish them. Typical actions include defacing websites—replacing the home page with a political slogan or graphic—flooding a company's site with traffic to knock it offline, or leaking internal emails to embarrass executives. What stands out in these cases is that the "payload" carries the message: the altered website or leaked data explicitly references a cause, a slogan, or a protest.

If you are the technician responsible for a company's public website, you might be the first to notice that the home page text and images have changed to a protest message. Or you might receive reports that the site is very slow or unreachable, and network monitoring reveals a massive volume of inbound traffic from around the world with no clear business reason. In these situations, clues like the content of the defacement or the nature of the target help you distinguish hacktivism from pure financial crime. A DDoS flood against an online banking portal with no messaging attached might be extortion by criminals; a DDoS flood against a controversial political organization's site, accompanied by social media posts from activists, points to hacktivism.

On the exam, you will often be asked to select between criminals and hacktivists when both could technically cause similar damage. The key difference is motive: if the scenario emphasizes public embarrassment, message spreading, or protest against the victim organization's beliefs or actions, hacktivism is usually the best fit, even if money is not mentioned at all.

Nation-States: Strategic, Sophisticated, and Patient

At the high end of capability are **nation-state** actors: teams that are sponsored or tolerated by governments and that operate in support of national interests. Their motivation is typically espionage, strategic advantage, or even sabotage. They may want to steal military secrets, gain access to critical infrastructure, copy advanced research, or weaken a rival country's economic position. Unlike criminals, they are not primarily after a quick profit, and unlike hacktivists, they are usually not looking for public attention. In fact, they often want to remain undetected for as long as possible.

Nation-state actors generally have the highest level of capability. They can hire skilled developers, invest in long-term research, and sometimes discover or purchase "zero-day" vulnerabilities—flaws that are not yet publicly known or patched. Their attacks are often described as advanced persistent threats (APTs): advanced because of their sophistication, and persistent because they maintain access over long periods, quietly exfiltrating data. Typical targets include government agencies, defense contractors, energy and transportation systems, and large enterprises with valuable intellectual property. However, these actors also go after smaller organizations that act as suppliers or partners, using them as stepping stones into larger, more protected networks.

As an entry-level technician, you are unlikely to be the one directly "fighting" a nation-state team. But you may still feel their influence. If your company works with government clients, handles sensitive research, or operates critical infrastructure, you will encounter stricter policies about patching, access control, logging, and incident reporting. Those policies are not there because anyone expects script kiddies to attack you; they are driven by the possibility of high-capability adversaries. You might see security tools flagging suspicious activity that your security operations center investigates in depth, while your job is simply to gather information, preserve evidence, and avoid taking actions that would destroy logs or artifacts.

In exam scenarios, clues that point to a nation-state include very sophisticated tools, long-term undetected access, targets with political or strategic value, and a lack of obvious financial motive. For example, if the question describes months of quiet data exfiltration from a government research lab with no ransom demand and no public leaks, espionage by a nation-state is a more plausible explanation than anything else.

Insiders: Threats from Within

So far, we have focused on outsiders who must cross a security boundary to cause harm. Some of the most dangerous threat actors, though, are people who are already inside those boundaries. **Insiders** are users with legitimate access to systems and data—employees, contractors, vendors, or partners—who misuse that access either intentionally or accidentally. What makes insiders so significant is not necessarily their technical skill, but the fact that the organization has already granted them trust: user accounts, passwords, physical badges, perhaps even elevated privileges.

Insider motivation can vary widely. Some insiders are malicious, acting out of revenge after a poor performance review or in anticipation of leaving for a competitor. Others are financially motivated, stealing customer lists or trade secrets to sell. Many insider-related incidents, though, are not truly malicious at all. They result from negligence or policy violations: a user copies sensitive data to an unencrypted USB drive to "work from home," or emails confidential reports to a personal account for convenience. From an impact standpoint, careless behavior can be just as harmful as deliberate sabotage, even if the law and HR policies treat them differently.

The "departing employee" scenario captures a realistic mix of technical and human clues. A user who is scheduled to leave the company soon asks you, as the technician, to "temporarily" restore access to a restricted project folder they no longer need for their current role. At the same time, you notice that this person has been downloading large quantities of data from multiple departments. Technically, they are inside: they have a valid account and can log in. Contextually, the timing and the unusual access pattern suggest a motive—perhaps taking data to a new job or planning to cause harm before departure. In that moment, your job is not to accuse them or investigate their motives, but to respect the principle of least privilege, refuse to bypass access controls without proper authorization, document what you have seen, and escalate according to policy.

Because insiders often "look normal" in the sense that they are using correct usernames and passwords, spotting insider threats depends heavily on context. You might see a user repeatedly trying to open documents unrelated to their job, someone asking you to disable logging "because it slows down the system," or a recently disciplined employee suddenly copying large numbers of files to an external drive. In each case, your awareness of insiders as a threat actor category should push you away from casual fixes and toward formal processes. You do not need to know whether the person is driven by revenge, greed, or simple carelessness—you only need to recognize that something is off and that others need to know.

Putting the Pieces Together

When you compare these threat actors side by side, patterns emerge that you can use to interpret scenarios quickly. Script kiddies sit at the low end of sophistication, often acting out of curiosity or immaturity, scanning broadly for any easy opportunity. Organized criminals are more focused and professional, turning technical access into financial profit through ransomware, fraud, or data theft. Hacktivists act for a cause, using defacements, leaks, and outages to send a message and attract attention. Nation-states pursue strategic goals, often with very advanced tools and long timelines, quietly targeting high-value organizations and their partners. Insiders, meanwhile, work from within, sometimes maliciously and sometimes carelessly, but always with the advantage of legitimate access.

As an IT support professional, you do not have to assign a perfect "actor label" to every incident. What matters is that you can read the signs: a ransom note and Bitcoin address signal financial crime; a politically charged message on a defaced web page suggests hacktivism; a quiet, long-term breach of government-related systems hints at espionage; a departing employee suddenly copying data looks like an insider issue. Once you start thinking in terms of who benefits, what the attacker seems to want, and how sophisticated the behavior appears, security alerts and odd user requests stop being random annoyances and start fitting into a coherent picture of human-driven threats that your organization's policies are designed to manage.

Knowledge Check

Question 1: A security log shows a large, automated scan from random IP addresses attempting to exploit an old, well-known web server flaw. The tools appear to be publicly available, and there is no sign the attacker is focused on this company in particular. Which threat actor type best fits this scenario?

A. Hacktivist group seeking to embarrass the organization
B. Nation-state conducting long-term espionage
C. Script kiddie using downloaded tools opportunistically
D. Malicious insider with elevated privileges

Question 2: An organization discovers that several file servers have been encrypted, and a note on each system demands payment in cryptocurrency to restore access. There is no political slogan or public statement, only payment instructions and a countdown timer. Which threat actor is most likely responsible?

A. Organized criminal group focused on financial gain
B. Hacktivist protesting the company's public policies
C. Script kiddie experimenting with a new exploit kit
D. Nation-state actor targeting critical infrastructure

Question 3: A company that provides cloud services to government agencies detects months of quiet data exfiltration from sensitive research environments. The attackers used a previously unknown vulnerability and left no ransom demand or public defacement. Which type of threat actor best matches these characteristics?

A. Script kiddie scanning for low-hanging fruit
B. Disgruntled insider seeking revenge
C. Nation-state engaged in espionage
D. Hacktivist leaking data to support a public cause

Question 4: A controversial organization's public website is defaced. The new homepage displays a political slogan, a manifesto criticizing the organization's beliefs, and links to social media accounts promoting a movement. What is the most likely primary motivation behind this attack?

A. Financial gain
B. Ideology and protest
C. Personal revenge
D. Accidental policy violation

Question 5: A departing employee with valid credentials suddenly starts downloading large volumes of files from multiple departments that are unrelated to their current role. They also ask the help desk to "temporarily" restore access to a restricted project folder they no longer need. Which threat actor description best applies?

A. External script kiddie with no legitimate access
B. Nation-state actor seeking strategic advantage
C. Hacktivist aiming to embarrass the company publicly
D. Insider potentially acting with malicious intent

Question 6: A junior IT technician notices that a user has copied confidential reports to a personal email account "to work from home faster," in violation of company policy. The user does not appear to have harmful intent but has exposed sensitive data. How should this user's behavior be classified as a threat?

A. Nation-state actor using advanced tools
B. Script kiddie abusing known exploits
C. Non-malicious insider causing risk through negligence
D. Organized criminal running a ransomware campaign

Question 7: An online retailer reports that many customers received realistic phishing emails that mimic the company's payment portal, tricking them into entering their credit card details. The stolen data is later sold on underground markets. Which primary motive from the FIRE-IP model is most evident in this attack?

- **A.** Immaturity or curiosity
- **B.** Revenge or personal grievance
- **C.** Espionage and national interest
- **D.** Financial gain

Question 8: A security analyst is trying to quickly categorize a newly observed threat actor. They start by asking, "Why are they doing this? How capable are they? Are they already inside or outside the organization?" Which concept from this chapter are these questions designed to clarify?

- **A.** The threat actor's motivation, capability, and opportunity
- **B.** The specific antivirus product needed
- **C.** The exact zero-day exploit being used
- **D.** The legal penalties for the attacker if caught

ANSWERS

1: Correct Answer: C
Rationale: Broad, untargeted scanning using public tools and exploiting well-known flaws with low sophistication aligns with script kiddie behavior.

2: Correct Answer: A
Rationale: Ransomware with clear payment instructions and no ideological message indicates organized criminals focused on financial gain.

3: Correct Answer: C
Rationale: Long-term, stealthy espionage, use of a zero-day, and a high-value government-related target strongly indicate a nation-state actor.

4: Correct Answer: B
Rationale: A politically charged defacement and manifesto reflect ideological motives typical of hacktivists—motivation is ideology/protest.

5: Correct Answer: D
Rationale: The person has legitimate access but is misusing it in a suspicious way near departure, fitting the profile of a potentially malicious insider.

6: Correct Answer: C
Rationale: The user is an insider violating policy without clear malicious intent, creating risk through negligence or convenience.

7: Correct Answer: D
Rationale: Stealing and selling payment data is clearly driven by financial gain, the "F" in the FIRE-IP motivation model.

8: Correct Answer: A
Rationale: Those questions map directly to identifying a threat actor's motivation, capability, and opportunity/access as described in the chapter.

2.2 Attack Vectors & Attack Surfaces

When you troubleshoot real systems, security problems rarely introduce themselves with labels like "phishing attack in progress" or "supply chain compromise detected." Instead, you hear things like "My laptop's been slow since I opened that invoice," or "I was on the café Wi-Fi and now my browser keeps opening strange sites." To make sense of situations like these, you need a mental map of how attacks actually reach users and devices, and where those attacks can take hold. That is exactly what the concepts of **attack vectors** and **attack surfaces** give you.

How Attacks Actually Get in

When security incidents are described in real life, they almost never arrive neatly labeled. No one reports that they "experienced an attack vector exploiting an expanded attack surface." Instead, you hear practical symptoms: files are suddenly encrypted, pop-ups appear out of nowhere, passwords stop working, or a system behaves strangely after a routine task. To understand what actually happened, and to respond in a way that makes sense, you need a way to reconstruct the path the attack took and the conditions that allowed it to succeed. That is where the concepts of **attack vectors** and **attack surfaces** become essential.

An **attack vector** is the path or method an attacker uses to reach a target and deliver an attack. It answers the question, "How did the attacker get in?" A phishing email that convinces a user to click a link, a malicious attachment opened from an unexpected invoice, a remote desktop service exposed to the internet, or a USB drive plugged into a workstation are all examples of attack vectors. The vector is not the malware itself and not the damage that follows; it is the delivery mechanism, the route the attacker chose to cross from the outside into your environment.

An **attack surface**, by contrast, is the total collection of points where an attacker could potentially interact with a system, user, or organization. It answers a different question: "What could be attacked here?" Every enabled service, open network port, user account, browser extension, wireless connection, cloud integration, physical access point, and even human habit becomes part of that surface. Attack surfaces exist whether or not an attacker is actively exploiting them. They are created by design choices, configuration decisions, and environmental realities, often long before any malicious activity occurs.

The most important thing to understand is that attack vectors and attack surfaces are tightly connected. An attacker cannot use a vector unless there is a corresponding surface available to receive it. A phishing email only becomes effective if users can receive email and are allowed to open links or attachments. A remote desktop attack only works if the service is enabled, reachable, and insufficiently protected. A malicious website can only deliver a payload if a browser is present and configured in a way that allows scripts, downloads, or plugins to run. In exam terms, incidents do not happen because attackers are clever alone; they happen because a chosen vector successfully intersects with an exposed surface.

A helpful way to think about this relationship is to imagine that every system lives inside a constantly shifting landscape of exposure. You rarely have control over the existence of attackers or their motivation, but you do influence how many paths are realistically available to them. Every unnecessary service left running, every default password not changed, every user granted more privileges than they need, and every unpatched system quietly increases the attack surface. As the surface grows, more vectors become viable. As the surface shrinks, many vectors still exist in theory, but far fewer of them work in practice.

CompTIA expects you to think in these terms when analyzing scenarios. Rather than asking you to name an attack type in isolation, questions often describe a sequence of events and ask which vector best explains what happened. For example, if a user reports that their files were encrypted shortly after opening an unexpected email attachment, the vector is the attachment delivered through email, while the attack surface includes the email client, the user's permissions, and the system's ability to execute the file. If several systems begin behaving oddly after connecting to public Wi-Fi, the vector may involve malicious network traffic or injected content, while the surface includes untrusted wireless networks, browser configurations, and the absence of protective controls like VPNs.

This mental model also explains why "fixing the problem" is not the same as "fixing the cause." Removing malware from a machine addresses the outcome, but it does not address the vector that delivered it or the surface that allowed it to run. From a security perspective, real improvement comes from understanding how the attack entered and adjusting the environment so that the same path is harder or impossible to use next time. That might mean tightening email filtering, disabling macros by default, enforcing least privilege, closing unused ports, or educating users to recognize suspicious messages. None of these actions eliminate attackers, but each one reduces the number of effective vectors available to them.

It is also important to recognize that attack surfaces are not purely technical. Human behavior is part of the surface. Trust relationships are part of the surface. Physical access is part of the surface. A locked-down server with perfect firewall rules can still be compromised if credentials are handed over through a convincing phone call or if someone props open a secure door for convenience. CompTIA scenarios often blend these elements, forcing you to look beyond software and consider people and processes as part of the security equation.

Social Engineering, Phishing, and Deception

Many of the most successful attacks do not begin with a technical exploit at all. They begin with a message, a conversation, or a carefully crafted request that persuades a user to do something they normally would not do. This category of attacks is known as **social engineering**, and it relies on manipulating human behavior rather than breaking software. For Security+, it is critical to recognize that social engineering is not a single technique but a family of related attack vectors that all depend on trust, authority, urgency, and familiarity. The technical systems involved may be perfectly patched and configured, yet the attack succeeds because a person becomes the entry point.

At the core of social engineering is **phishing**, which uses deceptive communication to trick users into clicking links, opening attachments, or surrendering credentials. The messages are designed to look legitimate and to trigger an emotional response that bypasses careful thinking. A user might receive an email claiming a package delivery failed, a bank account was locked, or an urgent security update is required. The details are often generic, but they are timed and worded to create pressure. In these cases, the attack vector is the message itself, and the immediate attack surface includes the **email client**, the **web browser**, and the user's ability to enter credentials or open files.

More targeted versions of phishing build on the same idea but add personalization. **Spear phishing** tailors the message to a specific individual or role, using details gathered from social media, company websites, or previous breaches. A message addressed by name, referencing a current project, or appearing to come from a known colleague feels far more credible than a generic scam. On the exam, spear phishing often appears in scenarios where the victim is not a random employee but someone with access to sensitive systems or financial authority. The attack surface here expands beyond the inbox to include the organization's internal trust relationships and communication patterns.

A particularly damaging form of this is **business email compromise**, where attackers impersonate executives, vendors, or finance staff to request wire transfers, gift card purchases, or changes to payment details. These messages may come from spoofed addresses or from real accounts that have already been compromised. The key recognition pattern is not a malicious attachment or link, but an unexpected request involving money, credentials, or confidential data, often accompanied by a sense of urgency or secrecy. Even though these scenarios feel more like fraud than hacking, CompTIA treats them as social engineering vectors because the attacker's success depends on manipulating a user into acting.

Social engineering is not limited to email. **Smishing** uses SMS or messaging apps to deliver short, urgent texts with links or callback numbers. These messages often exploit the limited screen space of mobile devices, making it harder for users to inspect URLs or notice subtle inconsistencies. A text claiming suspicious account activity or a missed delivery can push users to act quickly on their phones, where they may be less cautious than on a desktop system. The attack surface here includes **mobile devices**, mobile browsers, and the user's tendency to trust text messages as more personal or immediate than email.

Vishing takes the same manipulation into voice calls. Attackers pose as bank representatives, technical support staff, managers, or government officials, using scripted conversations to extract information or persuade victims to install remote access tools. In these cases, there may be no malicious link at all. The vector is the conversation, and the surface is the user's willingness to trust a voice claiming authority. Exam scenarios involving vishing often include details like caller ID spoofing, urgent warnings about account compromise, or instructions to bypass normal procedures "just this once."

Across all of these variations, the technical differences are less important than the shared patterns. Social engineering attacks often involve **unexpected communication**, **pressure to act quickly**, **requests for credentials or payment**, and instructions that discourage verification. They frequently rely on the victim believing they are helping resolve a problem or complying with authority. For Security+, recognizing these cues is more important than memorizing labels. If a scenario centers on persuasion, deception, or urgency rather than software flaws, social engineering should be at the top of your list.

From an attack surface perspective, these vectors thrive wherever communication and access intersect. Email systems, browsers, mobile devices, and **cloud accounts** are common entry points because they connect users directly to external parties. Cloud-based email and file-sharing platforms can amplify the impact if an account is compromised, allowing attackers to send convincing messages from a legitimate address or share malicious links that appear trustworthy. Once credentials are harvested, the attack surface expands further, because the attacker may now access additional systems without triggering immediate suspicion.

For an IT or security technician, the response to social engineering does not begin and end with cleaning up after the fact. When a user reports strange behavior after clicking a link or responding to a message, that report should be treated as a potential compromise, not as an inconvenience or a simple mistake. The appropriate mindset is to assume that credentials may be exposed, systems may be infected, or accounts may be abused until proven otherwise. That means escalating appropriately, resetting passwords, reviewing account activity, and advising users on what to do next rather than simply removing a pop-up or closing a browser window.

Browsers, Downloads, Services, and Exposure

Not every attack relies on persuasion or deception. Many succeed simply because software, services, and network access are exposed in ways that allow attackers to interact directly with systems. In these cases, the attacker does not need to convince anyone to trust them or act urgently; the environment itself provides the opportunity. For Security+, this category of attack vectors is especially important because scenarios often describe technical symptoms without explicitly naming the cause. Your task is to identify how the malicious activity arrived, not to jump straight to labeling the malware or the damage it caused.

Web browsers are one of the most common entry points in this category. Browsers are designed to interact with untrusted content all day long, which makes them a powerful but risky tool. **Malicious websites** and **drive-by downloads** exploit this reality. In a drive-by scenario, a user may simply visit a compromised or malicious site and have code executed or files downloaded without clearly approving it. The user might insist they "didn't download anything," yet the system begins showing symptoms shortly afterward. The vector here is the web session itself, and the attack surface includes the browser, its extensions or plugins, and the system's ability to execute downloaded content.

Closely related is **malvertising**, where attackers inject or place malicious advertisements on otherwise legitimate websites. A user might be browsing a well-known news site or blog when a pop-up suddenly claims their system is infected or urges them to install an urgent update. Because the site itself is familiar, the message feels credible. From an exam standpoint, the key detail is not what malware appears later, but that the initial contact came through an advertisement delivered inside a normal browsing session. The vector is the ad, not the website's main content, and the surface includes the browser's ability to run scripts and display third-party content.

Another common browser-based vector is the **fake login portal**. These attacks often overlap with phishing but can also appear through search results, malicious ads, or compromised websites. A user navigates to what appears to be a legitimate login page for email, cloud storage, or a business application, but the URL is subtly incorrect. The page captures credentials and then redirects the user to the real site, leaving the user unaware anything went wrong. In these cases, there may be no malware infection at all. The attack succeeds entirely through credential harvesting. CompTIA scenarios often test whether you can recognize that the browser and login process were the vector, even when the user reports no unusual system behavior afterward.

Email attachments and downloads remain a classic delivery mechanism, but here the emphasis is on execution rather than deception. A user opens an attachment or installs a file that contains malicious code. The attachment might be disguised as a document, an invoice, or a compressed archive, and it may prompt the user to enable macros or "allow content" to function properly. The important distinction is that the vector is the attachment itself, not the email in general and not the malware that eventually runs. Exam questions frequently describe performance issues or pop-ups appearing shortly after a file was opened, and the correct analysis hinges on recognizing that the initial entry point was a downloaded or attached file.

Untrusted installers and bundled software are another rich source of compromise. Users often download utilities, browser extensions, or "free" tools from third-party sites without realizing that the installer includes additional unwanted or malicious components. Adware, spyware, and potentially unwanted programs commonly arrive this way. In these scenarios, the user may honestly believe they installed legitimate software, because the program appears to work as advertised. The vector is the installer package, and the attack surface includes the user's ability to install software and the system's lack of application controls or restrictions. On the exam, clues like "installed a free tool" or "downloaded software from an unofficial site" should point you toward this category.

Beyond individual endpoints, network exposure plays a major role in how attacks arrive. Any service that listens for incoming connections contributes to the attack surface. **Open ports**, **exposed services**, and **unnecessary network-facing interfaces** give attackers something to talk to. Services like Remote Desktop Protocol, file sharing, web administration panels, and legacy protocols become vectors when they are accessible from untrusted networks and protected by weak or default credentials. In small office and home environments, it is common to find routers or devices with management interfaces exposed directly to the internet, often without strong authentication. In those cases, the vector is a direct network connection, not a user action.

Wireless configurations deserve special attention because they blur the line between user behavior and technical exposure. An **open Wi-Fi network** or one secured with weak or outdated encryption allows unauthorized users to join and observe traffic. In public Wi-Fi environments, attackers may operate as **man-in-the-middle**, injecting content, redirecting sessions, or capturing unencrypted data. Exam scenarios might describe multiple users experiencing strange browser behavior after working from a café or airport. The vector in such cases is not necessarily a specific website or email, but the untrusted network itself combined with browser activity. The attack surface includes wireless configuration, encryption strength, and user reliance on public networks without additional protections.

Remote access and management tools are another frequent vector when misconfigured. VPN gateways, remote desktop services, and remote monitoring agents are essential for support and administration, but when they are exposed to the internet without proper controls, they attract attackers. Weak passwords, lack of **multi-factor authentication**, and delayed patching make these services especially vulnerable. CompTIA often frames these scenarios with subtle hints, such as "remote access enabled for convenience" or "service reachable from the internet," followed by suspicious login activity or system compromise. The vector is the service itself, not the malware that may later appear.

When the Threat Isn't Online

Not every attack announces itself through suspicious network traffic, browser warnings, or malicious emails. Some of the most damaging security incidents begin far away from keyboards and firewalls, exploiting physical access, misplaced trust, or weaknesses in the supply chain. These vectors are easy to overlook because they do not fit the mental picture many people have of a "cyberattack," yet they can bypass technical defenses entirely. For Security+, it is essential to recognize that the attack surface does not stop at the network perimeter. It extends into offices, homes, vendors, and any place where devices, people, or updates intersect.

Removable media is one of the oldest and most reliable offline attack vectors, precisely because it feels mundane. USB flash drives, external hard drives, and memory cards move easily between systems, often without scrutiny. If autorun or autoplay features are enabled, simply inserting a device can trigger code execution. Even without autorun, a curious user opening a file from removable media can introduce malware into an otherwise well-defended environment. Attackers have exploited this behavior by deliberately leaving infected drives in parking lots or shared spaces, betting that someone will plug one in to see what it contains. In exam scenarios, when unusual behavior begins shortly after a device was connected, the removable media itself is often the vector, not the application that later crashes or the antivirus alert that appears.

Physical access to systems represents another powerful vector because it can render many logical controls irrelevant. An unattended workstation, an unlocked server room, or a laptop left on a desk provides opportunities that do not require network access at all. An attacker with physical access can install malicious software, connect hardware keyloggers, boot from external media, or remove storage devices for offline analysis. Even brief access can be enough. CompTIA frequently emphasizes that physical security underpins all other controls; if someone can touch the device, they may be able to bypass authentication, encryption, or monitoring measures that would otherwise stop them.

Closely related to this is **tailgating**, where an unauthorized person gains entry to a restricted area by following an authorized individual through a secure door. This vector relies entirely on social norms and convenience. No badge is cloned, no door is forced, and no alarm is triggered. Once inside, the attacker may have access to systems, workstations, or network ports that assume anyone in the space is trusted. On the exam, tailgating scenarios often test whether you recognize that the failure was not a broken access control system, but a breakdown in physical security awareness.

Lost or stolen devices are another category where attacks occur without any online interaction at first. Laptops, tablets, and smartphones frequently contain cached credentials, email access, VPN configurations, and sensitive data. If such a device is lost or stolen and lacks proper protections like full-disk encryption and strong screen locks, the attacker does not need to break into the network remotely. The device itself becomes the attack surface. CompTIA scenarios may describe a missing laptop followed by unusual account activity, and the key is recognizing that the vector was physical loss, not a remote exploit.

Hardware-based threats push this idea even further. **Hardware implants** and malicious peripherals can be introduced into environments under the guise of legitimate equipment. A compromised keyboard, charging cable, or network adapter can provide ongoing access or data capture without raising obvious software alarms. While these attacks are less common in everyday IT support, CompTIA includes them to reinforce the principle that trust in devices must be justified, not assumed. If hardware enters the environment through uncontrolled channels, it becomes part of the attack surface regardless of how well the network is defended.

Some of the most significant modern attacks fall under the category of **supply chain compromise**, where the attacker never interacts directly with your systems at all. Instead, they compromise a vendor, update mechanism, or service you already trust. A malicious software update, a tampered driver, or firmware preloaded on a device can introduce backdoors or malware during what appears to be a routine, legitimate process. From the user's perspective, nothing suspicious happened; they simply installed an update or deployed new hardware. On the exam, clues like "issues began after a routine update" or "multiple systems affected after installing the same software" should prompt you to consider a supply chain vector rather than isolated user behavior.

Untrusted vendors and low-quality hardware often introduce similar risks. Devices shipped with unnecessary services enabled, default credentials, or questionable preinstalled applications expand the attack surface the moment they are powered on. In some cases, what looks like a brand-new system already contains software that behaves more like spyware or adware than a useful utility. The vector here is not a malicious email or website, but the procurement decision itself. CompTIA uses these scenarios to highlight that security decisions begin long before a device is configured or connected to the network.

Third-party and **external service providers** represent another indirect vector. Cloud platforms, identity providers, managed service providers, and software-as-a-service applications often have deep integration into an organization's environment. If one of these providers is compromised, attackers may gain access to data or accounts without ever touching the organization's perimeter defenses. From an entry-level technician's perspective, the key responsibility is not to redesign vendor security, but to recognize patterns that suggest a shared external source of compromise and to escalate appropriately.

Knowledge Check

Question 1: A finance manager receives a convincing email that appears to be from the CEO, requesting an urgent wire transfer to a new vendor. Which BEST describes the attack vector in this scenario?

A. Business logic flaw in the finance application
B. Phishing message impersonating an executive
C. Compromised router performing man-in-the-middle
D. Malicious attachment embedded in a PDF invoice

Question 2: An administrator wants to reduce the number of ways an attacker can interact with a server. Which action MOST directly reduces the server's attack surface?

A. Disabling unnecessary services and closing unused ports
B. Enabling guest accounts for easier troubleshooting
C. Allowing users local administrator rights for flexibility
D. Moving the server into a different subnet without changing settings

Question 3: A user reports that after receiving an SMS stating "Your bank account is locked, tap here to verify," they tapped the link and entered their credentials on a mobile site. Later, they notice fraudulent transactions. Which type of attack vector does this BEST represent?

A. Vishing using automated voice calls
B. Smishing with a credential-harvesting link
C. Malvertising in a mobile web browser
D. Drive-by download from a compromised website

Question 4: Multiple users complain that while "just reading the news" on a popular website, a pop-up appeared urging them to "update your video player," after which their browsers began showing unwanted toolbars and redirects. What is the MOST likely initial attack vector?

A. Email attachment with embedded macros
B. Tailgating into a restricted office area
C. Brute-force attack against user passwords
D. Malvertising delivering a fake update

Question 5: A technician discovers that a small office router's web administration page is accessible directly from the internet using the factory default credentials "admin/admin." From a security perspective, what is the PRIMARY issue?

A. Misconfiguration that significantly expands the attack surface
B. Properly configured remote access but lacking user training
C. Social engineering that bypasses technical controls
D. Supply chain compromise of the router firmware

Question 6: Several workstations become infected with ransomware shortly after users install a free "PDF converter" downloaded from an unofficial website. Which component in this scenario is the attack vector?

A. The encrypted files on the file server
B. The user accounts with local administrator rights
C. The untrusted software installer downloaded from the internet
D. The company's shared network printer

Question 7: A user plugs a personal USB flash drive into a corporate laptop, after which malware is detected and the system begins running slowly. Autorun was enabled on the laptop. Which BEST explains how the malware reached the system?

A. Through a remote desktop session from an attacker's host
B. Through a phishing email that spoofed IT support
C. Through a compromised cloud file-sharing integration
D. Through removable media acting as the malware delivery vector

Question 8: After connecting to public Wi-Fi at a café, several employees report that their browsers are redirecting to strange websites and prompting unexpected "security updates." What is the MOST likely explanation?

A. Supply chain attack involving a malicious software update
B. Shoulder surfing that exposed their passwords
C. Malicious content injection over untrusted wireless as the attack vector
D. Tailgating that let an attacker into the office network closet

ANSWERS

1: Correct Answer: B
Rationale: The attacker uses a deceptive email that impersonates an executive to trigger a wire transfer. This is a phishing-based social engineering vector (business email compromise), not a technical flaw or attachment-based malware.

2: Correct Answer: A
Rationale: Disabling unnecessary services and closing unused ports directly reduces the number of reachable entry points, shrinking the server's attack surface. The other options either increase risk or do not change exposure.

3: Correct Answer: B
Rationale: The attack is delivered via SMS containing a malicious link that harvests credentials. This is smishing, which specifically uses text messages as the attack vector.

4: Correct Answer: D
Rationale: Users are infected after interacting with a fake update prompt while browsing a legitimate site, indicating malicious ads (malvertising) as the initial vector, not email, password attacks, or physical intrusion.

5: Correct Answer: A
Rationale: Exposing the admin interface to the internet with default credentials is a misconfiguration that greatly increases the attack surface by providing an easy remote entry point. No social engineering or supply chain issue is described.

6: Correct Answer: C
Rationale: The ransomware is introduced when users run a free, untrusted installer from an unofficial site. That installer is the malware delivery vector, not the encrypted files, user accounts, or printer.

7: Correct Answer: D
Rationale: The infection follows insertion of a personal USB drive with autorun enabled, so removable media is the attack vector that delivered the malware to the laptop.

8: Correct Answer: C
Rationale: On untrusted public Wi-Fi, an attacker can intercept or modify traffic, injecting malicious content and redirects. The wireless connection enabling this content injection is the likely attack vector, not supply chain, shoulder surfing, or physical access.

2.3 Vulnerability Types

If you think back to the previous sections on threats and attack vectors, you can picture an attacker, a path, and then some target at the other end. A **vulnerability** is what makes that target worth going after in the first place. Formally, a vulnerability is any weakness that could be exploited to harm confidentiality, integrity, or availability. The threat is who or what might cause the harm. The attack vector is how they reach you. The vulnerability is why, when they arrive, they can actually do damage. Once you start looking at systems this way, you realize that a huge part of an entry-level IT job is either quietly creating vulnerabilities through quick decisions, or quietly closing them through careful ones.

One way to keep things straight is to mentally label each element in a story. A phishing email is an attack vector. The fact that a user is not trained to recognize it is a vulnerability. The ransomware that runs after they click is the threat payload. That habit of separating the "how," the "who," and the "what's wrong" is exactly what CompTIA is looking for when it asks you to identify vulnerability types in short scenarios. In a help desk role, you are constantly touching the "what's wrong" side: configuring systems, choosing passwords, leaving doors locked or unlocked, and either reinforcing or undermining procedures.

Application and Operating System Vulnerabilities

Most people encounter vulnerabilities first in the context of operating systems and applications, because those are the tools they deal with daily. One of the most common and important software-related weaknesses is simply **unpatched or outdated software**. Every operating system and application ships with bugs. Over time, security researchers and attackers discover that some of those bugs can be abused to gain elevated privileges, execute code remotely, or read data they should not see. Vendors respond with security updates and patches. When those patches are not installed, the vulnerability remains open, sometimes for years.

On the exam, any reference to an **unsupported** or **end-of-life** operating system should set off alarms in your mind. An old server still running Windows 7, or a line-of-business app tied to an unpatched legacy Java version, is no longer getting fixes for newly discovered issues. That is different from a system that is technically supported but just a few months behind on updates, although both situations create risk. When a scenario says that "systems have not been updated in over a year" or that a printer, router, or IoT device has "never had its firmware updated since installation," you should recognize that as an age-related vulnerability. Attackers actively scan the internet for devices with known, unpatched flaws because they can often be compromised automatically with little effort.

Even when software is current, the way it is configured can introduce weaknesses. **Misconfigurations in software** are probably the most common vulnerability type you will create or fix in real life. Think about a file share where the permissions are set to "Everyone: Full Control" just to avoid dealing with group membership. Or a local application that is always run using an administrator account because otherwise it "doesn't work right." Or a technician who disables User Account Control (UAC) prompts on Windows because they are annoying. In all of these cases, the system works from a functional perspective, but the security boundaries the operating system is trying to enforce are being bypassed. On the exam, when you see defaults left unchanged, broad "Allow" settings, or security features disabled "to make things easier," you are looking at misconfiguration vulnerabilities, not clever optimizations.

Sometimes the vulnerability lies not in settings but in how the application itself handles data. Without going deep into programming, it is important to understand that **insecure input handling** is a classic category of flaw. Applications that do not properly validate what is typed into a form, a file field, or a network request can be tricked into crashing, overwriting memory, or executing unintended commands. As an entry-level technician, you are not expected to read source code, but you may notice symptoms: an app crashes consistently when a user pastes long or unusual text, or a security scanner flags a specific version of a web application as vulnerable to injection attacks. In those cases, no amount of changing local settings will fix the underlying problem; you need a vendor patch or update that corrects the code. Recognizing that the weakness is in the application logic, not your configuration, helps you know when to escalate.

Closely related are weaknesses in how applications handle identity and sessions. **Poor authentication and session management** can undermine all other controls. Imagine a web-based admin console that allows simple passwords like "1234" without any lockout after repeated attempts. Or an internal app where an entire department shares a single generic login, because creating individual accounts would "take too much work." Or a kiosk system in a clinic that automatically logs in a generic user and never times out or locks, no matter how long it is left unattended. Each of these patterns removes accountability and makes it easier for an attacker—or even just a curious insider—to gain or maintain access they should not have. When you read a scenario describing "no password changes ever required," "shared departmental accounts," or "sessions that never expire," you should immediately classify the core vulnerability as weak authentication and session control, even if the story mentions other details.

Network and Device Configuration Vulnerabilities

Stepping back from individual machines, network and device configurations define how systems talk to each other and to the outside world. Missteps at this layer often create broad exposure. One common pattern is enabling or leaving enabled network services that are not actually needed. **Insecure network services and ports** expand the attack surface unnecessarily. An older server may still be running Telnet or FTP even though no one legitimately uses them, or a remote desktop protocol (RDP) service might be open directly to the internet with no additional safeguards. In exam questions, a clue like "RDP exposed to the internet for convenience" or "unnecessary file shares accessible over Wi-Fi" is pointing you toward a network service vulnerability. The general rule is that if there is no clear business reason for a service to be reachable, it should be disabled or restricted.

Wireless settings provide another rich area of real-world vulnerabilities. **Weak wireless configurations** include access points set up with no encryption at all (open networks), outdated protocols such as WEP or WPA with TKIP, or a single, simple passphrase posted on the wall for everyone, including visitors. Sometimes, organizations keep legacy encryption methods enabled because they still have old devices that cannot support stronger options. When you see phrases like "to maintain compatibility with older handheld scanners, the warehouse Wi-Fi uses WEP," you should recognize that the accommodation for legacy equipment has created a known weakness. An attacker sitting in the parking lot can capture and crack WEP traffic quickly with freely available tools. From a Security+ perspective, the issue is not the presence of Wi-Fi itself, but the choice of insecure or mixed-mode encryption that leaves traffic exposed.

Network firewalls and access control lists are supposed to be your guardrails, but they can become vulnerabilities when they are loosened too far. A **firewall misconfiguration** might be as simple as a technician who, in desperation, turns off the Windows Defender Firewall on a workstation to get an app working and then forgets to turn it back on. At a larger scale, it might be a perimeter firewall with a rule that allows "any source, any destination, any service" for testing and then never gets tightened. You may also see management interfaces for routers, switches, and web applications exposed directly to the internet with no IP restrictions. These configurations are attractive to attackers because they offer direct access to high-value control points. On the exam, watch for language like "Allow All rule created to resolve connectivity," "firewall disabled for troubleshooting," or "web admin console reachable from the internet." Functionally, things may work, but the underlying vulnerability is an overly permissive, misconfigured barrier.

Another structural vulnerability is what is sometimes called a **flat network**. In a flat network, every device is on the same segment or VLAN with no meaningful separation between workstations, servers, printers, and sometimes even guest devices. From an attacker's perspective, once they compromise any one machine, they can scan and reach almost everything else with ease. Malware can spread rapidly because there are no internal chokepoints. While detailed network design is beyond the scope of A+, you should be comfortable recognizing that "all company systems, including point-of-sale devices and guest Wi-Fi, are on a single subnet" is not just an odd design choice—it is a vulnerability in segmentation. More secure environments deliberately isolate sensitive systems, but many small networks start out flat because it is easy, and that convenience carries risk.

Hardware, Firmware, and Physical Vulnerabilities

Even perfect software and network settings cannot save you if someone can walk up and touch the equipment. **Unsecured physical access** is one of the simplest and most powerful vulnerability types. Consider an "IT closet" that is really a broom closet with networking gear piled in, no lock on the door, and cleaning staff coming and going. Or a server room that is kept propped open "for airflow." On the desktop side, think of a receptionist's workstation that is logged in all day with no screen lock and sits near a public waiting area. In each of these cases, anyone who spends a few minutes in the area can plug in a rogue device, steal a laptop, reboot a machine from external media, or simply start browsing through open email and files. The underlying weakness is not a missing patch or poor encryption; it is the absence of physical controls. When exam scenarios mention unlocked doors, unattended logged-in devices, or "no policy requiring screen locks," you should classify the vulnerability as physical, even if software is mentioned.

Related to physical access is the configuration of the system firmware that initializes hardware and boots the OS. **BIOS/UEFI and firmware vulnerabilities** include leaving firmware unpatched and leaving protective features disabled or unset. Many organizations deploy systems with no firmware password at all, meaning anyone can restart a computer, enter the setup utility, and change the boot order to start from a USB stick. In some cases, **Secure Boot** is disabled unnecessarily, allowing untrusted operating systems or bootloaders to run. Network devices, printers, and IoT gear often run outdated firmware that has known security issues, because no one thinks to check for updates after initial deployment. From a support perspective, you may be the one configuring these devices, and you should be thinking, "Is there a firmware update? Have I set a management password? Is Secure Boot appropriate here?" When a question describes routers or access points with factory-default firmware and default admin credentials, recognize both the age and configuration aspects of the vulnerability.

Removable media and hardware interfaces are another physical-meets-logical weak point. Unrestricted USB ports on corporate systems create space for both data theft and malware introduction. A user might lose an unencrypted USB drive full of sensitive client data on public transportation. Someone with a malicious bent might plug in a USB device they found in the parking lot, not realizing it auto-runs malware or acts like a keyboard injecting commands. An attacker with brief access to a workstation could boot from an external drive and bypass the installed OS protections entirely. Organizations can mitigate these vulnerabilities by disabling unused ports, using device control software, and requiring encryption on approved removable media. For the exam, whenever you see "no restrictions on USB devices," "users regularly use personal external drives for work data," or "laptops can boot from any device by default," you should be thinking about removable media and interface vulnerabilities—not just careless users.

Human and Procedural Vulnerabilities

Technical vulnerabilities get a lot of attention, but in practice, people and processes are often the weakest link. One broad category is **susceptibility to social engineering**. This does not mean users are stupid; it means they are human. Attackers craft emails, phone calls, and in-person requests that exploit curiosity, fear, urgency, or respect for authority. A caller claiming to be "from the help desk" might pressure an employee into revealing their password "to fix an urgent issue." An email might appear to come from a senior executive demanding that a payment be sent immediately. The vulnerability here is not the phishing email itself, but the fact that users have not been trained or are under such pressure that they do not question unusual requests. When you read, "Employees routinely give out credentials over the phone to anyone claiming to be IT" or "Staff have never received security awareness training," recognize that the underlying weakness is human behavior and lack of preparation.

Password practices are another familiar human vulnerability. **Weak or reused passwords** make an attacker's job much easier. A single password used across work email, social networks, and a third-party service can lead to a cascade of compromises if one site's database is leaked. Shared accounts, where several people know the same credentials, eliminate accountability. Writing passwords on sticky notes attached to monitors or under keyboards helps anyone passing by. On an exam, if a scenario mentions that "users select their own passwords with no complexity requirements," or that "the accounting department shares one login, and the password is posted by the terminal," you should immediately identify credential management as the vulnerability, not just poor user judgment. Also distinguish between an individual user who chooses a bad password and an organization that has no policy or technical controls to prevent it; the latter is a systemic procedural issue.

Beyond specific behaviors, a **lack of training and poor security culture** can be thought of as a meta-vulnerability. In environments where security is treated as purely an IT problem, users improvise solutions that meet their immediate needs but bypass controls. This leads to "shadow IT," where staff sign up for personal cloud storage to move files, install unauthorized apps to collaborate, or forward work documents to personal email accounts. They are usually trying to get their jobs done, not break rules, but the effect is the same: data leaves protected systems and lands in places with unknown safeguards. When a question says, "Employees are responsible for deciding which cloud apps to use, and there is no formal security awareness training," the vulnerability to note is the absence of governance and education, not just the presence of cloud services.

Finally, many vulnerabilities stem from gaps in process and documentation. **Process weaknesses** might include no formal procedure to disable user accounts when employees leave, no defined patching schedule, or unclear ownership for backups and antivirus updates. From an attacker's perspective, a former employee account that remains active for months is an opportunity. From an operational perspective, a backup process that is never tested becomes a vulnerability to availability; you do not know if you can restore after an incident. In an entry-level role, you often encounter these issues firsthand. Perhaps you notice that terminated employees still show up in the Active Directory list, or that servers reboot unpredictably after updates because there is no change management. On the exam, the key is to read phrases like "no standardized process" or "responsibilities are not clearly assigned" and understand that these are not just management annoyances—they are security vulnerabilities in their own right.

As you work through practice questions and real-world situations, it can be helpful to run a quick mental check: Is this weakness primarily about a mis-set configuration, an aged or unpatched component, an overly open physical environment, or human behavior and procedures? That simple habit of naming the type of vulnerability turns vague unease into something concrete you can address yourself or escalate appropriately.

Knowledge Check

Question 1: A small business has several Windows 7 desktops still in daily use because a legacy accounting application will not run on newer operating systems. These systems have not received security updates for several years. Which vulnerability type is BEST illustrated in this scenario?

- **A.** Unsupported or end-of-life operating system
- **B.** Misconfigured firewall rules
- **C.** Weak wireless encryption
- **D.** Poor authentication and session management

Question 2: A security analyst discovers that a web-based HR application allows users to enter extremely long strings into a form field. When certain special characters are pasted into the field, the application crashes and the web server becomes unstable. No configuration changes on the server resolve the issue. Which vulnerability type does this MOST likely represent?

- **A.** Misconfigured file permissions
- **B.** Insecure input handling in the application
- **C.** Flat network architecture
- **D.** Weak password policy

Question 3: A retail store's network consists of a single subnet where point-of-sale terminals, office workstations, security cameras, printers, and guest Wi-Fi devices all share the same VLAN with no internal filtering. Once an attacker compromises one device, they can easily scan and access most others. Which vulnerability type BEST describes this design?

A. Insecure network service
B. Weak wireless configuration
C. Unpatched operating systems
D. Flat network with poor segmentation

Question 4: An organization configures its primary firewall with a temporary rule allowing "any source, any destination, any port" to troubleshoot a connectivity issue. The rule is never removed and remains in place for months, effectively bypassing most restrictions. What vulnerability type does this situation BEST represent?

A. Unsupported security appliance
B. Firewall misconfiguration with overly permissive rules
C. Weak session timeout settings
D. Legacy protocol compatibility

Question 5: A company's Wi-Fi network is configured to use WEP to support a set of older barcode scanners that cannot use stronger encryption. The same SSID is used for employees' laptops, tablets, and smartphones. Which vulnerability type is MOST clearly demonstrated here?

A. Weak wireless configuration using outdated encryption
B. Improper firmware update process
C. Insecure removable media usage
D. Poor physical access controls

Question 6: A help desk technician, frustrated that an internal application frequently prompts for elevated privileges, disables User Account Control (UAC) on several Windows workstations to "make things easier" for users. The systems otherwise remain fully patched. Which vulnerability type does this MOST accurately describe?

A. Unsupported operating system
B. Weak password complexity requirements
C. Misconfiguration that bypasses built-in security controls
D. Insecure network port exposure

Question 7: A receptionist's workstation near the lobby remains logged in all day and is never configured to lock the screen automatically. Visitors can easily reach the keyboard and mouse when the receptionist steps away briefly. Which vulnerability type is MOST relevant in this scenario?

A. Unsecured physical access to an unattended logged-in device
B. Insufficient application patch management
C. Poor session token handling in web apps
D. Misconfigured wireless access point

Question 8: During a security review, it is discovered that a department shares a single generic account for an internal web portal. The password is simple, never changes, and is posted on the wall near a shared terminal so everyone can log in quickly. What vulnerability type does this MOST clearly illustrate?

A. Insecure boot configuration
B. Unsupported browser version
C. Unnecessary network service exposure
D. Weak authentication and credential management

ANSWERS

1: Correct Answer: A
Rationale: Windows 7 is an end-of-life OS that no longer receives patches, so using it in production is an "unsupported or end-of-life operating system" vulnerability. The other options describe unrelated configuration or policy issues.

2: Correct Answer: B
Rationale: Crashes caused by long or special-character input indicate poor validation and sanitization, i.e., insecure input handling in the application. File permissions, network design, or password policy would not directly cause this behavior.

3: Correct Answer: D
Rationale: Putting all devices on one VLAN with no internal controls is a flat network with poor segmentation, allowing easy lateral movement. The issue is not specifically about services, wireless, or patching.

4: Correct Answer: B
Rationale: An "any-any" rule is a classic firewall misconfiguration with overly permissive rules, effectively removing most filtering. Appliance support status, session timeouts, or legacy protocols are not the core problem.

5: Correct Answer: A
Rationale: WEP is deprecated and easily broken, so using it for general Wi-Fi access is a weak wireless configuration using outdated encryption. Firmware, removable media, and physical controls are not the main vulnerability.

6: Correct Answer: C
Rationale: Disabling UAC removes a built-in security control and lowers the security posture, making this a misconfiguration that bypasses built-in security controls. The OS, passwords, and ports remain unchanged.

7: Correct Answer: A
Rationale: An unlocked, logged-in workstation in a public area is an unsecured physical access vulnerability, allowing anyone nearby to use the active session. Patching, web session tokens, or wireless settings are not the issue.

8: Correct Answer: D
Rationale: A shared, simple, static password posted on a wall reflects weak authentication and credential management. Boot settings, exposed services, or browser versions are unrelated to this specific risk.

2.4 Indicators of Malicious Activity

In a typical day on a help desk or junior security role, you almost never see the attacker. You see the aftermath. Someone calls and says their system suddenly "got really slow," or that files they were just working on now have strange names and won't open. A manager forwards an email that "looks weird" and wants to know if it's safe. The wireless network feels sluggish for everyone right before a big deadline. None of these observations say, "Hello, I am a cyberattack," but they are all potential **indicators of malicious activity**. Your value to the organization comes from recognizing when an everyday problem is just a glitch and when it might be evidence that something more serious is happening.

Security professionals use the phrase **indicator of compromise (IOC)** to describe any sign that a system, account, or network might have been attacked or misused. The idea is not that a single indicator proves anything beyond doubt; instead, you look at patterns and context. A single failed login might be fat-fingered typing. Dozens of failed logins from different IP addresses in a short period of time are something else entirely. In this section, the goal is not to turn you into a forensic analyst, but to build your ability to recognize suspicious patterns, avoid making the situation worse, and know when to escalate the issue to your security or incident response team.

You've already seen in earlier sections who the attackers are and the techniques they use. Now we shift to how those attacks show up in the real world from your vantage point. To make sense of what you see, it helps to think in three broad categories: how people and accounts behave, what individual devices do, and how the network as a whole looks. Those three lenses—behavioral indicators, host-based indicators, and network-based indicators—will come up again and again in both the exam and your day-to-day work.

Behavioral Indicators: When People and Accounts Act Strangely

Many incidents are first noticed not because a sensor fires an alarm, but because something about a user's behavior or account usage doesn't fit the usual pattern. Think of how a normal user account behaves in your environment. Most employees log in during their working hours, from a fairly small set of devices, on a predictable network. Their password resets are rare and usually follow a clear trigger: they forgot their password, their account locked out, or IT instructed them to change it. Against that baseline, certain patterns stand out.

One obvious red flag is unusual authentication activity. Repeated failed logins to multiple accounts from the same source can point to brute-force password guessing or credential stuffing, where an attacker tries a list of stolen usernames and passwords against your systems. If you see a legitimate user's account suddenly logging in at 3:15 a.m. when that user has a strict 8-to-5 schedule, you should be curious. If your logs show successful logins from IP addresses geolocated to regions where you have no offices and where that user has never traveled, the suspicion becomes stronger that the credentials have been compromised. When you combine odd timing, strange locations, and perhaps changes in the user's security settings—new multi-factor authentication devices registered or security questions changed without the user remembering doing it—you are no longer troubleshooting routine user error. You are looking at potential account compromise.

Permissions and access rights can also provide subtle but meaningful behavioral clues. In many organizations, help desk staff discover security problems when a user says, "I can suddenly see all the files in this confidential folder—am I supposed to?" or when a shared drive that used to be tightly controlled now lists "Everyone: Full Control" in its access control list. Similarly, a new local administrator account appearing on a workstation or server, without any corresponding change ticket or project, should immediately raise questions. Attackers who gain a foothold inside a network often perform **privilege escalation** and **lateral movement**, which almost always involve changing permissions or adding new accounts. Your job isn't to immediately rip out anything that looks unfamiliar; it's to verify whether a change was authorized and, if not, to treat it as a potential security event and escalate according to policy.

There is also the human side of behavioral indicators. Social engineering attempts are often first reported not by security tools but by skeptical employees. When several staff members start forwarding emails that claim to be from the CEO demanding urgent payment to a new vendor, or from "IT support" requesting that they "verify" their credentials on a strange website, that pattern itself is an indicator of malicious activity. Even a single user report can be important if the message instructs them to bypass normal processes—"Don't tell your manager, just do this quickly" or "Ignore the security training; this is an exception." Although the detailed mechanics of phishing and pretexting were covered earlier, recognize that multiple reports of similar suspicious messages should trigger a mental switch from "help this user decide if the email is safe" to "we may be seeing a broader phishing campaign against the organization."

Host-Based Indicators: When Devices Act "Off"

While behavioral clues often start the story, you will probably spend most of your time dealing with **host-based indicators**—the things individual desktops, laptops, mobile devices, and servers do when something is wrong. Not every odd behavior is malicious, of course, and you should always consider normal causes. The key skill is to recognize when the pattern of symptoms suggests malware or other hostile activity rather than simple misconfiguration or aging hardware.

Performance and stability are a common starting point. Users frequently open tickets because their machine has "suddenly become unusable." If a system that previously ran smoothly now shows sustained high CPU usage even with few applications open, or if its fans are constantly running at maximum while the user is only reading email, you should investigate what is consuming those resources. Task Manager, Activity Monitor, or similar tools can reveal unknown processes taking up a disproportionate share of CPU, memory, or disk I/O. Occasional freezes or blue screens can be explained by bad drivers or failing hardware, but when crashes begin right after a mysterious "required update" the user clicked from a website, or when multiple systems across a department begin locking up in similar ways, the probability of malware rises sharply.

The web browser is another rich source of clues. Unwanted pop-up windows advertising dubious products every time the user opens a page, especially on otherwise safe sites, often point to **adware** or a browser hijacker. If the homepage has changed to an unfamiliar search engine, or the default search results are suddenly filled with spam, and the user insists they didn't change anything, you are seeing typical symptoms of **potentially unwanted programs (PUPs)**. Redirections are particularly telling: when a user types a well-known URL into the address bar but is consistently taken to a look-alike phishing site or an unrelated advertising page, something is intercepting or manipulating their traffic. Often you will spot new browser toolbars or "helper" extensions that the user does not recall installing and that your organization doesn't approve. Even if these seem like mere annoyances, they indicate that software made it onto the system without proper controls, and they may coexist with more serious malware.

Beyond what the user can see, the underlying processes and services tell their own story. A workstation that has multiple instances of a browser process consuming high CPU when no browser windows are open invites closer inspection. Command-line utilities like PowerShell, cmd.exe, or bash running in the background on non-administrative user machines can be normal in some environments, but they are also favorite tools for attackers to execute scripts and download payloads. Processes with randomly generated names or ones that masquerade as legitimate system processes—like "svch0st.exe" instead of "svchost.exe"—are classic signs of malware trying to blend in. Services that are configured to auto-start and that do not correspond to any known or approved software in your environment should likewise raise concern. On the exam, you will often be given a description of resource-hungry unknown processes or suspicious command line activity and asked what this might indicate; map that quickly to spyware, keyloggers, or even cryptomining malware consuming CPU and GPU resources for the attacker's benefit.

Another reliable cluster of host-based indicators involves unexpected changes to security and system configurations. Many types of malware attempt to disable or degrade protections as soon as they infect a system. If antivirus or endpoint protection software suddenly stops updating, reports that its real-time protection is disabled, or disappears from the system tray without anyone having modified it, consider the possibility that a malicious program has interfered. Similarly, if the host firewall is turned off or shows new rules allowing inbound connections on unusual ports, and there is no related IT change, that may have been done by an attacker to open a backdoor. On Windows systems, missing System Restore points, altered Group Policy objects applied to only one user or machine, or strange additions in the registry's startup keys all fall into this category of configuration-level indicators.

Data and file anomalies can be some of the most dramatic signs, especially with modern ransomware. Imagine a user opening File Explorer and noticing that their familiar Word documents and spreadsheets now have odd extensions, such as ".locked" or ".encrypted," and that double-clicking them brings up an error or a ransom note demanding payment in cryptocurrency. Often, you will see a text or HTML file dropped into every folder with instructions and a threatening deadline. This combination—sudden file inaccessibility, changed extensions, and ransom notes—is the textbook pattern for a ransomware infection. Other data-level indicators can be more subtle, such as large, unexplained archive files appearing in user directories or shared drives, which may indicate that data is being staged for exfiltration. Rapidly disappearing files in sensitive directories or user reports that documents they know they saved last week have vanished might reflect destructive malware or an attacker covering their tracks.

Network-Based Indicators: When Traffic Looks Wrong

While host-based signs focus on a single device, **network-based indicators** tell you what is happening across systems and between your environment and the outside world. As an entry-level technician, you may not administer firewalls or intrusion detection systems directly, but you may receive alerts from them or have access to basic logs and utilization graphs. Learning to interpret those at a high level is an important skill.

Abnormal bandwidth usage is often a first hint that something is wrong. Under normal circumstances, network utilization follows a predictable rhythm: heavier during the workday, lighter at night, with occasional spikes for backups or software updates. When you observe a single workstation consistently pushing large volumes of outbound traffic, especially during off-hours, that should prompt questions. If users on several floors suddenly complain of slow internet access, and your monitoring tools show that a particular IP address is saturating the uplink, it could indicate data exfiltration, a system participating in a **botnet** launching attacks, or unauthorized cloud backups of sensitive data. The same concern applies when devices that should be relatively quiet, like printers or IoT hardware, start generating significant traffic to the internet.

Logs that describe which ports and protocols are in use can also reveal malicious activity. Organizations commonly expect most outbound traffic to use well-known ports such as 80 and 443 for web, 25 or 587 for email relay, and a handful of others based on business needs. If you see repeated outbound connections from a workstation to obscure external IP addresses on unusual ports, that could represent **command and control (C2)** traffic, where malware phones home for instructions. On the inbound side, a barrage of connection attempts from the same external IP address to multiple internal devices, or sequential scans of many ports on a server, strongly suggest scanning or an active attack. In authentication systems—VPNs, cloud services, or remote desktop gateways—logs that show repeated failed login attempts from foreign regions, followed by a successful login with those same credentials, essentially narrate an account compromise in progress.

Finally, pay attention to the presence of rogue or unapproved devices on the network. Attackers who gain physical access might install a small unauthorized wireless access point under a desk, bridging your internal network to the outside world. Users themselves may unintentionally create risk by plugging in personal routers or hot spots, or by connecting unapproved devices that then operate outside of your security baseline. Switch ports that unexpectedly show new, unknown MAC addresses, or Wi-Fi scans that reveal new SSIDs that mimic your corporate network, can all be indicators that your attack surface has silently grown. Even if no active attack is underway yet, these findings represent conditions that attackers often exploit.

Connecting Indicators to Threat Types and Responding Professionally

On the exam and in your work, you will rarely be asked to provide a forensic-level diagnosis. Instead, you will see descriptions of clusters of indicators and be expected to map them to broad categories of threats and choose appropriate next steps. For example, a user reporting relentless pop-ups, a browser homepage change, and unknown toolbars, along with an antivirus alert, points to adware or other malware infection. Taken together, multiple workstations showing high CPU usage, unknown processes, and constant outbound connections to strange IPs could indicate a botnet or cryptomining campaign. Widespread slowness of an externally facing website, with logs showing it is being flooded with requests from many different IPs around the world, matches the pattern of a distributed denial-of-service event.

Throughout all of these scenarios, your response must be guided by policy and by a professional mindset. That begins with verification: talk to the user, ask when they first noticed the problem, and whether they clicked on any unusual links or installed software. Compare their experience with others in the same department—are they the only one affected, or is the pattern broader? Use the basic tools available to you, such as Task Manager, Resource Monitor, event logs, and your organization's antivirus console, to confirm and document what you see. Do not, however, impulsively delete suspicious files, clear logs, or run random "cleanup" tools you found on the internet. Those actions can destroy evidence and may themselves introduce new risk.

Equally important is to preserve what you can and escalate according to your incident response procedures. Take screenshots of error messages, ransom notes, or suspicious settings. Note the time, the system name, the user involved, and the exact symptoms you observed. If your organization has an incident ticketing or reporting system, use it to hand off these details to the team responsible for deeper investigation. When the indicators suggest serious issues—such as ransomware encrypting files, clear signs of account takeover, or large unexplained data transfers—the correct reaction is almost always to stop further damage, avoid making changes beyond immediate containment if instructed, and get the incident into the hands of your security team quickly.

If you keep that mindset—always scanning for unusual behavior, host anomalies, and strange network activity, and then responding calmly, methodically, and within policy—you will be well prepared not only for Security+ questions in this domain but also for the kinds of real-world situations that make security work both challenging and rewarding.

Knowledge Check

Question 1: A user reports that all their documents suddenly have a new file extension like ".locked" and each folder contains a text file demanding payment in cryptocurrency. Which type of malicious activity do these indicators most strongly suggest?

A. Spyware infection capturing keystrokes
B. Adware and browser hijacking
C. Ransomware encrypting data
D. Rootkit masking system processes

Question 2: A workstation that was previously stable now shows sustained high CPU usage, its fan runs loudly even when few applications are open, and Task Manager reveals unknown processes with random-looking names consuming resources. Which of the following is the most likely explanation?

A. User error from incorrect software configuration
B. Routine operating system patching
C. Normal behavior for a system with many installed applications
D. Malware such as cryptomining or spyware running in the background

Question 3: An employee with a strict 8-to-5 schedule has log entries showing successful logins at 3:15 a.m. from a foreign country where the organization has no presence. What is the best interpretation of this situation?

A. The user's account has likely been compromised
B. The user is legitimately working remotely
C. The logs are most likely corrupted and can be ignored
D. This is normal behavior and needs no further action

Question 4: Multiple users report receiving emails that appear to be from the CEO, urgently demanding payment to a new vendor and instructing them not to follow normal approval processes. Several employees have forwarded these messages to the help desk. What should this pattern be considered?

A. A routine business process change
B. A misconfigured spam filter on the email server
C. An indicator of a broader phishing or social engineering campaign
D. A false positive due to user overreaction

Question 5: While examining a workstation, you notice the presence of a new local administrator account that does not match any documented change or ticket, along with user reports of suddenly having access to confidential folders they couldn't see before. What do these indicators most strongly suggest?

A. Unauthorized privilege escalation and potential lateral movement
B. Normal changes due to an operating system upgrade
C. A failed Group Policy update from the domain controller
D. Harmless misconfiguration that can be safely ignored

Question 6: A user reports that their browser homepage has changed to an unknown search site, they see persistent pop-up ads even on legitimate websites, and there are unfamiliar toolbars installed that they do not recall adding. Antivirus has also generated a low-severity alert. What is the most likely cause?

A. A complete hardware failure of the user's system
B. Adware or potentially unwanted programs (PUPs) installed on the host
C. A distributed denial-of-service (DDoS) attack against the organization
D. Normal browser behavior after clearing the cache

Question 7: While reviewing security logs, you see repeated failed login attempts from multiple IP addresses against various user accounts, followed by a successful login from one of those IPs. The affected user denies having logged in from that location. What type of malicious activity do these indicators best represent?

A. Normal variance in user behavior that requires no escalation
B. Benign scanning from an approved vulnerability assessment tool
C. Routine password reset activity by the help desk
D. Credential-based attack leading to account compromise

Question 8: Network monitoring tools show a single internal workstation sending large volumes of outbound traffic to unfamiliar external IP addresses on unusual ports during off-hours. Other users complain of slow internet connectivity, and the suspicious workstation is not a server or backup device. What is the most appropriate conclusion?

A. The user is legitimately uploading work files to an approved cloud service
B. The system is performing normal operating system updates
C. The workstation may be involved in data exfiltration or botnet activity
D. The issue is most likely a temporary Wi-Fi interference problem

ANSWERS

1: Correct Answer: C
Rationale: Sudden file extension changes plus ransom notes in each folder are classic indicators of ransomware encrypting data and demanding payment.

2: Correct Answer: D
Rationale: Sustained high CPU and unknown, resource-hungry processes with random names are strong host-based indicators of malware such as cryptominers or spyware.

3: Correct Answer: A
Rationale: Successful logins at unusual hours from foreign regions where the user has no activity are behavioral indicators of likely account compromise.

4: Correct Answer: C
Rationale: Multiple similar emails spoofing an executive and urging bypass of normal processes indicate a coordinated phishing/social engineering campaign.

5: Correct Answer: A
Rationale: An unexplained new local admin account and broadened access rights strongly suggest unauthorized privilege escalation and potential lateral movement.

6: Correct Answer: B
Rationale: Homepage changes, pop-ups, and unknown toolbars, along with AV alerts, match typical symptoms of adware or PUPs on the host.

7: Correct Answer: D
Rationale: Numerous failed logins from varied IPs followed by one success, with user denial, indicate brute-force or credential-stuffing activity leading to account compromise.

8: Correct Answer: C
Rationale: A single workstation pushing large outbound traffic on unusual ports during off-hours is a network-based indicator of possible data exfiltration or botnet participation.

2.5 Mitigation Techniques

Up to this point, you have looked at security mostly from the attacker's side of the chessboard. You have met different threat actors, walked through common attack vectors, and analyzed how vulnerabilities and indicators of compromise show up on real systems. Mitigation is where you finally move your pieces. It is the collection of concrete things you do on a daily basis to reduce the chance that an attack will succeed, and to limit the damage when something inevitably slips through.

In a typical entry-level support role, you will not be writing corporate security policy or designing enterprise architectures. Instead, you will be the person who actually implements those policies: configuring workstations, joining them to the domain, setting local options, installing and verifying endpoint tools, and working directly with users who are often the weakest link in the chain. Understanding mitigation techniques at this level means knowing which control to apply in which situation. Are you trying to stop malware, prevent unauthorized access, protect sensitive data if a laptop is stolen, or keep an attacker from moving laterally through the network? The answer drives what you do.

A useful way to think about this is in terms of two goals. First, you want to reduce the **likelihood** that an attack will succeed by shrinking the attack surface and raising the cost for the attacker. Second, you want to reduce the **impact** when something goes wrong by ensuring you can contain, recover, and learn from the incident. Practically, that translates into hardening individual systems, controlling accounts and access, deploying endpoint protections, securing network and remote access paths, protecting data itself, and following procedures that turn users from liabilities into partners. You have already seen what the bad outcomes look like; now you will see how day-to-day configuration decisions prevent or soften those outcomes.

System hardening: shrinking the attack surface

The term **system hardening** simply means configuring a device so it is less forgiving, less "friendly" to attackers and malware. Every extra service, open port, or unused application is one more thing that can go wrong. When you think back to the idea of an attack surface from earlier in the chapter, hardening is the act of deliberately shrinking that surface on each workstation, laptop, or mobile device you touch.

One of the most basic hardening steps is removing or disabling software and services that are not needed. A new Windows laptop, for example, might arrive with trial antivirus software, vendor-specific "support assistants," pre-installed games, and a grab bag of toolbars and synchronizers. Most of these programs do nothing to help the user do their actual work, yet every one of them is a potential vulnerability if it is poorly maintained or never updated. Attackers do not care whether the user ever opens that bundled photo-editing trial; if the software is installed and exposes a vulnerable component, it can be exploited. As a technician, you are often the one who decides whether to leave this clutter in place. In a managed environment, standard images and scripts will handle much of it, but you still need to recognize when a "helpful utility" from years ago has become a security liability and should be uninstalled rather than simply ignored.

Keeping operating systems and applications up to date is another cornerstone of mitigation. Many of the vulnerabilities you studied earlier—especially those used by worms and ransomware—are simply unpatched software flaws that have been public, with fixes available, for months or even years. On user systems, you will work with tools such as Windows Update, macOS Software Update, vendor patch utilities, or mobile device management (MDM) platforms that push updates to phones and tablets. The security logic here is straightforward: when a vendor releases a security patch, they are effectively telling the world, "Here is a hole we closed." Attackers analyze those patches, reverse-engineer them, and then build exploits targeting systems that have not yet been updated. That is why, although updates sometimes introduce bugs, security-related patches are almost always treated as urgent, with maintenance windows and staged rollouts used to balance stability and protection instead of indefinite delay.

Hardening also involves setting secure defaults at the operating system level. Simple configuration choices can close off entire classes of attacks. Disabling features such as AutoPlay or autorun for removable media, for instance, prevents a malicious USB drive from automatically executing malware as soon as it is plugged in. Configuring a screensaver timeout and requiring a password on wake helps prevent "walk-up" access when a user leaves a logged-in workstation unattended in a shared space. Even low-level firmware settings matter. In environments that care about physical security, you may be asked to set BIOS or UEFI administrator passwords and disable booting from USB or optical drives so that an attacker cannot simply bring their own bootable device, bypass the installed OS, and copy data.

Applications themselves need hardening as well. Web browsers are a common gateway for malware; they execute code from untrusted sites all day long. Disabling unnecessary plug-ins, blocking unsigned or outdated add-ons, and enabling built-in safe browsing features all raise the bar for drive-by downloads and malicious scripts. In many organizations, you will also configure document applications to treat macros cautiously, because macro-based malware delivered in office documents is still a very common attack vector. Setting macro security to disable unsigned or external macros by default directly mitigates that risk.

You can see how these ideas play out in a simple scenario. Imagine a user whose system keeps accumulating unwanted browser toolbars, search hijackers, and "system optimizer" tools after visits to questionable download sites. If you only clear the browser cache or reset the homepage, the problem will return. Effective mitigation would mean uninstalling the questionable software completely, resetting the browser to default, converting the user to a standard (non-admin) account so they cannot install arbitrary programs so easily, and tightening browser security settings. In one incident, you combine removal of current threats, hardening to prevent recurrence, and user guidance—all fundamental to mitigation.

Accounts and access: controlling who can do what

Even the most hardened system is not secure if anyone who reaches the keyboard can log in and do anything they like. **Access control** is the set of techniques used to ensure that the right people have the right permissions at the right time. At the workstation level, this begins with how you structure user accounts and continues through how you handle authentication and account lifecycle events.

A key idea you will encounter repeatedly is the **principle of least privilege**. In plain language, it means giving users only the access rights they need to do their job and nothing more. On a Windows desktop, that usually translates into standard user accounts for everyday work, with administrative rights used sparingly for tasks that truly require them. When a user runs as local administrator all the time, any malware they encounter also runs as administrator, with the ability to install itself system-wide, tamper with security tools, or modify critical settings. Many exam scenarios subtly hinge on this point: if malware was able to install drivers or change operating system files without resistance, you should suspect that the user had excessive privileges and that part of mitigation will be to correct that.

Authentication practices form another important layer. Strong password policies are the baseline in most organizations. As a technician, you do not design those rules, but you will help enforce them. You will ensure that password length and complexity settings are applied through group policy or local security settings, that account lockout thresholds are configured to slow down brute-force attacks, and that passwords are changed when policy requires it. More importantly, you will handle password resets, which is a social engineering hotspot. Secure behavior here means verifying the user's identity through approved procedures—such as callback to a known number, presentation of ID, or internal HR verification—before resetting a password, and never sharing one account's credentials between multiple people for convenience.

Increasingly, organizations rely on **multifactor authentication (MFA)** to mitigate the risk of stolen passwords. MFA combines something you know (a password), with something you have (a token, smartphone app, or smart card), or something you are (a biometric like a fingerprint). At the A+ level, your job is usually to help users enroll new devices, troubleshoot authentication app issues, or explain why logging in now requires an extra step. Linking this back to threats, MFA is one of the most effective countermeasures against phishing-based credential theft, because an attacker who steals a password still cannot log in without the second factor.

Managing accounts over their entire lifecycle is also part of mitigation. When an employee leaves the company or moves to a different role, their accounts should not linger with full access. Proper mitigation means promptly disabling their user account, revoking VPN tokens, and removing them from sensitive groups. Disabling rather than deleting accounts is often preferred, because it preserves logs and file ownership for investigation or handoff while preventing further access. Built-in guest accounts are typically disabled for the same reason: they are anonymous, cannot be tied to a specific person, and bypass the accountability that comes from named individual accounts.

Consider a case where HR informs you that a terminated employee still appears as "connected" in a VPN session report. That is a clear access control failure. Your immediate mitigation steps would be to disable the user's domain and VPN accounts, verify that any tokens or authentication apps are deactivated, and then coordinate with HR or security for further review. The technical actions—disabling accounts and revoking access—are what directly reduce the risk of an insider continuing to connect after departure.

Endpoint protection: guarding the device in real time

Hardening and access control reduce many risks, but you still need tools that actively watch for and stop threats as they occur. **Endpoint protection** is the collective name for software such as antivirus, anti-malware, host firewalls, and more advanced endpoint detection and response (EDR) agents that run on individual devices.

Traditional antivirus or anti-malware tools remain a staple mitigation technique. They monitor files and processes in real time, comparing them against **signatures**—patterns of known malicious code—or using heuristic and behavioral analysis to spot suspicious activity. As a technician, you ensure that these tools are installed, that their definition databases are updating, and that real-time protection has not been disabled by the user or by malware. When a user complains of pop-ups, suspicious toolbars, or unexplained slowdowns, part of your response is to run appropriate scans—quick scans to rapidly check common infection points, and full scans to thoroughly examine the system. It is important to recognize that detection alone is not full mitigation; removing the malware is only the start, and you will often need to combine cleanup with hardening to prevent re-infection.

Many businesses now deploy comprehensive endpoint protection suites that go beyond simple virus scanning. These agents may bundle antivirus, host-based firewalls, behavior analysis, device control (such as blocking unauthorized USB storage), and integration with a central management console or security information and event management (SIEM) system. You do not need to be an expert in all these components, but you are responsible for basic health checks: confirming that the agent is installed and reporting correctly, checking local logs or tray icons for alerts, and verifying that users have not disabled protections in an attempt to "speed up" their devices.

The host firewall component deserves special attention. A **host firewall** runs on the endpoint itself and monitors inbound and outbound network connections. On Windows systems, you will see different profiles—private, public, and domain networks—each of which applies different rules. On a public Wi-Fi network, for example, the firewall should default to a more restrictive stance, blocking unsolicited inbound connections that could be used to probe or attack the device. When a user calls from a hotel complaining that their firewall is off and asking if it is safe to leave it that way "just to get online," the mitigation answer is clear: re-enable the firewall immediately, then troubleshoot connectivity within that secure baseline. Turning off fundamental protections to "fix" a problem almost always increases risk rather than resolving the underlying issue.

Network and remote access: protecting the path

So far, the focus has been on individual devices and the people using them. Mitigation also has to address the paths over which data travels. Many of the attack vectors you studied—man-in-the-middle attacks, eavesdropping, session hijacking—depend on weaknesses in network and remote access configurations that you will often help implement and support.

Wireless networks are one of the easiest places to see this. An **open** Wi-Fi network, with no password, transmits traffic in cleartext, making it trivial for an attacker on the same network to capture unencrypted data. Using strong Wi-Fi encryption such as WPA2 or WPA3 is a basic mitigation. In small environments, that might mean WPA2-Personal with a strong pre-shared key; in enterprises, WPA2-Enterprise or WPA3-Enterprise with user-specific credentials and a RADIUS backend. You do not have to design the authentication infrastructure for the A+ exam, but you should be able to recognize that "open Wi-Fi" and "WEP-secured Wi-Fi" are indicators of poor security, whereas modern WPA2/WPA3 configurations are the default choice for mitigating wireless eavesdropping and unauthorized access.

Remote access is another area where secure configuration matters. Tools like Remote Desktop Protocol (RDP), VNC, and various remote support solutions are essential for managing systems and assisting users, but they are also prime targets for attackers who scan the internet for exposed remote login services. Safe practice requires that these services use encrypted channels, require strong authentication, and are not left directly open to the internet without additional protections such as VPNs or secure gateways. When a user asks you to "just leave RDP open on my workstation so I can get in from home," they are asking you to create an attack surface that is widely abused by brute-force tools and credential-stuffing attacks. Mitigation, in this case, means explaining that remote access should be done through a VPN connection to the corporate network or via an approved remote access gateway, keeping RDP closed to the broader internet.

VPNs themselves act as an important mitigation technique, especially for remote workers. A **virtual private network** creates an encrypted tunnel between a user's device and the organization's network over an untrusted medium like public Wi-Fi. When configured and used correctly, this mitigates many forms of interception and tampering. As a support technician, you will assist users with installing VPN clients, configuring server addresses and authentication methods, and verifying that they connect successfully. If a user reports that their VPN is not working on airport Wi-Fi and proudly tells you they disabled the firewall and antivirus to "get around it," you can see how deeply mitigation and troubleshooting are intertwined. You would guide them to re-enable host protections, verify the network they have joined is the legitimate airport SSID and not an evil twin, and then work through VPN client logs or captive portal steps without sacrificing core protections.

Data protection and technician-level containment

No matter how well you harden systems, manage accounts, deploy endpoint tools, and secure networks, you can never drive risk to zero. Devices will still fail, users will still lose laptops, someone will eventually click the wrong link. Mitigation therefore has to include strategies that limit the damage when prevention fails.

Data protection begins with **backups**. From a mitigation perspective, a backup is not just a copy of data; it is a tested ability to restore that data after loss or corruption. You will encounter various backup schemes—full, incremental, differential—but what matters most at the A+ level is that backups occur regularly, are stored in a way that is not easily affected by the same incident (such as offline or off-site), and can actually be restored when needed. In a ransomware scenario, for example, having recent, offline backups can mean the difference between paying a ransom for decryption keys and simply wiping affected systems and restoring from clean copies. Technicians contribute by configuring backup clients on workstations, verifying that scheduled jobs succeed, and performing periodic test restores so that the first restore attempt does not happen in the middle of a crisis.

Encryption is another crucial mitigation tool, especially for mobile devices and laptops that are easily lost or stolen. **Disk encryption** technologies such as BitLocker on Windows or FileVault on macOS encrypt the contents of the drive so that, without the proper authentication, the data is unreadable even if the physical drive is removed and attached to another system. At your level, you will often be the one enabling encryption according to organizational policy, ensuring that recovery keys are backed up to a secure location like Active Directory or an MDM platform, and educating users about why bypassing encryption—by, for example, storing sensitive data on unencrypted external drives—is not acceptable. To relate this to a real situation, imagine a sales representative's laptop containing customer information is stolen from their car. If the drive was properly encrypted and protected by strong authentication, the incident is largely a hardware loss. If not, it may become a reportable data breach with serious legal and reputational consequences.

Finally, mitigation involves what you do the moment you suspect something is wrong. While full incident response processes are covered elsewhere, there are technician-level containment actions that are both exam-relevant and critical in practice. If you believe a workstation has been compromised by malware or is participating in an active attack, one of the most effective immediate steps is to isolate it from the network—disconnect the Ethernet cable, turn off Wi-Fi, or use a network isolation feature in your endpoint agent. This reduces the attacker's ability to move laterally or exfiltrate data. At the same time, you should avoid overreacting in ways that destroy evidence, such as reimaging the system or deleting logs without approval, especially in organizations with formal incident response teams. Your role is often to contain, document what you observed and what you did, and escalate according to procedure.

Throughout all of these mitigation techniques, you are constantly balancing security, usability, and customer service. Users will often push back against restrictions that slow them down or require extra steps. Your effectiveness as a professional depends not only on knowing which settings to configure but also on being able to explain, in plain language, why those measures are necessary and on finding secure ways to meet business needs rather than taking insecure shortcuts. When you encounter exam questions with two answers that both seem functional, look for the one that aligns with this mindset: least privilege over convenience, secure defaults over ad-hoc exceptions, containment and escalation over quick but incomplete fixes.

Knowledge Check

Question 1: A technician wants to reduce the chance that malware can automatically execute when users plug in USB flash drives. Which mitigation step best addresses this risk on Windows workstations?

A. Enabling guest accounts for temporary users
B. Allowing users to run as local administrators
C. Disabling the host firewall on public networks
D. Disabling AutoPlay/autorun for removable media

Question 2: A support technician is configuring user accounts on new laptops. To follow the principle of least privilege while still allowing software installations when needed, how should the accounts be set up?

A. Create standard user accounts for daily work and use admin credentials only when required
B. Make all users local administrators so they can install needed tools
C. Use a single shared local administrator account for multiple users
D. Enable the built-in guest account for users who need occasional access

Question 3: A salesperson's company laptop containing sensitive client data is stolen from a car. Which preexisting mitigation control would most effectively ensure the data remains protected even if the drive is removed from the laptop?

A. Daily quick antivirus scans
B. A host-based firewall blocking inbound connections
C. Strong password complexity requirements
D. Full-disk encryption such as BitLocker or FileVault

Question 4: An organization wants to improve wireless security on its office Wi-Fi network. Which configuration provides a stronger mitigation against unauthorized access than an open or WEP-secured network?

A. Leaving the SSID hidden but using no encryption
B. Using WPA2 or WPA3 with strong authentication
C. Using MAC address filtering without encryption
D. Lowering the transmit power of the access point

Question 5: A remote user on hotel Wi-Fi reports that their VPN client will not connect, so they disabled the host firewall and antivirus "to make it work." From a mitigation perspective, what is the most appropriate first step for the technician to direct the user to take?

A. Uninstall and reinstall the VPN client software
B. Connect to any open wireless network with a stronger signal
C. Re-enable the host firewall and endpoint protection, then troubleshoot within that baseline
D. Disable multifactor authentication to simplify the login

Question 6: A user calls the help desk asking for a password reset. To mitigate social engineering risk during this process, what should the technician do first?

- **A.** Verify the user's identity using an approved method before resetting the password
- **B.** Immediately reset the password to restore the user's access as quickly as possible
- **C.** Email the new password to the address the caller provides over the phone
- **D.** Ask the caller to share their current password to confirm their identity

Question 7: A workstation appears to be infected with malware and may be communicating with an attacker's command-and-control server. What is the most appropriate immediate technician-level mitigation action?

- **A.** Immediately reimage the workstation to a clean baseline without notifying anyone
- **B.** Isolate the workstation from the network while preserving system state and logs
- **C.** Power off the workstation by unplugging it from the wall to stop all activity
- **D.** Disable antivirus to prevent interference while the user completes urgent work

Question 8: A company wants to be able to recover quickly if user data is encrypted by ransomware. Which preparation best mitigates the impact of such an incident?

- **A.** Requiring users to change their passwords every 30 days
- **B.** Enabling AutoPlay for removable drives to streamline backups
- **C.** Allowing users to store critical files only on local unencrypted drives
- **D.** Maintaining regular, tested backups stored offline or off-site

ANSWERS

1: Correct Answer: D
Rationale: Disabling AutoPlay/autorun prevents removable media from automatically executing code, directly mitigating malware that leverages automatic execution from USB devices. The other options do not address automatic execution and can increase risk.

2: Correct Answer: A
Rationale: Least privilege means using standard accounts for daily work and elevating to admin only when needed, reducing the impact of malware or user error. Making users admins, sharing admin accounts, or using guest accounts all violate least-privilege principles.

3: Correct Answer: D
Rationale: Full-disk encryption protects data at rest; even if the laptop or drive is stolen, the data remains unreadable without the decryption key. Antivirus, firewalls, and password complexity do not prevent offline access to data on a removed drive.

4: Correct Answer: B
Rationale: WPA2/WPA3 with strong authentication provides robust encryption and access control, mitigating eavesdropping and unauthorized access. Hidden SSIDs, MAC filtering, or reduced power without encryption are easily bypassed and do not provide strong protection.

5: Correct Answer: C
Rationale: Core protections like host firewalls and endpoint security should remain enabled; the user should restore these defenses and then troubleshoot the VPN within that secure baseline. The other options either weaken security further or address the wrong problem.

6: Correct Answer: A
Rationale: Verifying identity with approved procedures before resetting passwords mitigates social engineering attempts to gain unauthorized access. Resetting immediately, emailing to an unverified address, or asking for the current password are insecure practices.

7: Correct Answer: B
Rationale: Network isolation contains the threat and prevents lateral movement or data exfiltration while preserving evidence for analysis. Reimaging or hard power-off can destroy evidence, and disabling antivirus while continuing work increases risk.

8: Correct Answer: D
Rationale: Regular, tested offline or off-site backups allow systems to be wiped and data restored without paying ransom, greatly reducing ransomware impact. Password changes, AutoPlay, and local unencrypted storage do not provide effective recovery capability.

CHAPTER 3

Architecture Models & Security Implications

3.1 Architecture Models & Security Implications

When you strip away the buzzwords and vendor marketing, architecture really comes down to two simple questions: where does the stuff live, and how do we decide whether to trust whoever is trying to use it? "Stuff" here means applications, data, and services. In a modern organization, those might be running on a server in a closet down the hall, in a hyperscale data center on the other side of the world, or split between the two. As an IT support professional, you are not expected to design these architectures from scratch, but you are absolutely expected to recognize them when you see them, understand their security habits and weaknesses, and adjust your troubleshooting and user guidance accordingly.

A good way to orient yourself in any scenario is to pause and mentally ask three quick questions. First, **where are the resources located**—are the key systems and data on local servers, in a cloud service, or in both? Second, **how do users connect** to those resources—over the local network, via a VPN, directly over the Internet, or through some conditional access system? Third, **who controls which security settings**—is the organization responsible for everything, or are some layers handled by a cloud provider? Once you train yourself to see those three dimensions, you'll find that many exam scenarios almost solve themselves. The architecture clues tell you where the likely failure points are, whose security responsibilities are in play, and which controls make the most sense to recommend.

On-premises architecture: everything in your own house

The classic model most people picture when they think "IT department" is the **on-premises** environment. Imagine a small company in a single building with a locked server room in the back. In that room, you'd see domain controllers providing Active Directory, a file server with shared folders, a print server, maybe an internal web application server, and a rack of switches and a firewall. Most employees work on desktops or laptops that rarely leave the office, and those devices are joined to the domain so group policies can manage their settings. Users access almost everything over the local area network, and if someone needs to work from home, they start a VPN client that "tunnels" them into the internal network first.

That setup has an intuitive appeal: if the servers are in your building, behind your locks and network gear, it feels like you have full control. From a security perspective, there are real advantages. The organization decides who can physically enter the server room. The IT team chooses how to configure the operating systems, what host-based firewalls to run, which antivirus product to deploy, and how to segment the internal network using VLANs and internal firewalls. If finance data needs to be isolated, you can literally put those servers on their own subnet and restrict which workstations can talk to them. Nothing is exposed directly to the Internet unless you intentionally open it up.

Control, however, always comes with responsibility. In an on-premises architecture, the organization owns almost every security task end to end. If domain controllers, file servers, and endpoints are not patched regularly, there is no provider in the background quietly doing that for you; those unpatched systems turn into attractive targets for attackers. If the only domain controller is in that single server room and the power fails or a disk dies and there's no redundancy, the entire company might lose the ability to log in or access data. If the building floods and wipes out the server rack, and no one ever configured off-site or cloud backups, that "local control" turns into catastrophic data loss.

On-premises environments are also more exposed to **insider threats** and physical issues. A disgruntled employee with a keycard and enough permissions can delete shared folders, disable accounts, or plug unauthorized devices into the network. Even well-intentioned staff can do damage by copying confidential data to unencrypted USB drives or accidentally changing group memberships. It is easy to fall into the trap of thinking "inside the network is safe," which leads to weak internal access controls and too much trust attached to a device being on the LAN.

For an A+-level technician, this environment defines a lot of your daily work. You will join endpoints to the domain and check that the correct group policies—password complexity rules, screen lock timers, software restrictions—are being applied. You will help users connect VPN clients when they are remote, and you'll immediately recognize that if the VPN is down, access to internal file shares and line-of-business apps will usually fail. You will field access requests for shared folders and printers, and you need to understand why "give everyone full control" is not an acceptable solution. In an on-prem world, enforcing **least privilege** really does mean carefully checking which group has which file permissions and explaining to employees that broad, unrestricted access is a security risk, not a perk.

Cloud architecture: someone else's data center, your configuration

At the other end of the spectrum is **cloud architecture**. Here, the servers and storage are no longer in your building. Instead, they live in data centers owned by providers like Microsoft, Google, Amazon, or any number of SaaS vendors. The practical face of this, at the A+ level, is usually software-as-a-service. Users open a browser or a dedicated client to access Microsoft 365, Google Workspace, a CRM system, or cloud storage. They sign in with an account, and behind the scenes the provider's infrastructure handles the computing, storage, and much of the underlying security.

A common misconception is that "it's in the cloud, so the provider handles security." The reality is more nuanced and appears on Security+ as the **shared responsibility model**. The provider secures the physical data centers, the hypervisors, the core network infrastructure, and often the base operating systems of the service. They keep their environment patched, control access to the physical hardware, and usually offer secure protocols such as HTTPS/TLS by default. But the customer—the organization using the service—controls and is responsible for security decisions **in** that cloud environment: user accounts and passwords, multi-factor authentication settings, group and role assignments, whether data is shared publicly or internally, and sometimes the configuration of virtual networks or firewalls when using infrastructure-as-a-service.

Once you view it that way, a lot of real-world incidents make more sense. If a company's Microsoft 365 mailbox is compromised because the user chose "Password123!" and the administrator disabled MFA for convenience, that is not Microsoft failing to secure their platform. The weakness is in the customer's configuration choices. Similarly, if someone creates a shared cloud storage folder and uses "anyone with the link can view" for sensitive financial documents, and those links leak, that is again a customer misconfiguration, not a cloud infrastructure breach.

Cloud services do bring real security benefits. You don't have to worry about replacing aging server hardware or manually patching an Exchange server every month, because the provider does that for the backend. Data is often replicated across availability zones, so a single disk or server failure does not take the service down. Users can connect from virtually anywhere with an Internet connection, typically over encrypted sessions. For small organizations especially, moving email and collaboration to the cloud can instantly improve uptime and baseline security compared to a single under-maintained on-premises server in a closet.

The new risks are mostly about identity and configuration. Accounts are reachable from anywhere on the Internet, which makes them attractive targets for phishing and credential stuffing. Weak passwords, lack of MFA, and over-permissive sharing become much more dangerous. Because users often access SaaS services through a browser, malware that steals cookies or saved passwords can directly compromise cloud accounts. Another subtle risk is data resilience: many organizations assume their cloud data is automatically backed up forever, but in practice a deleted mailbox or file may only be recoverable for a limited time unless separate backup or retention policies are configured.

As a support technician, your responsibilities shift from maintaining local servers to managing identity and settings in admin consoles. You help users enroll in MFA, reset passwords, and recover locked accounts. You check that a user is in the right Azure AD or Google Workspace group to receive the correct licenses and permissions. When someone complains they cannot see a shared document, you check the cloud sharing settings rather than local NTFS permissions. You are also the one who has to explain, in simple terms, why they cannot just disable MFA to "make things easier," and how cloud access from any device, anywhere, means the organization must be stricter about account security.

Hybrid architecture: the messy middle ground

Most organizations do not flip from pure on-prem to pure cloud overnight. Instead, they live in a **hybrid architecture**, where some workloads remain on-premises and others are in the cloud. A very typical pattern is to keep legacy line-of-business applications and large file shares on local servers while moving email, office productivity, and collaboration into a SaaS platform. Identity often bridges both worlds: an on-premises Active Directory remains the primary directory, and tools such as Azure AD Connect synchronize accounts and passwords to a cloud identity service like Microsoft Entra ID. A user might log into their Windows laptop with domain credentials, then use that same username and password—now synchronized—to access cloud apps.

Hybrid architectures introduce more moving parts, and with them, more places where security can go wrong. There are now at least two environments to secure and monitor: the on-prem network and systems, and the cloud services. Integration points—VPNs from the corporate office to the cloud, directory synchronization agents, single sign-on configurations—have to be hardened, updated, and monitored just like any other critical component. Policies also need to be consistent. It is confusing and risky if on-premises policies demand 15-character passwords but the cloud policies allow eight-character ones, or if group membership controls access to on-prem file shares but separate, unaligned roles govern access to cloud storage.

The flip side is that hybrid gives organizations flexibility. Very sensitive systems can remain under direct on-prem control, perhaps even segmented onto isolated networks, while less sensitive or more collaborative services can take advantage of cloud scalability and resilience. From a security transformation standpoint, hybrid is often a stepping-stone: an organization can implement modern identity protections like MFA and conditional access for cloud services first, then gradually extend those concepts back into the on-prem environment.

For you as a technician, hybrid mainly means you must think in two directions at once when troubleshooting. If a remote user reports that they can open their cloud email and CRM but cannot access the project shared drive, you immediately suspect that the share lives on an on-prem file server and requires a VPN connection, even though the cloud services do not. If a user's login fails only in cloud apps but works fine at the Windows logon screen, you recognize that the problem might lie in the synchronization process or cloud account configuration, not in the on-prem domain controller. You also need to know where to check for different things: some group memberships are managed in local AD, while license assignments and cloud-app-specific roles live in a SaaS admin portal.

Zero trust: never trust, always verify

Overlaying all of these architectures is a modern security philosophy called **zero trust**. Zero trust is not a specific product or a magic switch you can flip; it is a way of designing access that assumes no user, device, or network segment is trusted by default. Being "on the internal network" or "inside the VPN" is no longer considered adequate proof that something should be allowed. Instead, every access request is evaluated based on who the user is, how they are authenticating, what device they are on, where they are located, and what they are trying to reach. The system asks: should this specific combination be allowed, and if so, with how much privilege?

You have already seen pieces of zero trust in day-to-day tools. When a user gets an MFA prompt every time they access email from a new device, that is zero trust in action: identity is re-verified beyond just a password. When a cloud service blocks a login attempt from a country your company never does business in, even though the username and password are correct, that is a **conditional access policy** enforcing location-based rules. When a mobile device management (MDM) system refuses to let a laptop connect to corporate resources because its operating system is out of date or its disk is not encrypted, that is a **device compliance** check aligned with zero trust. Even network design can reflect zero trust through micro-segmentation: separating guest Wi-Fi, IoT devices, servers, and workstations onto different VLANs with tight firewall rules between them, so compromise in one area does not easily spread.

The security benefits are substantial. Password theft, which used to be enough to break into many systems, is blunted by MFA and behavioral checks. Malware that compromises a single workstation has a harder time moving laterally if internal systems do not automatically trust each other, and if admin privileges are tightly limited. Frequent verification and logging of access attempts produce a rich trail of data that security teams can analyze for anomalies. This is why many organizations are willing to accept a bit more friction in the user experience: a few extra prompts or restrictions in exchange for greatly reduced risk of large-scale breaches.

From the user's point of view, zero trust can feel like the network "doesn't like them" anymore. They may be prompted for MFA when they are traveling, blocked from logging in from personal devices, or told that their home PC is "non-compliant" and therefore cannot access certain resources. That frustration often lands in your queue. Supporting users in a zero trust environment requires you to understand not just that access was denied, but why. Was it a device compliance failure that can be resolved by enrolling the device and enabling disk encryption? Was it a location-based block that requires use of a corporate VPN to appear from an allowed IP range? Was it a conditional access policy requiring MFA enrollment?

Communicating the "why" is just as important as fixing the immediate issue. When a sales employee complains about being forced to use an authenticator app for cloud email, you need to explain in plain language that their mailbox is accessible from any web browser in the world, and that simple passwords are too easy to steal. Position MFA and conditional access as protections for them and their customers, not arbitrary barriers. When a remote engineer forgets to start the VPN and then cannot reach an on-prem project share, you can use that moment to reinforce the idea that different resources live in different places and may require different security paths: cloud apps over the Internet with identity-based controls, and internal file servers over a secure tunnel.

Whether the resources are on-premises, in the cloud, or spread across both, and whether the organization has fully embraced zero trust or is just starting to move that direction, your value as a technician comes from being able to look at any scenario and quickly orient yourself. Where does this application or data actually reside? How is the user supposed to reach it? Which security controls should be in play at that boundary—VPN, MFA, conditional access, group policies, or some combination? Once those questions become second nature, you are not just clicking buttons; you are thinking like a security-aware professional operating within whatever architecture the organization has chosen.

Knowledge Check

Question 1: A technician is supporting a small organization where all servers are in a locked room onsite, users primarily access resources over the LAN, and remote users must start a VPN client before reaching internal file shares. From a security responsibility perspective, what is MOST true of this environment?

- **A.** The cloud provider patches all servers, but the organization manages endpoint security.
- **B.** The ISP is responsible for firewall configuration and access control lists.
- **C.** The organization is responsible for nearly all security tasks from endpoints to servers and network devices.
- **D.** Security responsibilities are evenly split between the ISP, hardware vendors, and the organization.

Question 2: A company moves its email and collaboration platform to a SaaS provider but keeps legacy file servers and a line-of-business app in its data center. Users log on to Windows with domain credentials and then access cloud apps with the same username and password, which are synchronized. What architecture model does this BEST describe?

- **A.** Pure on-premises
- **B.** Community cloud
- **C.** Multitenant SaaS only
- **D.** Hybrid

Question 3: In a cloud environment following the shared responsibility model, which task is typically the CUSTOMER's responsibility rather than the provider's?

A. Enforcing multi-factor authentication and appropriate role assignments for users
B. Patching the underlying hypervisors
C. Securing physical access to the data center
D. Maintaining power and cooling for the server hardware

Question 4: A user can access their cloud-based email and CRM from home without a VPN, but cannot open the organization's shared project drive unless connected to the corporate VPN. What is the MOST likely explanation?

A. The cloud provider is blocking SMB traffic from external IP addresses.
B. The user's MFA token has expired for all cloud services.
C. The user's device is out of compliance with the MDM policy.
D. The shared drive is hosted on an on-prem file server that is only reachable over the internal network or VPN.

Question 5: In an on-premises architecture, which risk is MOST directly associated with over-trusting anything "inside the network"?

A. Increased dependency on cloud provider misconfigurations
B. Weak internal access controls that can be abused by insiders or compromised devices
C. Excessive reliance on MFA and conditional access policies
D. Lack of Internet connectivity for external partners

Question 6: A security analyst notices that a user's login from an unfamiliar foreign country is blocked, even though the correct username and password were used. The organization has not changed any firewall rules, but a cloud identity service is enforcing location-based policies. Which security approach does this behavior MOST closely reflect?

A. Perimeter-only defense relying on network firewalls
B. Single sign-on without additional controls
C. Zero trust with conditional access evaluating context for each request
D. Air-gapped network segmentation based on VLANs alone

Question 7: A user complains they are being forced to enroll in an authenticator app before accessing a cloud storage service that can be reached from any browser worldwide. From a security perspective, what is the BEST explanation a technician should provide?

A. MFA is needed to protect against stolen or guessed passwords.
B. The authenticator app is required only for on-prem file shares.
C. The authenticator app is needed because on-prem networks are inherently untrusted.
D. The authenticator app replaces the need for passwords entirely.

Question 8: An organization is adopting a zero trust model. Which change BEST aligns with this philosophy?

A. Allowing all devices on the internal LAN to access every server without additional checks
B. Disabling VPN access and relying solely on perimeter firewalls
C. Trusting any device that has previously connected successfully to the network
D. Requiring device compliance checks and MFA before granting access to sensitive resources, even from internal networks

ANSWERS

1: Correct Answer: C

Rationale: This is an on-premises environment with VPN for remote access. The organization owns and manages physical security, servers, network devices, and endpoints, so it is responsible for nearly all security tasks. ISPs and vendors provide services and hardware but do not manage day-to-day security.

2: Correct Answer: D

Rationale: Some services (email, collaboration) are in the cloud while others (file servers, line-of-business app) remain on-prem, with synchronized identities. This mix of cloud and on-prem resources is a hybrid architecture.

3: Correct Answer: A

Rationale: Under the shared responsibility model, the provider secures physical facilities and core infrastructure, while the customer secures identities, MFA, and role assignments. Physical security and hypervisor patching are provider tasks; power and cooling are also provider responsibilities.

4: Correct Answer: D

Rationale: Cloud apps are exposed securely over the Internet, so they are reachable without VPN. Traditional shared drives on on-prem file servers are usually only routable on the internal network, so a VPN is required to access them remotely.

5: Correct Answer: B

Rationale: Assuming everything inside the LAN is trusted often leads to weak internal controls and flat networks. This increases the risk that insiders or compromised devices can move laterally and abuse access to internal resources.

6: Correct Answer: C

Rationale: Blocking a login based on location and other context, even with correct credentials, reflects zero trust with conditional access. It goes beyond perimeter firewalls or basic SSO by evaluating each request's risk.

7: Correct Answer: A

Rationale: A cloud storage account is reachable globally, so if a password is stolen or guessed, an attacker could log in from anywhere. MFA via an authenticator app adds a second factor, significantly reducing this risk.

8: Correct Answer: D

Rationale: Zero trust's "never trust, always verify" approach requires continuous checks such as device compliance and MFA, even for internal users accessing sensitive resources. The other options maintain implicit trust in the internal network.

3.2 Infrastructure Security Design

When most people think about security, they picture alarms going off, malware alerts popping up, or someone frantically trying to remove a virus. In real environments, the most effective security work happens long before anything goes wrong. It happens when someone decides where to place the router, how to configure the wireless network, which settings to leave at their defaults, and which ones to lock down. For an entry-level technician, this is the day-to-day reality of security: you are often the person physically plugging things in and clicking through those "quick setup" wizards. The choices you make in those moments either build a resilient, well-segmented environment or leave an attacker with a straight path to everything.

A useful mindset is to keep two questions in your head whenever you touch infrastructure. First, if this system is compromised, what else can be reached from here? Second, if a user or device does not truly need an access path, can I remove it or at least restrict it? Those questions connect directly to the principles you saw earlier: **least privilege**, **segmentation**, and **defense in depth**. Least privilege pushes you to give each user and device only the access it needs to do its job, nothing more. Segmentation encourages you to break your network into zones so that a problem in one zone does not automatically become a problem everywhere. Defense in depth reminds you that no single protection is perfect, so you layer controls at the perimeter, on the network, and on each host.

From Simple SOHO Networks to Layered Designs

It helps to begin with something familiar: a typical small office/home office network. You have an ISP modem, often combined with a basic router provided by the service provider. Behind that you usually see a **SOHO router** that combines router, switch, firewall, and wireless access point in one box. Everything—desktops, laptops, phones, smart TVs, printers—connects either by Ethernet or Wi-Fi to that single device. Out of the box, the router might have a default admin username and password, a default Wi-Fi network name, and a single wireless network that everyone uses. In far too many environments, nobody changes those defaults.

On the surface, this seems to work fine. Machines get on the internet, email flows, streaming services play. But from a security perspective, this typical flat design has several weaknesses. With one undivided LAN, every device can try to talk to every other device. If an attacker compromises one weak link—say, an unpatched smart TV or a guest's infected laptop—they can scan the rest of the network, probe the shared NAS that holds company files, or try to reach management interfaces. The router's built-in firewall blocks unsolicited traffic from the outside, but it does almost nothing to control what happens inside the LAN. This is where design decisions matter: you want to shape the network so that internal compromise is harder to achieve and easier to contain.

Strengthening the perimeter is usually the first step. The edge router or firewall should still provide **NAT** and stateful packet filtering, blocking unsolicited inbound connections from the internet. However, you also need to remove the easy paths an attacker can use to bypass that protection. Changing the default router admin username and password is a basic but critical control. Leaving them at "admin/admin" or "admin/password" means that any attacker who can reach the management interface—especially if remote administration is enabled from the internet—has an open door. Disabling unnecessary remote administration is just as important. Many consumer routers expose their management page to the WAN so the owner can "log in from anywhere." That convenience means that anyone on the internet can try common passwords or exploit known vulnerabilities in the router's firmware if it is not up to date.

Imagine an exam question that describes a SOHO router with remote management enabled, default credentials left in place, and no firmware updates applied. The primary risk here is not that local users might abuse the router, but that someone on the internet could log in directly, change DNS settings to redirect traffic, open inbound ports, or even join the internal network through VPN-like features. Recognizing that risk leads directly to the recommended changes: unique admin credentials, remote management disabled or tightly restricted, and firmware updated to close known holes.

Once the perimeter is reasonably hardened, the next step is to stop thinking of the internal side as a single flat space. Instead, you begin to separate devices and services into logical zones based on their risk and trust level.

Segmentation: DMZs, Guest Networks, and VLANs

Segmentation sounds like an advanced enterprise topic, but in practice you use it any time you create a **guest Wi-Fi** separate from your main network. The idea is simple: untrusted or less-trusted devices—such as visitors' phones or a smart TV—should not sit in the same broadcast domain as your workstations and file servers. Many SOHO routers provide an option to enable a guest network with isolation. When this is turned on, devices on that guest SSID can reach the internet but are prevented from accessing computers and shares on the main LAN. Some models also implement "AP isolation," which stops guests from talking to each other. That way, if a friend's laptop is infected when they join your guest network, it cannot start probing your office PC or the NAS holding client data.

In small businesses that host public-facing servers, you will sometimes encounter a **DMZ**, or demilitarized zone. Conceptually, a DMZ is a separate network segment where you place systems that must be reachable from the internet, such as web servers or mail gateways, while keeping them away from the internal LAN. In a simple implementation, the perimeter firewall or router has one interface connected to the ISP, another interface for the internal LAN, and a third for the DMZ. Firewall rules allow inbound web traffic from the internet to the web server in the DMZ, and limited or no direct access from the DMZ to the internal LAN. If the public web server is compromised, the attacker still does not automatically gain full access to internal accounting systems and workstations.

In exam scenarios, students often mix up DMZs with other forms of segmentation, especially **VLANs**. A VLAN, or virtual LAN, is a way to create logically separate networks on the same physical switch infrastructure. Devices in different VLANs act as though they are on different switches; they cannot talk to each other directly unless a router or layer-3 device forwards traffic between them. In a small office, you might place all employee PCs on one VLAN, IoT devices such as cameras and smart TVs on another, and perhaps management systems on a third. The important distinction is that a DMZ is about isolating public-facing servers from your internal environment, while VLANs are a more general tool to carve up internal traffic. In many real networks, a DMZ is implemented using VLANs plus firewall rules, but on the exam you want to keep the purpose of each clear in your mind.

Guest networks fit in the same family of ideas but serve a different purpose. Where a DMZ protects the internal LAN from internet-facing servers, a guest network protects the internal LAN from untrusted users. Patients in a clinic, clients in a law office, or friends visiting your house fall into this category. You expose the guest network only to the internet, not to your server shares, printers, or management consoles. Understanding which zone each device belongs in—internal LAN, guest, or DMZ—often leads you to the most secure design option offered in a question.

Wireless Design and Its Security Tradeoffs

Wireless networks are where many environments first show weakness. Configuring Wi-Fi is often treated as a convenience step—pick a name, set a password, and move on—but wireless choices have major security implications. The encryption mode is your starting point. Modern best practice is to use **WPA3-Personal** where available, falling back to **WPA2-PSK with AES** when needed for compatibility. Older options like WEP or original WPA are considered broken and should be avoided. Some access points offer "mixed" modes that support both old and new clients; while convenient, these modes may weaken security by allowing legacy protocols.

In smaller environments, most wireless networks use a pre-shared key. Everyone who needs access enters the same passphrase. That model is simple, but it also means that if a visitor learns your staff Wi-Fi password, they can join the same network as sensitive systems. For larger organizations, an enterprise mode that uses RADIUS and individual accounts is preferred, but that is beyond what you will configure day-to-day as an A+ technician. What you should recognize on the exam is the relative strength of encryption schemes: WPA3 or WPA2-AES is hard to crack with current methods, whereas WEP and open networks are trivial to exploit.

SSID design introduces another dimension. Using a single SSID for everything—staff laptops, guest devices, IoT hardware—makes management simple but security poor. A more secure pattern is to have at least two SSIDs: one "main" network for trusted, managed devices and another for guests and other untrusted equipment. Many SOHO access points allow you to map each SSID to a different internal network or VLAN. When properly configured, the guest SSID becomes its own segment with internet-only access. Some administrators attempt to hide their SSID, thinking that if the network name is not broadcast, attackers will not see it. This is mostly **security by obscurity**. Wireless tools can easily discover hidden SSIDs by watching the traffic when legitimate devices connect. On the exam, answers that rely on hiding SSIDs instead of using real encryption and segmentation are usually wrong or, at best, incomplete.

Physical and radio placement of wireless access points also has a security angle. If you place an AP in a front window with maximum transmit power, your network may be available from the parking lot or the street. For many small businesses, it is better to position APs more centrally and, when possible, adjust transmit power so that signal strength falls off outside the building. You cannot make the signal vanish at the property line, but you can avoid projecting an unnecessarily strong beacon for attackers. Again, this is not your primary defense—that is still strong encryption and good segmentation—but it narrows the coverage footprint.

Finally, remember that the wireless router or AP is itself a device needing protection. Its **management interface** should use strong, unique credentials that are distinct from any Wi-Fi passphrase. Firmware updates should be applied periodically to close vulnerabilities, particularly because routers are a common target for mass exploitation campaigns. Some organizations restrict management access to wired connections or a specific management VLAN so that regular wireless users cannot even reach the admin page. From an A+ perspective, you should at least recognize that allowing management over the internet on plain HTTP with default credentials is a highly insecure design, while restricting it to HTTPS on the internal network with strong credentials is much better.

Endpoints as Part of the Infrastructure

It is easy to think of infrastructure as just the routers, switches, and access points, but every workstation, laptop, smartphone, and printer is part of the security surface. The network design can limit where an attacker can move, but if endpoints are misconfigured, they can still be taken over easily. Organizations increasingly rely on **secure baselines** for endpoints: standardized, approved configurations that all machines of a particular type should have. A baseline might specify that the operating system must be fully patched with automatic updates enabled, that a **host firewall** must run with specific rules in place, that unnecessary services and startup programs are disabled, and that an approved antivirus or endpoint detection agent is installed and kept current.

When you deploy new machines according to a baseline, you reduce guesswork and inconsistencies. If every laptop leaves the help desk with updates applied, firewall enabled, local administrator accounts restricted, and endpoint protection running, it becomes much harder for routine malware to establish itself or spread. This is where **defense in depth** shows up at the host level. The network firewall at the perimeter filters unwanted inbound traffic, but the host firewall protects the device even when it is away from the office on public Wi-Fi. If a user takes a laptop to a coffee shop, the office router's firewall no longer shields it; the only line of defense is what runs on the device itself.

Distinguishing between network and host firewalls is a frequent exam theme. A **network firewall** sits between networks—typically between your LAN and the internet, or between VLANs—and makes decisions about traffic passing through. A **host firewall** runs on a single device, deciding which inbound and outbound connections to allow for that host. You rarely choose "one or the other." Proper design uses both. If an attacker compromises a machine inside the network, the network firewall might not block the lateral traffic they generate, because from the firewall's perspective it is just internal-to-internal communication. The host firewalls on the potential targets, however, can still deny unexpected inbound connections, slowing or stopping lateral movement.

Placement of shared resources also plays a role in infrastructure security. A file server or NAS holding sensitive documents should not sit on the same easily accessible guest segment as untrusted devices. Externally, a NAS should never be directly reachable from the internet with open ports unless it is behind an appropriate firewall and configured for secure remote access. Internally, you should configure file shares with appropriate permissions rather than simply granting "Everyone: Full Control." Even in small offices, it is common to see printers or "all-in-one" devices that ship with web-based management interfaces. Leaving those on the default password and placing them on segments visible to guests can allow anyone to access print jobs, change fax forwarding numbers, or pivot deeper into the network through vulnerabilities in the embedded firmware.

IoT devices deserve special suspicion. Security cameras, smart thermostats, televisions, and similar gear often run minimal, rarely updated operating systems. Treat them as less trustworthy. In many designs, you place them on a dedicated VLAN or on a guest-like network isolated from your business-critical hosts. If a camera needs to upload footage to a cloud service, you allow that outbound connection while still blocking direct access to your internal servers. The exam often tests this reasoning indirectly: if a scenario describes smart lighting and surveillance devices sharing a network with finance systems, you should recognize segmentation as an important improvement.

Remote Access and Management Paths

Modern environments almost always require some form of remote access, whether for employees working from home or for administrators managing devices. At an A+ level, you should understand the difference between using a **VPN** and exposing remote desktop services or management interfaces directly to the internet. A VPN creates an encrypted tunnel from the remote user's device into the internal network. Once connected, the user behaves (from the network's point of view) as if they are physically on the LAN, and internal firewalls and access controls still apply. This is typically the safer approach for remote work.

By contrast, some small offices configure port forwarding on their router, mapping an external port to an internal computer's **Remote Desktop Protocol (RDP)** port. This means that anyone on the internet can attempt to reach the login prompt of that internal machine. Even with strong passwords, direct RDP exposure is a frequent target for brute-force attacks and exploits. A better design is to require VPN access first, then allow RDP only from inside. When you see an exam scenario describing RDP open to the world via port forwarding, you should think "high risk" and consider answers that move remote access behind a VPN or at least limit the source addresses that can connect.

In the same way, network device management should not be broadly exposed. Ideally, routers, switches, and access points are administered only from internal, trusted networks, or from a management VLAN that ordinary users cannot reach. When remote administration is absolutely required, it should use secure protocols such as HTTPS or SSH, not unencrypted HTTP or Telnet. Knowing those protocol names is usually enough at this level; you are not expected to configure complex SSH keys, but you should be able to recognize that Telnet transmits credentials in clear text and is not appropriate for secure management.

Designing with Containment in Mind

Finally, good infrastructure design assumes that, sooner or later, something will go wrong. A workstation will be infected, an IoT device will be compromised, or an employee will fall for phishing. Your goal is not to pretend that perfect prevention is possible, but to ensure that a single failure does not become a disaster. Segmentation—whether through VLANs, DMZs, or guest networks—acts as a firebreak, limiting how far an attacker can move. Secure baselines and standardized builds make it faster to wipe and reimage a compromised machine without having to guess about what software or settings it should have. When you understand the intended layout of a secure environment, you are also in a better position to spot misconfigurations in diagrams and scenario descriptions, which is exactly what many A+ exam questions ask you to do.

Consider again the law office where the router uses default credentials, remote admin is enabled, staff and guests share one SSID, and the NAS sits on the same flat network. Simply telling them to "run antivirus" does little to fix the underlying exposure. A design-focused response changes admin credentials, disables or tightly restricts remote management, creates a properly isolated guest SSID, moves the smart TV and visitors onto that guest network, and ensures the NAS is reachable only from the trusted LAN with proper share permissions. In a small clinic with open Wi-Fi for everyone, an improved design creates a secured staff SSID using WPA3 or WPA2-AES, keeps a separate patient SSID with isolation, and ensures wireless printers and medical workstations join only the secure staff network. As you practice reading exam scenarios, train yourself to see these structural weaknesses and to imagine how a slightly different layout or setting choice could drastically change the organization's risk.

Knowledge Check

Question 1: A small office uses a single flat LAN where staff PCs, smart TVs, IoT cameras, and a NAS with client data all share the same network. According to secure infrastructure design principles, what change would most reduce the risk of an attacker moving from a compromised IoT device to the NAS?

A. Enable SSID hiding on the wireless network to prevent outsiders from seeing it
B. Replace the SOHO router with a higher-bandwidth model from the ISP
C. Segment IoT devices onto a separate VLAN or guest-like network isolated from the NAS
D. Disable automatic updates on the NAS to avoid unexpected reboots

Question 2: A technician is configuring a new SOHO router. Remote web management from the internet is enabled by default, the admin username is "admin," and the password is set to the factory default. What is the primary risk of leaving these settings unchanged?

A. Attackers on the internet could log in and reconfigure the router
B. Local users will be unable to access the router's wireless network
C. The router will no longer perform NAT correctly for internal clients
D. Internal devices will be prevented from reaching the internet

Question 3: A clinic wants to offer Wi-Fi for both staff and patients. Staff laptops access electronic medical records, while patients only need internet access. Which design best follows the principle of least privilege?

A. One WPA2-PSK SSID for everyone, with the same password shared with staff and patients
B. A secured staff SSID mapped to the internal LAN and an isolated guest SSID with internet-only access for patients
C. A single open (unencrypted) SSID so that staff and patients can connect without needing a password
D. A hidden SSID for staff and a visible SSID for patients, both mapped to the same internal LAN

Question 4: A small business hosts a public web server and an internal accounting server. The administrator wants to reduce the impact if the web server is compromised from the internet. Which infrastructure design choice best achieves this goal?

A. Place both servers on the same internal LAN but enable SSID hiding on the wireless network
B. Use a stronger administrator password on the web server while keeping the same flat network
C. Configure port forwarding from the router directly to both the web and accounting servers
D. Place the public web server in a DMZ separated from the internal LAN by a firewall

Question 5: A technician is reviewing wireless configurations in a small office. Which of the following is the most secure approach for protecting the staff wireless network while still allowing visitors to connect to Wi-Fi?

A. Use WEP encryption for compatibility and share the key with everyone
B. Use WPA3 or WPA2-AES for a staff SSID mapped to the internal LAN and a separate guest SSID mapped to an isolated segment
C. Hide the SSID so that only staff who already know it can connect
D. Use a single WPA3 SSID and post the passphrase on a sign in the lobby

Question 6: A remote employee needs access to an internal file server from home. Currently, the administrator has configured the router to forward TCP port 3389 from the internet directly to a workstation using RDP, where the file share is mounted. Which change would most improve the security of this remote access design?

A. Require users to connect through a VPN first, then allow RDP only from the internal network
B. Change the RDP port from 3389 to a high-numbered port to avoid scans
C. Disable the host firewall on the workstation to prevent RDP connection issues
D. Enable Telnet access to the router so the admin can monitor RDP sessions remotely

Question 7: An organization wants to improve containment if a workstation on the internal network becomes infected with malware. Which control most directly helps limit the malware's ability to initiate unexpected inbound connections to other internal hosts?

A. A stronger pre-shared key on the wireless network
B. Hiding the SSID of the internal Wi-Fi network
C. Properly configured host firewalls on endpoints with restrictive inbound rules
D. Enabling AP isolation on the guest wireless network

Question 8: A technician is tasked with hardening the wireless router in a law office. Which combination of settings best reflects a secure infrastructure design for the router itself?

A. Enable remote management over HTTP from any IP and use the same password as the Wi-Fi network
B. Allow management from the internet only and disable local management from the internal LAN
C. Use Telnet for management with default credentials so support staff can easily log in
D. Use a unique admin username and strong password, apply firmware updates, and restrict management to HTTPS from the internal network only

ANSWERS

1: Correct Answer: C
Rationale: Segmenting IoT devices onto a separate VLAN or guest-like network isolates them from sensitive assets such as the NAS, limiting lateral movement from a compromised device and aligning with least privilege and network segmentation.

2: Correct Answer: A
Rationale: With remote management exposed and default credentials, attackers on the internet can easily authenticate and change critical settings (DNS, port forwarding, passwords), effectively taking control of the router and the network.

3: Correct Answer: B
Rationale: A dedicated, secured staff SSID mapped to the internal LAN and a separate, isolated guest SSID with internet-only access ensures patients cannot reach internal systems, enforcing least privilege and proper segmentation.

4: Correct Answer: D
Rationale: Placing the public web server in a DMZ separated from the internal LAN by a firewall isolates it from internal systems; if the web server is compromised, the attacker does not automatically gain access to the accounting server.

5: Correct Answer: B
Rationale: Using strong encryption (WPA3 or WPA2-AES) for a staff SSID on the internal LAN and a separate guest SSID on an isolated segment provides robust protection for staff traffic while safely accommodating visitors.

6: Correct Answer: A
Rationale: Requiring a VPN first creates an encrypted, authenticated tunnel into the internal network and allows RDP only from inside, avoiding direct RDP exposure to the internet, which is a common and high-risk attack vector.

7: Correct Answer: C
Rationale: Properly configured host firewalls with restrictive inbound rules on each endpoint block unsolicited inbound connections from other internal hosts, limiting malware's ability to spread laterally within the network.

8: Correct Answer: D
Rationale: A unique admin account with a strong password, up-to-date firmware, and restricting management to HTTPS from the internal network hardens the router's management plane and minimizes its attack surface.

3.3 Data Protection Strategies

When you think about security architecture, it's easy to picture firewalls, VPNs, and hardened servers. Those are all important, but in practice organizations are not trying to protect "servers" for their own sake. They are trying to protect the information that lives on and moves through those systems. That shift in focus—from systems to data—is what this section is about. Even in a well-designed infrastructure, with networks segmented and devices locked down, data can still be exposed if it is copied to the wrong place, sent over an insecure connection, or handled carelessly. Modern security architecture layers specific **data protection strategies** on top of the infrastructure so that the information itself is controlled, labeled, encrypted, and monitored wherever it goes.

As an entry-level technician or analyst, you will feel this at a very practical level. You might be the person imaging laptops with full-disk encryption, helping a user understand why an email attachment is blocked, or answering a question about whether a spreadsheet can be saved to a USB drive. You won't be writing the company's data protection policy, but you will be expected to follow it and often to enforce it in your daily work. Exam questions in this area are really testing that mindset: do you recognize what kind of data you are dealing with, what state it is in, and which control is appropriate for that situation?

Classifying Data: Knowing What You're Dealing With

Before you can protect data, you need to know what you are protecting and how important it is. Organizations solve this problem with **data classification**. Not all information is equal. A public press release is not in the same category as a database of customer Social Security numbers, and it would be wasteful and frustrating to treat them as if they were. So most businesses define a small number of classification levels and then build handling rules around them.

You will see different labels in different companies, but the pattern is usually similar. At the lowest level, you have **public** information: material that is intended to be shared broadly, such as website content, marketing brochures, or job postings. These still need integrity and availability—you don't want your public website defaced or offline—but confidentiality is not a concern. A step above that is some form of **internal** or **private** classification, covering documents meant only for employees and contractors. Internal procedures, staff directories, or non-public meeting minutes might fall here. It would be embarrassing and possibly harmful if this information leaked, but it's not usually catastrophic.

The stakes rise when you reach **confidential** or **sensitive** categories. This is where you typically find customer lists, supplier contracts, non-public financial reports, and many operational documents. Exposure could result in financial loss, damage to reputation, or competitive disadvantage. Access to this category is usually restricted by need-to-know, and encryption becomes a normal requirement both in storage and during transmission. At the top end is often a **highly confidential** or **restricted** classification. These are the crown jewels: trade secrets, authentication secrets, high-risk personal data, and sometimes pre-announcement financials or merger information. Access is tightly limited, extensively audited, and encryption is expected everywhere, including backups and archives.

Within those broad levels, you will often see specific labels for **types of sensitive data** that are regulated or especially risky. **Personally identifiable information (PII)** is any data that can identify an individual, especially when elements are combined: names, addresses, national IDs, birthdates, phone numbers, and similar details. **Protected health information (PHI)** refers to health-related data tied to a person, such as diagnoses, treatment history, or insurance records. Payment environments focus on **payment card data**, like primary account numbers (PANs), expiration dates, and security codes. Whether or not you work directly in healthcare or payment processing, you should recognize these terms, because company policies and exam scenarios will often say, "The file contains PII" or "The system stores cardholder data," which is your cue that strict handling requirements apply.

Classification drives concrete rules. A policy might say that confidential or higher data must not be stored on personal devices or unencrypted USB drives, that PHI must only be accessed across a VPN from corporate-managed endpoints, or that customer PII in printed form must be shredded rather than tossed into regular trash. As a technician, you are not inventing these rules, but you will be asked to apply them. When a user asks whether they can email a spreadsheet of customer addresses to their personal Gmail so they can work on it at home, the correct answer depends entirely on recognizing that this is at least confidential data, likely PII, and that policy almost certainly prohibits sending it to unmanaged personal accounts.

This is where it helps to build a habit: whenever a scenario describes data, pause and mentally classify it. Is it public, internal, confidential, or highly sensitive? Does it contain PII, PHI, financials, or payment card data? That quick mental "label" step sets up the right instinct for which protections are required and which behaviors are not acceptable.

The Three States of Data: Ready-Transit-Use

Once you know what kind of data you have, the next question is: what is the data doing right now? A simple way to keep this straight is to think in terms of three states—data at rest, data in transit, and data in use. The same file may move through all three states in the course of a day, and different controls apply at each point.

Data at rest is information that is stored somewhere: on a laptop's SSD, a server's hard drive, a mobile device, a backup tape, or a cloud storage bucket sitting idle in a provider's data center. To protect confidentiality in this state, organizations rely heavily on encryption. At the device level, that usually means **full-disk encryption (FDE)**, using tools like BitLocker on Windows or FileVault on macOS. When FDE is enabled and properly configured, the contents of the drive are unreadable if someone steals the device or removes the disk and connects it to another computer. Only when the user authenticates and the system boots does the disk become accessible. You may be the one turning on BitLocker during laptop provisioning, storing recovery keys in a management system, and later troubleshooting what happens when a user forgets their password and can't unlock the device.

Sometimes the protection needs to be more granular than a whole disk. On shared servers, for example, organizations may use **file- or folder-level encryption** to protect specific directories that contain confidential documents, while leaving less sensitive data unencrypted. Similarly, backup systems often include options to encrypt backups at rest. A lost backup tape or misplaced portable drive could represent a major breach if the data is unencrypted; with strong backup encryption, the physical loss is still a problem but does not automatically mean data exposure.

Data in transit is information that is moving across a network. Every time someone browses a website, connects to a cloud app, syncs email, uses remote desktop, or uploads a file, data is transiting. The main threat here is eavesdropping: someone in a position to capture network traffic, such as on an open Wi-Fi hotspot or a compromised router, could read or modify the data if it is not protected. The standard defense is to use encryption at the transport layer, most commonly **TLS**, which you encounter as HTTPS for web traffic. The difference between `http://` and `https://` in a browser URL bar is not cosmetic; HTTPS means the client and server have established an encrypted tunnel, so credentials, forms, and file contents cannot be read by network intermediaries.

The same principle extends beyond web browsing. Remote workers connect back to the corporate network over **VPN tunnels**, which wrap all their traffic in encryption between their device and the VPN endpoint. File transfers can use secure protocols such as SFTP or FTPS rather than older cleartext options. Email servers can use TLS to encrypt messages in flight between systems, and some environments go further with end-to-end encryption so only the sender and recipient can decrypt the content. When you see a scenario describing someone sending sensitive information over public Wi-Fi, the correct instinct is to ask: is this protected with HTTPS, a VPN, or another form of encryption in transit? If not, that is the control that needs to be added.

Data in use is easier to overlook but equally important. At some point, even if data is encrypted at rest and in transit, the system has to decrypt it so that an application can process it or a human can read it. When a customer record is open on a screen or being manipulated in a spreadsheet, that is data in use. Technically, it lives in RAM, CPU registers, and application memory. This state is less about cryptographic controls and more about **endpoint and access controls**. Screen lock policies ensure that if someone walks away from a workstation, it will automatically lock after a short period, preventing passersby from viewing open records. Role-based access controls limit which users can open particularly sensitive files or application views. Privacy screens on monitors and simple awareness about shoulder surfing protect against nearby observers.

From an exam perspective, a key point is not to confuse these states. Full-disk encryption is a control for data at rest; it does nothing for data once a user is logged in and using a file, and it does nothing for data sent across the network. HTTPS or a VPN protect data in transit; they say nothing about how data is stored at either end. Auto-locking screens and strict permissions help with data in use; they are not substitutes for encryption at rest or in transit. When you read a scenario, ask yourself: where is the data at this moment—stored, traveling, or being used—and then choose the control that matches that state.

Tokenization, Masking, and Anonymization

So far, we have looked at encrypting data and controlling who can access it. There are additional techniques that change how data is stored or displayed so that even if it is accessed, the sensitive parts are shielded. These become especially important in environments like payment processing, healthcare, and analytics, and CompTIA expects you to recognize them and distinguish them from simple encryption.

Tokenization is a strategy in which a system replaces a sensitive value with a meaningless substitute, called a token. The token has no mathematical relationship to the original data and is only useful inside systems that know how to map tokens back to real values. A classic example is credit card processing for an e-commerce site. When a customer enters their card number, the site sends it securely to a payment processor. The processor stores the actual card data in a highly secured vault and returns a token—perhaps a random-looking string of characters. The merchant's systems store only that token. The next time they need to charge the card, they send the token to the processor, which looks up the true card number and completes the transaction. If an attacker breaches the merchant's database, they see only tokens, not usable card numbers. On the exam, if a question describes a system that can process payments without storing actual card numbers, tokenization is probably the answer CompTIA is looking for.

Masking is about how data is presented to humans. Instead of storing an alternative value, the system hides part of the actual data when it is displayed. You see this constantly in user interfaces: only the last four digits of a card number are shown, or a Social Security number appears as *--1234. The underlying database still holds the full value (often encrypted), but the application masks it on screen to reduce the chance of accidental exposure through screenshots, shoulder surfing, or unnecessary viewing by staff who do not need the full value. If you work on a help desk system, you might notice that you can see a customer's name and last four digits of their card, but nothing else. That is data masking at work. It is important not to confuse masking with encryption or tokenization—masking is about partial hiding in the user interface, not fundamentally changing the stored value.

When organizations want to analyze data without exposing individual identities, they may use **anonymization** or **pseudonymization**. With anonymization, the goal is to remove or alter data so individuals cannot be re-identified at all. Direct identifiers like names and email addresses are stripped, and often quasi-identifiers such as exact birthdates or addresses are generalized or aggregated. If done correctly, no one can link the records back to specific people. Pseudonymization, in contrast, replaces identifiers with pseudonyms—codes, numbers, or artificial IDs—but maintains a separate mapping somewhere secure. That means re-identification is still possible if you have access to the mapping table. A research dataset might use pseudonyms so that, if a critical issue is found later, investigators can go back to the original records. The exam will not dive into legal subtleties here; what you need to remember is that anonymized data cannot be reversed, whereas pseudonymized data can be linked back with the right key or mapping.

All of these techniques differ from straightforward encryption. Encryption transforms data in a reversible way using a key; given the key, you can recover the original. Tokenization substitutes unrelated values and depends on a separate lookup system; there is no decryption algorithm that can turn a token back into a card number. Masking hides part of a value on screen but does not change what is stored. Anonymization, if done properly, destroys the ability to identify individuals at all. In scenario questions, this distinction matters. If you see "a placeholder value that lets the system process payments without holding real card data," think tokenization. If you see "show only last four digits on screen," think masking. If you see "dataset where no one can be re-identified," think anonymization.

Data Loss Prevention: Watching the Exits

Even with classification, encryption, and smart storage techniques, sensitive data can still leak through ordinary user behavior. Someone might try to copy a confidential report to a USB drive, upload it to a personal cloud account, or email it to the wrong recipient. To reduce this risk, many organizations deploy **Data Loss Prevention (DLP)** systems, which act as a kind of safety net. DLP tools inspect data as it is used or moved, looking for patterns that indicate sensitive content—things like credit card number formats, national ID numbers, or specific keywords—and then apply policies to block or warn about risky actions.

DLP can sit in several places. **Endpoint DLP** uses agents installed on laptops and desktops to monitor activity locally. These agents can detect when a user tries to copy files containing PII to a USB drive, print documents marked confidential, paste sensitive content into a chat application, or upload certain file types through a browser. If the action violates policy, the DLP agent can block it outright or at least warn the user and log an incident for review. From your perspective at the help desk, this might appear as a pop-up that says "Copy operation blocked due to data protection policy" when a user drags files to a removable drive.

Network DLP focuses on traffic as it leaves the organization's network. Deployed at email gateways or perimeter devices, it inspects outgoing email messages and attachments, web uploads, and other protocols, scanning for sensitive content. If a user tries to email a spreadsheet of customer SSNs to an external address, a network DLP system might quarantine the message, strip the attachment, or route it for encryption. In cloud-centric environments, **cloud DLP** capabilities—often delivered through a Cloud Access Security Broker (CASB) or built into SaaS platforms—monitor and control data stored and shared in cloud services like Microsoft 365 or Google Workspace. Policies can prevent files labeled confidential from being shared with "anyone with the link," for instance, or alert administrators when PHI appears in a chat channel.

From an IT support standpoint, you don't have to design these policies, but you do need to recognize DLP behavior when you see it and respond appropriately. If a user complains, "Outlook keeps saying 'Sending blocked due to policy' when I attach this customer list," the mention of a policy and the nature of the data are strong clues that DLP is involved. The right next steps are to ask what is in the file, mentally classify that content, and then explain that the organization's tools are preventing sensitive data from being sent in an unapproved way. Instead of disabling the DLP client or trying to work around it, you point the user toward approved methods, such as accessing the file remotely via VPN or using a secure, company-managed file-sharing service. If the user insists that this is an urgent business need, you escalate to the security team or management rather than attempting to override protection on your own.

You will also encounter DLP from the troubleshooting angle. Suppose a user reports that yesterday they could email a particular report to a partner, but today the attempt is blocked with a "policy violation" message. Your job is to verify that the DLP agent is running, that the system is up to date, and to check whether there have been recent policy changes communicated by security. You might gather logs or screenshots and attach them to a ticket for the security team to review. On the exam, descriptions of blocked attachments, prevented uploads, or messages referencing "sensitive data" or "pattern match (credit card number)" are reliable indicators that DLP is the control at play, not antivirus, not a firewall, and not simple file permissions.

All of this reinforces a central point: protecting data is not just about turning on encryption and walking away. It is an ongoing combination of labeling information, applying the right protections at rest, in transit, and in use, transforming or hiding data when appropriate with techniques like tokenization and masking, and then watching how that data moves so that mistakes and policy violations are caught before they turn into breaches. In day-to-day IT work, you will find yourself in the middle of these controls—not necessarily designing them, but making sure they are present, functioning, and not casually bypassed because someone wants a faster way to send a spreadsheet.

Knowledge Check

Question 1: A help desk technician is provisioning new laptops that will be used by sales staff traveling frequently. Management's primary concern is that if a laptop is lost or stolen, the data on its drive cannot be accessed by an attacker who removes the drive and connects it to another system. Which control best addresses this requirement?

- **A.** Full-disk encryption using a tool such as BitLocker or FileVault
- **B.** TLS encryption for all web browsing sessions from the laptop
- **C.** Network DLP inspection at the corporate email gateway
- **D.** Screen lock timeout configured to 3 minutes of inactivity

Question 2: A security analyst is reviewing a web application that allows customer service agents to see only the last four digits of a customer's credit card number (e.g., **** **** **** 1234), even though the full card number is stored securely in the backend database. Which technique is being used to limit what the agents can see on screen?

- **A.** Tokenization
- **B.** Anonymization
- **C.** Masking
- **D.** Full-disk encryption

Question 3: A research team wants to share a dataset with an external university. The organization requires that the data be transformed so that records cannot be linked back to specific individuals under any circumstances, even by internal staff. Which data protection technique best meets this requirement?

- **A.** Tokenization with a lookup table stored in a secure vault
- **B.** Masking direct identifiers such as names and email addresses
- **C.** Encrypting all PII fields using strong symmetric cryptography
- **D.** Anonymization that removes or generalizes identifiers so re-identification is not possible

Question 4: A user asks if they can email a spreadsheet containing customer names, home addresses, and phone numbers to their personal Gmail account so they can work from home. As an entry-level technician following company policy, what is the most appropriate response?

- **A.** Explain that the file contains PII and likely confidential data, so it must not be sent to unmanaged personal email
- **B.** Allow them to send the file as long as they password-protect the spreadsheet
- **C.** Approve the request if they promise to delete the email after downloading the file
- **D.** Tell them to remove names from the spreadsheet and send the remaining data to Gmail

Question 5: A company's classification policy defines four main levels: public, internal, confidential, and highly confidential. Which of the following is the best example of data that should be labeled as highly confidential or restricted?

A. Trade secrets and authentication secrets used to access core production systems
B. Marketing brochures that will be posted on the public website
C. Internal staff directory with employee names and office extensions
D. Non-public meeting minutes about upcoming social events

Question 6: A user connects to an open Wi-Fi network at a coffee shop to access a cloud CRM application that uses HTTPS. The data being viewed and edited in the browser is best described as which state at the moment it is traveling across the internet between the user and the cloud service?

A. Data at rest
B. Data in use
C. Data in transit
D. Data tokenized

Question 7: A credit card processor stores actual card data in a highly secured vault. Merchant systems only store randomly generated values that are meaningless outside of the processor's environment but still allow future charges to the same card when sent back to the processor. Which technique is primarily being used to protect the card data at the merchant?

A. Masking
B. Tokenization
C. Anonymization
D. Full-disk encryption

Question 8: A user reports that when they try to copy a document containing customer Social Security numbers to a USB drive, a pop-up appears stating, "Copy operation blocked due to data protection policy." Which type of control is most likely responsible for this behavior?

A. Network firewall with strict egress rules
B. Endpoint Data Loss Prevention (DLP) agent
C. TLS encryption on the local network
D. Role-based access control (RBAC) on the file share

ANSWERS

1: Correct Answer: A
Rationale: Full-disk encryption protects data at rest on the laptop's drive so a stolen or removed drive cannot be read without proper authentication. TLS, DLP, and screen locks address data in transit, data exfiltration, or casual access, not offline drive access.

2: Correct Answer: C
Rationale: Masking hides part of a sensitive value in the user interface (such as showing only the last four digits) while the full value remains stored. Tokenization replaces the entire value with a token, anonymization removes identifiability, and full-disk encryption protects storage, not display.

3: Correct Answer: D
Rationale: Anonymization removes or generalizes identifiers so that records cannot be linked back to individuals, even by insiders. Tokenization and encryption are reversible with the mapping or key, and masking only obscures what is shown, so they do not meet the "no re-identification" requirement.

4: Correct Answer: A
Rationale: Customer names and addresses are PII and at least confidential, and policy typically forbids sending such data to unmanaged personal email. The technician should deny the request and direct the user to approved remote-access methods; password protection, promises, or partial removal are insufficient.

5: Correct Answer: A
Rationale: Trade secrets and authentication secrets are highly sensitive "crown jewels" that warrant a highly confidential or restricted label. Marketing brochures are public, the staff directory is usually internal, and social event minutes are low-sensitivity internal information.

6: Correct Answer: C
Rationale: When data is moving across networks between client and server, it is data in transit. HTTPS (TLS) protects its confidentiality during transit; data at rest is stored, data in use is being processed on a host, and tokenization is a separate protection technique.

7: Correct Answer: B
Rationale: Tokenization replaces sensitive card numbers with unrelated tokens stored by merchants, with only the processor able to map tokens back to real data. Masking only obscures display, anonymization removes identifiability, and full-disk encryption protects stored data, not this payment flow.

8: Correct Answer: B
Rationale: An endpoint DLP agent inspects content on the host and can block copying sensitive data (such as SSNs) to USB, displaying a policy pop-up. Firewalls control network traffic, TLS encrypts communications, and RBAC governs access to resources, not USB copy operations.

3.4 Resilience, Redundancy & Recovery

If you walk into almost any business and quietly unplug the "wrong" system, you will find out very quickly how important resilience really is. Maybe it is the point-of-sale server in a small retail store, the file server in a design studio, or the single router that connects an entire branch office to the internet. Within minutes, people stop working, customers get frustrated, and managers start asking hard questions. At that moment, no one cares which brand of hardware is in the rack. They care about one thing: how quickly they can get back to normal. This is the world of resilience, redundancy, and recovery—the operational side of security architecture that turns theory into business continuity.

A useful way to frame this topic is to start with a simple question: what happens to the business if this system suddenly stops working or this data disappears? The answer is rarely "nothing." Even in a small shop, downtime and data loss have real costs: lost sales, angry customers, missed deadlines, and in some industries, regulatory trouble. In earlier chapters you saw how we protect the confidentiality and integrity of data. Resilience adds the third leg of the stool: **availability**. A secure system that is constantly down is not really serving the organization. As an entry-level IT professional, you are expected not only to fix individual broken devices but to think one level higher and ask, "How do we design things so that a single problem does not bring everything down?"

Resilience, Fault Tolerance, and Redundancy

You will see the word **resilience** used as an umbrella term for an organization's ability to keep operating and to recover quickly from disruptions. Resilient systems anticipate that hardware will fail, that people will make mistakes, and that occasionally something truly bad—like a flood or ransomware outbreak—will happen. Instead of pretending failures are rare, resilience assumes they are normal and designs for that reality.

A core building block of resilience is **fault tolerance**. A fault-tolerant system is designed so that when one component fails, the overall service keeps running, usually with little or no noticeable impact to users. Think of a server with two cooling fans. If one fan dies, you do not want the entire server to overheat and shut down; the remaining fan should be able to keep it within safe operating temperatures until maintenance can replace the failed unit. Or consider a storage system that uses multiple disks: if one drive fails, you want the data to remain accessible, not vanish instantly. Fault tolerance does not eliminate failures; it changes the outcome from "service completely down" to "service continues in a degraded but usable state."

To achieve fault tolerance, we usually rely on **redundancy**, which is the deliberate use of duplicate components or systems. In practice, this can be as simple as putting two power supplies into a server instead of one, so that if either fails, the machine still has power. It can mean having two identical switches connecting different parts of a network, so the loss of one path does not isolate users. It can even be as low-tech as having an extra external drive ready to plug in if the primary backup drive fails. Redundancy always has a cost in hardware, licensing, or complexity, so organizations reserve the highest levels of redundancy for systems that are truly important to operations.

Storage is a classic example where redundancy and fault tolerance come together, and this is where **RAID** enters the picture. RAID, or Redundant Array of Independent Disks, spreads data across multiple physical drives to improve performance, resilience, or both, depending on the configuration. Understanding the main RAID levels is essential at the A+ level because exam questions often describe symptoms of a RAID setup and expect you to infer which level is being used.

When you see **RAID 0**, associate it with striping and performance, but absolutely no protection. Data is split across at least two disks so read and write operations can be faster, but there is "zero protection in RAID 0." If either disk fails, the striped data set is effectively destroyed. This is why using RAID 0 on its own for important business data is almost always a mistake.

In contrast, **RAID 1** uses mirroring. The same data is written to two drives, so if one fails, the other still has a complete copy. Storage capacity is effectively cut in half, but you gain the ability to survive a single-drive failure. This is a common, relatively simple choice for small servers where ease of understanding and straightforward recovery are more important than maximizing capacity.

RAID 5 combines striping with parity information, which is essentially extra data that allows the system to reconstruct the contents of a failed drive on the fly. It requires at least three disks, and if one fails, the array continues to operate while you replace and rebuild the bad drive. The catch is that rebuilds can be slow and stressful on the remaining disks, especially with large modern drives. A useful phrase to keep in mind is "five has parity to survive" one disk failure. You might also hear about RAID 10 (or 1+0), which stripes across mirrored pairs of disks. At this level, you only need the conceptual idea: RAID 10 aims to combine the performance of striping with the redundancy of mirroring, at the cost of requiring more disks.

It is critical not to confuse RAID with backups. RAID protects against certain hardware failures—primarily drive failures—but it does not protect you from accidental deletion, malicious encryption by ransomware, or corruption that gets replicated across all disks. If a user deletes a folder on a RAID 1 array, it vanishes from both mirrored drives. If malware encrypts the shared volume on a RAID 5 system, the parity does not save you. For those situations, you need backup and recovery strategies, which we will return to shortly.

Power and Network Resilience

Fault tolerance is not limited to storage. Power is another area where a little planning can make the difference between a forgettable blip and a major outage. Most technicians are familiar with surge protectors, which primarily defend against voltage spikes that can damage sensitive electronics. A **UPS**—an Uninterruptible Power Supply—goes a step further. It provides short-term backup power from a battery, along with line conditioning that smooths out smaller fluctuations. In a small office, a UPS attached to the main file server, router, and switch can keep them running through brief outages or brownouts and give you time to shut systems down gracefully during longer ones. Without that cushion, you may see sudden shutdowns, corrupted files, and reboot loops that are traced back not to malware or bad RAM, but simply unstable power.

Larger environments may pair UPS systems with generators so that, after a short gap, critical equipment can run for hours or days. Inside key devices like enterprise servers and core switches, **redundant power supplies** are common. Each power supply may be fed from a different electrical circuit, so even if one circuit trips a breaker, the equipment remains on. As a technician, you might not design the electrical layout, but you should recognize how these features contribute to resilience and why unplugging the "spare" power cable from a running server is not a harmless act.

Network and connectivity resilience follow similar principles. A critical server may have multiple network interface cards configured in a team, so that if one port or cable fails, traffic transparently switches to another. A small business that cannot tolerate internet downtime might contract with two different ISPs and connect them to separate routers, so a fiber cut to one provider does not isolate the entire office. Even at the wireless layer, some organizations deploy overlapping access points so that if one fails, nearby APs can take over coverage. At the A+ level, you are not expected to configure complex failover routing, but you should understand that a single router, single switch, and single internet link represent single points of failure, and that adding redundancy in these areas increases availability.

High Availability and Service Expectations

When we combine redundancy, fault-tolerant design, monitoring, and rapid failover processes, we are aiming for **high availability**. High availability is really about setting and meeting uptime targets. You will hear phrases like "three nines" (99.9% uptime) or "four nines" (99.99% uptime), which translate into specific amounts of allowable downtime per year. For systems like e-commerce websites, hospital records, and payment processing, even an hour of unscheduled downtime can be a serious incident. For a test lab file server, the tolerance might be much higher.

The key idea is that high availability is proactive. You design the system so that if one component fails, users either do not notice at all, or notice only a short, controlled interruption while another component takes over. This might involve clustering multiple servers, deploying load balancers, or running services in multiple data centers or cloud regions. For A+ purposes, keep it conceptual: high availability uses redundant systems and fast failover to minimize unplanned downtime, and it is tied to explicit service-level expectations that the organization agrees on in advance.

Backups and Recovery: Getting Back Up

No matter how resilient your architecture is, some events will go beyond its design. A fire can destroy a server room. A ransomware attack can encrypt every disk in the building. A user can overwrite an important database with bad data that replicates happily across your fault-tolerant cluster. When resilience fails to "stay up," you move into **recovery**—getting back up. This is where **backups** become the cornerstone of both everyday operations and formal **disaster recovery**.

At its core, a backup is a second (or third, or fourth) copy of data stored separately from the original, with the explicit purpose of being able to restore it later. The simplest approach is the **full backup**, which copies all selected data every time it runs. Full backups are straightforward to understand and restore: if last night's full backup completed successfully and a user deletes a file today, you restore that file from the latest backup set. The trade-off is that full backups take longer and consume more storage, especially as data grows.

To manage this, organizations often combine full backups with **incremental** and **differential** backups. An incremental backup copies only the data that has changed since the last backup of any type. If you run a full backup on Sunday and incrementals on Monday, Tuesday, and Wednesday, each weekday backup contains only that day's changes. This keeps backup windows short and storage usage "minimal," but the restore process can be more involved. To recreate the state as of Wednesday, you need Sunday's full plus the Monday, Tuesday, and Wednesday incrementals, applied in order. If any of those sets are missing or corrupted, you may not get a complete restore.

Differential backups use a slightly different reference point. A differential backup copies all data that has changed since the last full backup. Using the same Sunday full example, Monday's differential includes Monday's changes since Sunday, Tuesday's includes everything changed since Sunday (Monday plus Tuesday changes), and so on. The daily backup sizes "grow daily" until you do another full backup, but restores are simpler. To recover Wednesday's state, you need only Sunday's full and the latest differential. Exam questions often hinge on this difference, so when you read a scenario, ask yourself: is this method referencing the last backup of any type (incremental) or specifically the last full backup (differential)?

Beyond file-based backups, many environments use **image-based** or system-level backups. These capture an entire system, including the operating system, applications, configuration, and data, in a single image. If a server's system drive fails or the OS becomes badly corrupted, you can restore the image to new hardware or a virtual machine and bring the system back quickly, sometimes in less time than it would take to reinstall and reconfigure everything manually. For critical workstations, like a CFO's laptop or a specialized design workstation, image-based backups can dramatically reduce downtime after hardware failure or theft.

Where you store backups matters just as much as how you create them. **On-site** backups—such as an external drive attached to a backup server—are fast to write and fast to restore from. They are convenient for common incidents like accidental deletions. However, if the building suffers a fire, flood, or theft, both the primary systems and the on-site backups can be lost together. To address this, organizations use **off-site** backups, where media like tapes or removable drives are physically moved to another location, or they use **cloud backups** that send encrypted copies over the internet to a provider's data center. Cloud backups have the advantage of geographic separation and the provider's own resilience features, but they depend on internet bandwidth and availability, especially when you need to restore large amounts of data.

You will sometimes hear the **3-2-1 backup rule** mentioned as a best-practice guideline: keep at least three copies of your data, on two different types of media, with at least one copy off-site. For example, the original data on your file server, a backup copy on a local NAS, and another copy in the cloud. You are not required to quote this rule on the exam, but it is a useful mental model when evaluating backup designs in scenarios.

Backup Procedures, Verification, and Disaster Recovery

Setting up a backup job once is not enough. Organizations establish schedules—daily incrementals, weekly fulls, monthly archives—and rotation schemes for media. They decide what needs to be backed up: user home directories, shared project folders, databases, critical configuration files, and sometimes full system images. Many will encrypt backup sets, especially when they leave the premises or go to the cloud, to protect sensitive data if a tape or drive is lost in transit. Encryption introduces its own operational risk: if the encryption key or password is lost, the backup becomes useless. From a support perspective, this is not an abstract issue; you may be the one trying to restore from an encrypted backup, only to discover that no one documented the decryption credentials.

One of the most neglected aspects of backups in real environments, and a common theme in exam questions, is **verification**. A backup job that reports "success" only means that data was written somewhere; it does not guarantee that you selected the correct folders, that the media is readable, or that the restore process works correctly. Silent failures are more common than people like to admit. A company might think it has been backing up a new department's shared drive for months, only to discover after a crash that the drive was never added to the backup job. The professional approach is to perform periodic test restores, deliberately recovering sample files or even whole systems to verify that backups are valid and that staff know how to execute the procedure. When an exam scenario asks what to do after configuring backups for a new server, "perform a test restore" is often the best next step.

All of these practices feed directly into **disaster recovery**, or DR. Disaster recovery planning asks, in a structured way, "If something serious and disruptive happens—far beyond a single disk failure—how do we restore services and data?" Two concepts help translate business needs into technical requirements: **RPO** and **RTO**. The **Recovery Point Objective** defines how much data loss, expressed in time, the business can tolerate. If the RPO for a financial system is four hours, that means the organization is willing to risk losing at most four hours of transactions; in practice, you would need backups or replicas at least every four hours. The **Recovery Time Objective** defines how long a system can be down before the impact becomes unacceptable. An RTO of eight hours for that same system implies that, from the moment of failure, you have up to eight hours to restore it to a usable state.

These values differ depending on the system. A retailer's point-of-sale database might have a very low RPO and RTO; losing more than a few minutes of sales data or being unable to take payments for an hour could be devastating. An internal archive of past marketing materials may tolerate an RPO of one day and an RTO of two days without serious consequences. When the exam gives you hints like "the business cannot lose more than one day of data" or "the server cannot be offline for more than 30 minutes," it is effectively giving you RPO and RTO targets and expecting you to choose backup and recovery methods that fit.

From your perspective in an entry-level role, you are usually not designing the entire DR strategy; you are executing and supporting it. That means you follow the documented DR plan, rather than improvising. If a data center goes down, the plan will specify which systems to bring back first, who authorizes failover to a secondary site or to cloud-hosted services, and how to communicate status to managers, end users, and possibly external partners. It is common to restore core services like directory authentication and DNS first, because many other systems depend on them, then move on to email, file services, and line-of-business applications. You may coordinate with other teams—network, security, vendor support—each following their part of the plan.

It is also important to recognize that high availability and disaster recovery are related but distinct. High availability focuses on minimizing unplanned downtime through redundant, fault-tolerant designs so that many failures are almost invisible. Disaster recovery assumes that something has happened that overwhelms those protections—a major power loss, natural disaster, or widespread compromise—and focuses on rebuilding and restoring, often to a different location or platform. In conversations and exam scenarios, a phrase like "automatic failover between clustered nodes" should make you think of high availability, while "restore services at an alternate site using off-site backups" should make you think of disaster recovery.

Finally, real environments are full of trade-offs. A small non-profit might not have the budget for elaborate clustering or duplicate data centers, but it can still be reasonably resilient by using RAID 1 for its main server, putting that server and its networking gear on a UPS, and scheduling regular encrypted cloud backups of critical data. The ideal technical solution is not always the best fit if it is too expensive or complex for the organization to maintain. As you gain experience, you will find yourself balancing these constraints, advocating for essential protections like tested backups and clear DR procedures, and educating users and managers about why occasional maintenance windows or failover tests are necessary. The mindset shift is from "How do I fix this break once?" to "How do we make sure this kind of failure has minimal impact next time it happens?"

Knowledge Check

Question 1: An administrator needs to ensure that a storage system can continue operating even if a single drive fails, while also maximizing usable space. Which RAID level BEST meets this requirement for a minimum of three disks?

A. RAID 0
B. RAID 1
C. RAID 1+0 (RAID 10)
D. RAID 5

Question 2: A company's financial application has an RPO of 1 hour and an RTO of 4 hours. Which statement BEST describes what the RPO requirement means?

A. The business can tolerate losing up to 1 hour of data.
B. The business must restore service within 1 hour.
C. The system can be offline for up to 1 hour.
D. The system must fail over to a secondary site in under 1 hour.

Question 3: A technician implements a backup scheme where a full backup runs every Sunday, and Monday through Saturday backups only capture files that changed since the last backup of any type. What type of weekday backups is the technician using?

A. Incremental
B. Differential
C. Image-based
D. Continuous data protection

Question 4: A retailer wants its e-commerce website to remain available during a single server failure with little or no noticeable downtime to customers. Which approach BEST aligns with a high availability design?

A. Performing nightly full backups and weekly test restores
B. Configuring RAID 0 on the web server's storage
C. Using a single powerful server on a UPS
D. Clustering multiple web servers behind a load balancer for automatic failover

Question 5: A small business runs a full backup every Sunday and a differential backup each weekday. If a file is deleted on Wednesday and must be restored, which backup sets are required to restore the system to its state as of Wednesday?

A. Sunday full, Monday incremental, Tuesday incremental, Wednesday incremental
B. Sunday full and Monday differential only
C. Sunday full and Wednesday differential
D. Wednesday differential only

Question 6: A technician is asked to improve resilience for the company's main file server. Management wants protection from power fluctuations and brief outages without investing in a generator. Which solution BEST meets this requirement?

A. Add a second internal hard drive in RAID 0.
B. Connect the server and core networking gear to an Uninterruptible Power Supply (UPS).
C. Move all backups to an off-site cloud provider.
D. Implement weekly image-based backups of the server.

Question 7: After a major flood destroys the primary server room, the IT team follows the documented plan to restore services at a secondary location using off-site backups. Which concept does this scenario MOST clearly illustrate?

- **A.** High availability
- **B.** Fault tolerance
- **C.** Load balancing
- **D.** Disaster recovery

Question 8: An administrator configures RAID 1 on a critical database server. Which risk is RAID 1 specifically designed to address in this context?

- **A.** Single disk hardware failure
- **B.** Ransomware encrypting all data
- **C.** Users accidentally deleting records
- **D.** Loss of the entire data center due to fire

ANSWERS

1: Correct Answer: D
Rationale: RAID 5 uses striping with parity, requires at least three disks, can continue operating after a single drive failure, and provides more usable capacity than mirroring-based RAID levels.

2: Correct Answer: A
Rationale: RPO (Recovery Point Objective) defines the maximum acceptable amount of data loss measured in time; an RPO of 1 hour means losing up to 1 hour of data is tolerable.

3: Correct Answer: A
Rationale: Incremental backups copy only data changed since the last backup of any type (full or incremental), which matches the described weekday backup behavior.

4: Correct Answer: D
Rationale: High availability relies on redundancy and rapid failover; clustering multiple web servers behind a load balancer allows automatic failover with minimal or no visible downtime.

5: Correct Answer: C
Rationale: Differential backups store all changes since the last full backup. To restore to Wednesday's state, you need the Sunday full plus the latest differential, which is Wednesday's.

6: Correct Answer: B
Rationale: A UPS provides conditioned power and short-term backup during brief outages, protecting against power fluctuations and short interruptions without the cost of a generator.

7: Correct Answer: D
Rationale: Moving operations to a secondary site and restoring from off-site backups after a flood is a classic example of disaster recovery, not routine high availability or load balancing.

8: Correct Answer: A
Rationale: RAID 1 mirrors data across drives so that if one disk fails, another holds an identical copy, directly mitigating the risk of a single disk hardware failure.

CHAPTER 4

Security Operations I

4.1 Secure Configuration & Hardening

When you take a brand-new laptop out of the box and power it on for the first time, it feels clean and fresh. For many users, that first-boot state also feels safe. For a security-minded technician, though, it's the opposite: a starting point that still needs serious work. Vendors ship operating systems and devices configured for easy setup, flashy features, and broad compatibility, not maximum protection. That "just works" experience usually includes extra software, open services, permissive defaults, and sometimes even weak or well-known credentials. The process of turning that default install into something you would trust with company data is what we mean by **secure configuration and hardening**.

A good way to think about hardening is to imagine every feature, service, and open port as another window in a building. The more windows, the more places an intruder can try to get in, and the harder it is to watch all of them. A hardened system has fewer windows, stronger locks, and better rules about who can open them. In IT terms, you are deliberately reducing the **attack surface** by turning off what you don't need, tightening how the rest works, and aligning the system with a documented **baseline**—a known-good set of settings that meets your organization's standards. That baseline might be called "standard office workstation" or "lab PC" or "remote sales laptop," but the idea is the same: you aren't improvising security on each new machine; you are repeatedly aiming for the same secure configuration.

At the A+ level, you are often the person actually putting hands on those systems. You image new PCs, join them to a domain or workgroup, create local accounts, and install or remove software. Every one of those actions either supports the baseline your organization wants or pulls the device away from it. Thinking like a professional means constantly asking, "Is what I'm doing making this system easier to attack or harder?" Once that mindset clicks, most configuration decisions become much clearer.

Why We Harden: Core Principles Behind the Settings

Before diving into specific operating systems and devices, it helps to anchor your thinking in a few core principles. These are the "why" behind nearly every hardening step you'll take.

The first is **least privilege**. This is the idea that users, applications, and services should have only the access they need to do their job, and no more. On a Windows workstation, that might mean creating a standard user account for everyday work instead of letting someone run everything as an administrator. The practical impact is huge: if malware executes under a standard account, it is confined to what that account can touch. It might corrupt that user's files, but it is less likely to install system-wide drivers, tamper with security controls, or spread laterally. Least privilege also applies to services and applications, such as running a web service under a dedicated low-privilege account rather than using a full admin context.

The second principle is **attack surface reduction**. Every running service, open port, browser plugin, background agent, or unused application is another place a vulnerability might exist. You will often see "feature-rich" systems that are also fragile and hard to secure precisely because too much is allowed to run. Reducing the attack surface is not about randomly turning things off; it is about systematically identifying what is not required for this role and disabling, uninstalling, or tightly restricting it. Disabling Remote Desktop on systems where no one ever remotely connects, removing a bundled trialware suite that opens its own network listener, or turning off unnecessary file-sharing protocols all fall under this concept.

The third principle is **secure defaults and defense in depth**. Users will sometimes make mistakes, click things they shouldn't, or forget to lock their screens. A hardened configuration anticipates that and builds in layers of protection that do not rely on perfect user behavior. Enforcing an automatic screen lock after a short period of inactivity, keeping the built-in firewall enabled, turning on full disk encryption, and requiring automatic updates are all examples of setting secure defaults. If one layer fails—say, someone clicks a malicious link—the others are still there to limit the damage.

With those principles in mind, it's easier to see why specific settings matter. Disabling an unneeded service is more than just "tuning"; it follows attack surface reduction. Running users as standard accounts is more than an HR policy; it enforces least privilege. Enabling a host-based firewall isn't just a checkbox; it's a key layer in defense in depth.

Hardening Desktop and Laptop Operating Systems

Most of the systems you will touch early in your career run Windows, macOS, or a Linux distribution. While their interfaces and tools differ, the hardening logic is remarkably similar: tighten accounts and permissions, keep software current, enable built-in protections, and strip away what isn't needed.

A natural starting point is how you handle **account types and local security settings**. On a Windows system, you can choose between administrator, standard user, and guest accounts. macOS offers admin and standard accounts as well. The secure configuration is nearly always to reserve administrator or admin roles for IT staff and occasional elevated tasks, while users operate day-to-day under standard accounts. Enabling a guest account on a business machine, especially one without a password, is a textbook example of an insecure configuration; anything done under that account is anonymous, and there is no way to tie actions back to a person. When you create named user accounts instead of sharing a generic "Admin" login, you gain both accountability and control. You can disable or lock a specific user without affecting others, and you can trace activity in logs to an actual person.

Password policies sit alongside account types. A hardened machine will require passwords of sufficient length and complexity, enforce history so users can't just flip between "Password1" and "Password2," and lock accounts temporarily after several failed attempts to slow brute-force guessing. In Windows, you might configure these using Local Security Policy or the Settings app for a standalone machine, or through domain policies in an enterprise. While you don't need to memorize every dialog box for the exam, you do need to recognize the outcomes that represent secure baselines: passwords that are long and not trivially guessable, lockout thresholds that are strict enough to deter attackers while still allowing legitimate users to recover via the help desk, and the absence of automatic logon to privileged accounts.

Once accounts and passwords are under control, the next layer is keeping the operating system and applications patched. A securely configured system does not run years behind on updates with automatic updating turned off "to avoid reboots." Instead, it has **automatic OS updates** enabled on a schedule that fits business needs, and critical applications such as web browsers, office suites, and common plugins are kept current. For Windows, that often means configuring Windows Update and verifying that updates are installing successfully. On macOS, it involves ensuring system and App Store updates are enabled. On Linux, you may use package managers to keep system and core tools up to date. On the exam, when you see a scenario describing an outdated OS or an unsupported version (such as an end-of-life Windows release still in use), proposing an update and patching plan is almost always part of the correct hardening answer.

With the operating system current, attention turns to **built-in security features**, especially firewalls and antivirus or endpoint protection. A **host-based firewall** monitors and controls network traffic to and from that device. At minimum, your baseline should have it enabled, with only necessary exceptions allowed. If file and printer sharing is needed for a particular subnet, you might create a narrow rule that allows that protocol only for that network, rather than a broad "allow all inbound" rule. Windows includes Windows Defender Firewall, integrated with Windows Security; macOS offers its own application firewall; Linux distributions frequently use iptables, nftables, or distribution-specific front-ends. When exam questions contrast "firewall off because it was blocking something" and "firewall on with a specific exception," you should instinctively favor the option that keeps the firewall active and refines the rule set.

Antivirus and broader **endpoint protection** tools are your next line. On modern Windows systems, the built-in Microsoft Defender Antivirus is often sufficient for baseline protection, provided its real-time scanning and automatic signature updates are enabled. macOS includes Gatekeeper and XProtect, which restrict untrusted software and scan for known malware in the background. Linux environments may rely more heavily on strict permissions, minimal services, and careful patching, but many organizations still deploy antivirus on Linux systems that handle sensitive data or interact with untrusted files. As a technician, your role is to ensure these tools are active, updated, and not trivially disabled by users. If a user insists they turned off antivirus "because it slowed their game down," your job is to re-enable it, tune where appropriate, and explain that performance tweaks cannot come at the expense of basic protection.

Reducing the attack surface on desktops and laptops also involves dealing with **services, startup programs, and unnecessary software**. Many new systems ship with "bloatware": preinstalled trial security suites, cloud backup tools, vendor utilities, and even games. Each of these can introduce vulnerabilities, run background services, and nag users into clicking things they don't understand. A hardened baseline typically includes removing unneeded software and ensuring only approved applications remain. On Windows, Task Manager's Startup tab or tools like System Configuration can help you see what launches on boot. The goal is not to strip so aggressively that the system breaks, but to be deliberate. Before disabling a service, you research what it does. If you identify something clearly unnecessary—perhaps a third-party remote-control tool that no one uses—you remove or disable it. You also avoid the opposite mistake of "turning things off for performance" with no security rationale and no understanding of the impact.

It is easy to forget that many attacks start in the browser, not in the core operating system. Basic **browser and application-level hardening** can dramatically lower risk. On users' primary browsers, you might configure stricter controls on third-party cookies, limit or block pop-ups except from trusted sites, and remove extensions that are not required for work—especially anything that came from unknown sources or promises free coupons and deals. You might set the homepage and default search engine according to policy to prevent rogue toolbars from hijacking these settings. In organizations with specific web usage requirements, these configurations may be enforced centrally, but even in a small office or home environment, you can implement them manually as part of your baseline. When you see scenario questions about multiple suspicious browser toolbars, constant redirect pop-ups, and unexplained search behavior, one of your hardening steps should be cleaning up the browser environment and locking it down.

Hardening Mobile Devices and SOHO Environments

Security doesn't stop at laptops and desktops. Modern work relies heavily on smartphones, tablets, and small office/home office (SOHO) networks. Attackers know this, and exam scenarios increasingly include them. Fortunately, the same core principles apply: least privilege, attack surface reduction, and secure defaults.

On **mobile devices**, a secure configuration begins with access control. Every smartphone or tablet that touches company data should have a screen lock enabled—whether that's a strong PIN, a complex password, a pattern combined with a secondary factor, or biometric options like fingerprint and facial recognition. Pair that with an automatic screen timeout so that, after a short period of inactivity, the device locks itself. Most modern devices also implement **device encryption** automatically when a lock method is set. This means that if a device is lost or stolen, the data on it remains protected as long as the attacker cannot unlock it. For corporate environments, mobile device management (MDM) platforms can enforce these settings remotely, but even in smaller environments, you may find yourself walking users through enabling these options manually.

Another crucial mobile hardening step is controlling where apps come from and what they can do. On Android, that usually means keeping the "install from unknown sources" or sideloading options disabled unless there is a very specific, approved business need. On both Android and iOS, reviewing and limiting app permissions—such as access to location, microphone, camera, and contacts—helps reduce the blast radius of a malicious or compromised app. Many organizations also require enabling "Find My Device" or similar services, which support remote locate and remote wipe. If a sales representative leaves a phone in a taxi, you want to be able to erase the company email and documents on it without having physical access to the device.

SOHO routers and Wi-Fi access points are another common weak spot and a favorite exam topic. Securing these devices starts with the management interface. Leaving the **default administrator username and password** in place is equivalent to leaving a key under the doormat; these defaults are widely published and regularly scanned for by attackers. As part of hardening, you log into the router's admin console, change those credentials to a strong, unique combination, and make sure remote management from the internet is disabled unless truly necessary. From there, you turn to wireless settings. For any environment that handles sensitive data, you should be using **WPA2** at a minimum, and **WPA3** where available. Older options such as WEP, or even open networks with no encryption, are simply not acceptable for secure deployments, no matter how convenient they seem.

Configuring a strong, unique passphrase for the Wi-Fi network is another baseline step. It should not be a default printed on the label that has already been leaked online, nor something easily guessed from the company name and a birth year. Many routers offer WPS (Wi-Fi Protected Setup), which promises easy device onboarding via a push-button or PIN method. Unfortunately, WPS implementations have a history of vulnerabilities and brute-force weaknesses. Some organizations explicitly require WPS to be disabled as part of hardening. Router firmware should also be updated periodically, just like operating systems, to receive security fixes for discovered vulnerabilities. In a small business scenario, you might be the one logging into the router, checking for updates, and planning a brief maintenance window so you can apply them.

Keeping Systems Hardened: Baselines and Configuration Management

Hardening one system carefully is useful. Hardening every system consistently is where real security gains appear. This is where **configuration management** ideas start to matter, even at the A+ level. Instead of configuring each machine from scratch based on memory, organizations define **baselines** and use images or templates to apply them. A baseline for a "standard office workstation" might specify that users have only standard accounts, full disk encryption is enabled, certain approved software is installed, the firewall is on with a defined rule set, and specific services are disabled. That baseline can then be captured in a golden image and deployed to new machines so that each one starts life from the same secure foundation.

Of course, systems change over time. Users install applications, settings get tweaked, and troubleshooting steps introduce exceptions. This gradual drift away from the baseline is known as **configuration drift**. To manage it, even small organizations benefit from some form of change awareness or "change control lite." The idea is simple: do not treat security-relevant changes as casual experiments. If you need to disable a firewall rule to test a connectivity issue, you document what you changed, why you changed it, and how you will restore the original configuration afterward. If a user needs a specific application that normally isn't part of the baseline, you make sure it is approved and you note that their workstation now differs from the standard. In many exam questions, when you are asked what to do next after making a significant configuration change, the secure answer often includes documenting the change rather than silently walking away.

Verification completes the loop. Periodically, you compare systems against the baseline. In a larger environment, that might be done via centralized tools that report on which machines have out-of-date antivirus or disabled firewalls. In a smaller shop or a home office context, you might rely on checklists and spot checks. Regardless of scale, the mindset is the same: configuration is not "set and forget." People, software, and threat landscapes change. A machine that was hardened last year might be exposed today if no one has checked its settings, updated its software, or confirmed that users haven't quietly made themselves local administrators "to make installs easier."

Seeing all of these pieces together—accounts, updates, protection tools, stripped-down services, mobile and Wi-Fi security, and consistent baselines—gives you a practical mental framework when you're faced with a scenario on the job or on the exam. When you encounter a new or inherited system and need to harden it, you can walk through the same sequence in your head: lock down accounts and permissions, apply updates and patches, protect with built-in security tools, and strip away unnecessary features. Over time, this becomes second nature, and "out-of-the-box" will no longer look safe to you; it will simply look like the starting line.

Knowledge Check

Question 1: A technician is configuring a new Windows laptop for a standard office user. Which action best enforces the principle of least privilege during daily use?

A. Allow the user to share the built-in local Administrator account with IT
B. Enable the guest account with no password for convenience
C. Create a named standard user account and reserve administrator access for IT tasks
D. Configure automatic logon to an admin account so the user never needs credentials

Question 2: An organization wants to reduce the attack surface of new workstations. Which action most directly supports this goal?

A. Enabling Remote Desktop for all users to support remote work
B. Uninstalling unnecessary trialware, disabling unused services, and limiting startup programs
C. Allowing automatic installation of all browser extensions requested by users
D. Creating one shared admin account for all technicians to simplify management

Question 3: A user frequently disables the Windows Defender Firewall because it "blocks some apps." As part of hardening, what should the technician do?

A. Re-enable the firewall and create specific, narrow rules for required applications
B. Permanently disable the firewall and rely only on antivirus software
C. Enable full administrative rights for the user so they can manage firewall settings
D. Replace the firewall with a browser pop-up blocker

Question 4: A newly imaged laptop is being prepared as a "standard office workstation." Which of the following best describes using a security baseline for this system?

A. Letting each technician configure settings based on personal preference
B. Applying only default vendor settings without additional hardening
C. Following a documented set of required security settings applied consistently to similar systems
D. Allowing users to choose their own password and firewall settings during first logon

Question 5: A security analyst notices that employees are sharing a single "Admin" account to log into their PCs. From a hardening perspective, which change should be made first?

A. Replace the shared account with individual named user accounts and restrict admin use
B. Shorten all user passwords so they are easier to remember
C. Enable automatic logon to the Admin account for all workstations
D. Disable account lockout policies to prevent accidental lockouts

Question 6: A SOHO router is being hardened for a small business. Which combination of changes best improves its security posture?

A. Enable WEP, keep the default admin password, and turn on WPS for easy connections
B. Leave Wi-Fi open to avoid password issues and disable the router's firewall
C. Enable remote management from the internet and publish the Wi-Fi key to staff
D. Change default admin credentials, disable WPS, and use WPA2 or WPA3 with a strong passphrase

Question 7: A mobile device used for company email is lost. Which previously configured control would best protect the data stored on the device?

A. Allowing sideloading of apps from unknown sources
B. Enabling device encryption + screen lock + remote wipe capability
C. Disabling the screen lock to improve usability
D. Installing multiple third-party game apps to keep the OS updated

Question 8: Over time, several workstations have accumulated unapproved software and changed security settings. This deviation from the original secure template is best described as which concept?

A. Configuration drift
B. Patch management
C. Defense in depth
D. Least privilege

ANSWERS

1: Correct Answer: C
Rationale: A named standard user account for daily work enforces least privilege and accountability, while reserving admin rights for controlled IT tasks. The other options either weaken security or violate least privilege.

2: Correct Answer: B
Rationale: Removing unnecessary software, disabling unused services, and limiting startup programs directly reduce the attack surface by minimizing exposed components. The other options increase risk or do not address attack surface.

3: Correct Answer: A
Rationale: Keeping the host firewall enabled and adding precise exceptions maintains protection while allowing required apps. Disabling the firewall, granting full admin rights, or using a pop-up blocker do not provide equivalent host-based network protection.

4: Correct Answer: C
Rationale: A security baseline is a documented, known-good configuration applied consistently to systems with the same role. The other choices describe ad hoc, default, or user-driven settings, not a baseline.

5: Correct Answer: A
Rationale: Replacing a shared admin account with individual named accounts improves accountability and supports least privilege; admin access should be limited. The other options weaken authentication or remove important safeguards.

6: Correct Answer: D
Rationale: Changing default admin credentials, disabling WPS, and using WPA2/WPA3 with a strong passphrase are standard SOHO hardening practices. The other options use weak or no security and expose the router to attack.

7: Correct Answer: B
Rationale: Device encryption, a strong lock, and remote wipe best protect data on a lost device. The other options either reduce security or are unrelated to data protection.

8: Correct Answer: A
Rationale: Configuration drift is the gradual deviation from the original hardened baseline due to unapproved changes over time. Patch management, defense in depth, and least privilege are different security concepts.

4.2 Asset Management & Lifecycle

If you spend a day shadowing a busy help desk, you quickly notice a pattern. On the surface, it looks like you're just fixing "a laptop" or "a printer," but the more mature the organization, the more every action is framed around something bigger: assets. Someone will ask for the asset tag, want to know who the device is assigned to, check whether its warranty is still active, or insist that you log a ticket before you even touch it. That can feel like paperwork for its own sake—until you see what happens in environments where this discipline is missing: lost equipment, mystery software, unknown devices on the network, and, eventually, data breaches and audit failures. Asset management and lifecycle are about making sure that every piece of hardware, software, and data has a controlled story from the moment it enters the organization until the moment it leaves.

At its simplest, an **IT asset** is anything of value to the organization that IT is expected to support, protect, and track. The most visible category is hardware: desktops under desks, laptops in backpacks, servers and storage arrays in racks, smartphones and tablets, network switches and wireless access points, printers and multifunction copiers, point-of-sale terminals and kiosks, USB drives and external hard disks. Then there are **software assets**: operating systems, office suites, email clients, line-of-business applications, security tools, virtualization platforms, cloud-based subscriptions, and even the firmware that runs on network appliances. Finally, perhaps the most important category is **data assets**: customer records, financial spreadsheets, intellectual property, HR files, log archives, configuration backups, email archives, and all the other information that keeps the organization running. When a company issues you a laptop, what they're really doing is giving you a bundle of assets: a hardware chassis, licensed software, and access to data that could be very costly to lose or leak.

From a support technician's point of view, asset management matters because it underpins almost everything you do. Security teams need it so they know what to protect and patch. You need it to troubleshoot effectively, because knowing the exact model, OS build, and configuration history of a device makes it much easier to diagnose problems. Management and auditors need it to prove that the organization is in control of its equipment and its data. Finance cares because assets cost money; unused licenses and forgotten hardware sitting in closets are real budget leaks. The recurring theme is simple: if you can't identify or locate an asset, you can't secure it, fix it, or make smart decisions about it. Many exam scenarios quietly assume this; when you see a question about an "unknown device" on the network or "unlicensed software" found during an audit, you're really being tested on whether you understand the consequences of weak asset management.

One way to make sense of all this is to think of each asset as having a life story with recognizable stages. Different organizations may use different labels, but a simple model works almost everywhere: you **request** something, you **acquire** it, you **deploy** it, you **maintain** it during its active life, you eventually **retire** it from service, and then you **dispose** of it or repurpose it. If you keep that Request–Acquire–Deploy–Maintain–Retire–Dispose sequence in your head, it becomes easier to decide what you should and should not be doing at any given moment.

Imagine the lifecycle of a laptop. A manager decides a new hire needs a machine, submits a request, and once it's approved, procurement buys it. That's the request and acquisition side, and you might not be heavily involved there, though in smaller organizations technicians sometimes help choose models or check compatibility. When the laptop arrives, your work starts in earnest. In the deployment stage, you unbox it, record its serial number, apply an **asset tag** sticker, image it with the standard OS and applications, apply security hardening from the previous chapter, and assign it in the inventory system to a specific user and location. At that moment it transitions into active use, and your focus shifts to maintenance: patching, responding to tickets, replacing a failed SSD, maybe upgrading RAM, adjusting its configuration as the user's role changes. Years later, when it becomes unreliable or can't run the current OS securely, it moves into retirement: you remove it from active service, migrate the user's data to a replacement, and update the record. Disposal comes last: secure wiping or physical destruction of the drive, and recycling or donation of the chassis according to policy.

On the exam, you will often have to infer which lifecycle stage a scenario is describing. A "newly issued laptop" is clearly in deployment, so the right actions emphasize imaging, hardening, tagging, and documentation. A question that starts with "an employee is leaving the company next week" is pushing you toward retirement and reassignment decisions: backing up and transferring required data, removing the user's access, wiping and reimaging the device, and updating ownership records. When you see mention of a server that is "no longer supported by the vendor and cannot receive security updates," you should immediately think about retirement and secure decommissioning rather than heroic attempts at repair. The lifecycle lens prevents you from treating every situation as just another break/fix problem.

To keep all of this under control, organizations need reliable ways to identify and track assets. The most basic tool is an asset tag: a unique identifier, usually on a barcode or QR-code sticker, physically attached to the device. This tag is different from the manufacturer's serial number stamped on the chassis, and it's also distinct from network identifiers such as an IP address or MAC address. The asset tag belongs to the organization and follows its own logic, so that a help desk technician can ask a user, "What's the asset tag on the sticker near your keyboard?" and immediately pull up the correct record. Those records live in some form of inventory system or **Configuration Management Database (CMDB)**. In a small office, that might be a simple spreadsheet listing make, model, serial number, asset tag, location, assigned user or department, OS version, and warranty dates. In a larger environment, automated discovery tools such as Remote Monitoring and Management (RMM) agents, Mobile Device Management (MDM) platforms, or Endpoint Detection and Response (EDR) consoles feed data into a central CMDB.

From your perspective, the most important part of an asset record is that it tells you three things: who currently has the device or owns it, how it is supposed to be used, and where it sits in its lifecycle. If you can answer those questions—who, usage, lifecycle—you're much less likely to make choices that conflict with policy. Before you walk across campus to look at a printer, you can check its record and see its model, age, warranty status, whether it has a known firmware bug, and whether it's handled in-house or by a vendor contract. When a user reports "my computer is acting up," asking for the asset tag lets you pull up its entire history, including past repairs or repeated incidents that might point to a systemic problem. In many exam questions, the best first step is something like "verify the device's asset information and review its history" rather than jumping straight into ad hoc troubleshooting.

Hardware is only half of the picture. Every significant application in your environment is also an asset, and software comes with its own set of responsibilities. Licenses can be tied to individual devices, to individual users, to a pool of seats, or to a subscription account, but in all cases the organization needs to know what it owns and where it is installed. If users install whatever they like, using personal copies or "free" downloads without approval, you have both legal and security problems. Licensing terms are often monitored during audits, and if an auditor finds more installations than purchased licenses, fines and forced true-ups can get expensive quickly. At the same time, from a security standpoint, untracked software makes patch management and vulnerability remediation almost impossible. You cannot fix a vulnerable version of a database client or browser plugin if you don't even know it exists.

You don't need to become a licensing lawyer for the exam, but you do need to internalize a few behaviors. Installing software is never just a technical task; it is also a policy and licensing decision. When a user says, "Just install this tool I found online, it will solve my problem," the safe response is to check whether the software is approved and licensed rather than grabbing the first download link. When an employee leaves the company, reclaiming their software licenses is part of the offboarding process, especially for expensive productivity or creative suites. Removing or reassigning those licenses, and updating the software inventory to reflect the change, protects the organization and keeps you compliant.

Underneath both hardware and software is the real crown jewel: data. The physical laptop that fails in the finance department can be replaced; the customer financial data it holds might be irreplaceable or regulated. Data can reside on internal hard drives, external USB disks, smartphones, tablets, network shares, backup tapes, and cloud storage. Some of it is routine and low-risk, but other data qualifies as personally identifiable information, protected health information, trade secrets, or confidential contracts. When you're making asset lifecycle decisions, you always have to think of the data component, not just the hardware. A dead hard drive from a server is not "just trash"; depending on what was stored there, it may need to be securely wiped or physically destroyed even if it no longer functions properly.

This perspective becomes critical during common support tasks like moves, adds, and changes. Suppose you're reassigning a laptop from one employee to another. It is not enough to hand it to the new person after deleting a few obvious files. Good practice—and what the exam expects—is that you back up any organizational data the old user still needs, remove them from ownership in the inventory and access control systems, then wipe and reimage the laptop with the standard build before assigning it to the new user. That protects against leftover personal data, cached credentials, or configuration drift. You update the device's record to show its new user, its new physical location if relevant, and any change in its intended use. The same goes for physical moves, like relocating a printer or a wireless access point. Moving equipment between departments or buildings without updating the inventory inevitably leads to "ghost assets" that no one can find on paper, even though they are happily running in a forgotten corner, unpatched and unmanaged.

In more sensitive situations, you may also encounter the concept of **chain of custody**. This is just a formal way of recording who has possession of a device at each handoff and for what purpose. If a laptop is suspected of containing evidence of policy violations or is involved in a security incident, you cannot treat it like a normal break/fix job. You might be instructed to power it down, label it, and log in a ticket exactly when you took it, then hand it to an investigator or security team member who signs for it. Each transfer is recorded, so later no one can claim that the device was tampered with or that evidence was mishandled. Even outside of investigations, basic "who had it, when, and why" tracking is valuable when devices are shipped to vendors for repair or loaned between departments.

Eventually, every asset reaches the end of its useful life, and this is where asset management and security intersect most visibly. There are many reasons to retire a device: it may be out of warranty and unreliable, incompatible with current software, using an operating system that is no longer supported with security patches, or simply obsolete due to an upgrade project. The retirement process typically starts by removing the asset from active monitoring tools and inventory as a live device, while still keeping a record of what it was. You back up or migrate any needed data, remove or transfer software licenses, and prepare the hardware for disposal or reuse.

At this point, **data sanitization** becomes the key security concern. Logical wiping methods involve overwriting storage with new data or using built-in secure erase functions. For traditional hard disk drives (HDDs), multi-pass overwrites have been common, though in practice a single thorough pass using approved tools is usually sufficient for most organizations. Solid-state drives (SSDs) work differently internally; their wear-leveling mechanisms can make traditional overwrites less reliable, so secure erase commands and the use of full-disk encryption are often preferred. In mobile environments, factory reset combined with device encryption and, if necessary, an MDM-issued remote wipe can be used when devices are lost or decommissioned. For the highest assurance, especially with drives that held very sensitive data, physical destruction is used: shredding, crushing, drilling, or working with a certified e-waste vendor who can show proper destruction procedures. And don't overlook less obvious storage: network printers and copiers often have internal storage that caches print jobs, scans, and faxes. Those, too, must be wiped or have their drives removed before resale, recycling, or lease return.

Supporting all of this workflow are the tools you interact with daily. Ticketing or IT service management systems tie incidents and service requests to specific asset records, so when you close a ticket you can also update the device's status. MDM platforms keep track of smartphones and tablets, letting you see which user is associated with which device, push configuration profiles, and issue remote wipes for lost or stolen units. RMM and EDR agents installed on endpoints feed health, patch level, and software inventory back to central consoles, which in turn support vulnerability management and incident response. In smaller environments that rely on spreadsheets or simple databases, you have to be especially disciplined, because those records only stay accurate if technicians actually update them after moves, repairs, and decommissions.

In the end, working well with asset management comes down to professional behavior and alignment with policy. It can be tempting to bypass procedures in the name of speed—handing out any working laptop without logging it, installing unapproved software to solve a user's immediate problem, tossing a dead drive into the trash because "it's broken anyway." Those shortcuts almost always show up on the exam as the wrong choices. When two answers are technically plausible, the better one is usually the option that respects documented processes, protects data throughout the asset's lifecycle, and leaves a clear trail of what changed. As you practice, make it a habit to pause and ask yourself not just "Can I fix this?" but "Where is this asset in its lifecycle, who owns it, what data does it hold, and how do policy and security shape what I should do next?"

Knowledge Check

Question 1: A technician is preparing a newly issued laptop for an employee who starts tomorrow. Which action best aligns with the deployment phase of the asset lifecycle?

- **A.** Negotiating the purchase price of the laptop with the vendor
- **B.** Removing the device from active monitoring and inventory tools
- **C.** Imaging the laptop with the standard OS, applying hardening, and assigning an asset tag
- **D.** Performing secure destruction of the internal storage prior to recycling

Question 2: During an internal audit, the security team discovers several unlicensed applications installed on user laptops. Which control would have most directly reduced the likelihood of this issue?

- **A.** A centralized software inventory and enforcing approved software lists
- **B.** Requiring local administrator rights for all end users
- **C.** Implementing full-disk encryption on all laptops
- **D.** Mandating that users store all data on network shares instead of local drives

Question 3: A server is running an operating system that is no longer supported by the vendor and cannot receive security updates. What is the most appropriate next step from an asset lifecycle perspective?

- **A.** Increase the frequency of log reviews on the server and continue using it
- **B.** Disable all nonessential services and leave it in production indefinitely
- **C.** Plan for retirement and secure decommissioning, including data migration and sanitization
- **D.** Block all outbound traffic from the server while allowing normal internal use

Question 4: A help desk technician receives a call: "My computer is acting up." To follow good asset management practice before troubleshooting, what should the technician do first?

- **A.** Immediately remote into the system and start running diagnostic tools
- **B.** Ask the user for the device's asset tag and review its record in the CMDB
- **C.** Physically visit the user's desk to inspect the device in person
- **D.** Reimage the system to the standard corporate build

Question 5: An employee leaves the company, and their laptop will be reassigned to a new hire. Which action is the best practice before handing the laptop to the new user?

- **A.** Back up needed organizational data, wipe and reimage the device, and update ownership records
- **B.** Delete the previous user's personal documents folder and change the hostname
- **C.** Change only the local username and password, leaving applications and data intact
- **D.** Disable the wireless adapter until the new user signs the acceptable use policy

Question 6: A storage array containing highly sensitive customer records is being decommissioned. The organization requires the highest assurance that data cannot be recovered. Which method best meets this requirement?

- **A.** Performing a single-pass logical overwrite of the disks using a software tool
- **B.** Issuing a factory reset command from the storage array's management interface
- **C.** Removing the disks and placing them in a locked cabinet for five years
- **D.** Physically destroying the drives through shredding or crushing using a certified vendor

Question 7: A laptop suspected of containing evidence of a policy violation is turned over to IT. What is the most appropriate action for the technician to take to preserve chain of custody?

- **A.** Log in as an administrator and collect screenshots of suspicious activity
- **B.** Perform a full malware scan and then return the laptop to the user
- **C.** Immediately reimage the device to prevent further misuse
- **D.** Document the time and reason for seizure, label the device, and record each handoff to investigators

Question 8: A multifunction network printer leased from a vendor is being returned at the end of the lease. It has an internal hard drive that stores print and scan jobs. What should the organization do before shipping it back?

- **A.** Only remove network cables and power it off to prevent further access
- **B.** Wipe or remove the internal storage according to data sanitization policy before return
- **C.** Change the printer's IP address and DNS name to prevent it from being found
- **D.** Disable color printing features and restore factory default paper settings

ANSWERS

1: Correct Answer: C
Rationale: The deployment phase includes preparing the device for use: standard imaging, security hardening, tagging, and adding it to inventory. The other options relate to procurement, disposal, or retirement.

2: Correct Answer: A
Rationale: A centralized software inventory with enforced approved software lists (allowlisting) directly addresses unlicensed and unauthorized software. The other options do not control what software is installed.

3: Correct Answer: C
Rationale: An unsupported OS is a trigger for retirement. Proper lifecycle management is to plan decommissioning, migrate needed data, and securely sanitize the system rather than keep it in production.

4: Correct Answer: B
Rationale: Confirming the asset tag and checking the CMDB provides configuration, ownership, and history, aligning with good asset management before technical troubleshooting begins.

5: Correct Answer: A
Rationale: Before reassignment, organizational data should be backed up, the device wiped and reimaged to remove prior user data and drift, and records updated to reflect new ownership.

6: Correct Answer: D
Rationale: For highly sensitive data, physical destruction by a certified vendor provides the highest assurance of non-recoverability. Overwrites, resets, or storage-only retention offer less assurance.

7: Correct Answer: D
Rationale: Chain of custody requires documenting seizure details, labeling the device, and recording each transfer to maintain an auditable record of evidence handling. Accessing or reimaging the system can compromise evidence.

8: Correct Answer: B
Rationale: Printers can store sensitive documents; wiping or removing internal storage per data sanitization policy is required before return. Merely powering off or changing network settings does not protect stored data.

4.3 Vulnerability Management

If secure configuration and hardening give your systems a strong starting point, vulnerability management is how you keep them strong over time. In real environments, nothing stays static. New software is installed, users change how they work, vendors discover bugs, and attackers constantly probe for weaknesses. As an entry-level technician, you will not be designing corporate security strategies, but you will be right in the middle of the day-to-day work of finding and closing holes before someone else finds them first. That ongoing, practical effort is what we mean by **vulnerability management**.

Understanding Vulnerabilities in Context (Vulnerability vs Threat vs Exploit)

Before you can manage vulnerabilities effectively, you need a clear and practical understanding of the language used to describe them. In security conversations, the words **vulnerability**, **threat**, and **exploit** are often used together, and in casual discussion they are sometimes used interchangeably. On the Security+ exam, that confusion is costly. CompTIA expects you to recognize that these terms describe different parts of the same story, and that most of your day-to-day work as a technician lives firmly in one part of that story, long before anything actually goes wrong.

A **vulnerability** is a weakness or flaw in a system, configuration, or process that could be used to compromise security. It exists whether anyone is actively abusing it or not. An operating system missing a security patch, a web application running an outdated library, a router still using its default administrative password, or a shared folder with overly permissive access rights are all vulnerabilities. They are conditions, not actions. In many cases, systems can run for months or years with vulnerabilities present and appear perfectly normal, which is exactly what makes them dangerous. From a vulnerability management perspective, the most important idea to internalize is that vulnerabilities are almost always present *before* any incident occurs.

A **threat**, by contrast, represents the potential source of harm. It answers the question, "Who or what might take advantage of this weakness?" Threats can be human, such as cybercriminal groups, malicious insiders, or opportunistic attackers scanning the internet. They can also be non-human, such as environmental events or accidental actions that trigger failure. A threat does not automatically cause damage; it simply has the capability or motivation to do so. On the exam, threats are often implied rather than named directly. A scenario might mention "external attackers," "unauthorized users," or "actors scanning the network," all of which point to the existence of a threat rather than a vulnerability itself.

An **exploit** is the specific technique, method, or code used to take advantage of a vulnerability. It is what turns a theoretical weakness into a real compromise. Exploits might be highly technical, such as a crafted network packet that triggers a buffer overflow, or relatively simple, such as logging in with a default password that was never changed. In many support roles, you will never see exploit code directly. You may only see the result: a system behaving strangely, files being encrypted, or unauthorized access being discovered after the fact. This is an important distinction for Security+, because the exam does not expect entry-level technicians to write or analyze exploits, but it does expect them to understand that exploits exist and that vulnerabilities make them possible.

A useful way to keep these concepts straight is to think in terms of sequence. A vulnerability is the open door. A threat is someone willing to try that door. An exploit is the act of opening it. If there is no vulnerability, the exploit fails. If there is a vulnerability but no threat, nothing happens. Incidents occur only when all three line up. This mental model helps you avoid one of the most common mistakes on the exam: treating the presence of a vulnerability as proof that an attack has already occurred.

In real IT environments, technicians spend most of their time dealing with vulnerabilities, not threats or exploits. When you apply operating system updates, you are closing known vulnerabilities. When you disable an unnecessary service, change default credentials, or restrict file permissions, you are reducing vulnerabilities. You are not reacting to an attack; you are performing preventive work. Even when a system appears to be functioning normally, vulnerability management is still happening in the background through patching, configuration reviews, and routine maintenance.

This distinction also clarifies why vulnerability management is not the same as incident response. If a user reports that their system is acting strangely after opening an attachment, you may be dealing with an exploit that has already occurred, and incident response procedures come into play. But when you review a scan report that lists missing patches or insecure configurations, you are looking at vulnerabilities that exist *before* any exploit. The correct response is not to hunt for malware, but to prioritize and remediate those weaknesses so they cannot be used in the first place. On the exam, scenarios that describe known weaknesses without evidence of compromise are testing your understanding of vulnerability management, not your ability to clean up an infection.

CompTIA frequently tests whether you can correctly identify which of these elements a scenario is describing. A question might mention a newly disclosed software flaw with a vendor advisory but no signs of exploitation. That is a vulnerability. Another might describe attackers actively scanning systems for open ports. That is a threat. A third might describe a specific attack technique being used to gain unauthorized access. That is an exploit. If you confuse these concepts, it becomes much harder to choose the best next step, because the appropriate action depends on which part of the chain you are dealing with.

Understanding vulnerabilities in context also reinforces the idea that security is proactive by nature. Waiting until an exploit is visible means the organization is already responding to damage. Effective vulnerability management focuses on identifying and addressing weaknesses while systems are still healthy. This is why patch management, configuration hardening, and routine reviews are such a large part of everyday IT work, even though they may not feel dramatic or urgent. They quietly reduce the number of opportunities attackers have and limit the impact if a threat does appear.

The Vulnerability Management Lifecycle: Identify, Prioritize, Remediate, Verify

Vulnerability management is not a task you complete once and then move on from. It is an ongoing process that runs quietly in the background of almost all IT work, repeating itself as systems change, software evolves, and new weaknesses are discovered. For Security+, it helps to think of vulnerability management as a **continuous lifecycle** rather than a checklist. The same four phases appear again and again: **identify**, **prioritize**, **remediate**, and **verify**. Most exam questions in this area are really testing whether you can recognize which part of that cycle you are in and what the appropriate next step should be.

The cycle begins with **identification**, which is simply the act of discovering that a vulnerability exists. In day-to-day work, this often happens in ways that feel routine rather than dramatic. An operating system prompts for a critical security update. A browser notifies the user that it is out of date. A vulnerability scan report lists missing patches or insecure configurations. A vendor publishes a security advisory describing a newly discovered flaw in a widely used application. All of these are identification events. At this stage, no decision has been made yet about urgency or action; the key point is awareness. You now know that a weakness exists somewhere in the environment.

Technicians also encounter identification indirectly. A user reports strange pop-ups, unexplained toolbars, or browser redirects, and investigation reveals that their system was several updates behind. In that case, the vulnerability was not discovered through a scanner or advisory but through operational symptoms. Even though incident response may be happening at the same time, the underlying issue is still part of vulnerability identification: recognizing that an unpatched system created an opening that should not exist elsewhere. For the exam, understanding that identification can come from tools, vendors, or user reports helps you avoid assuming that scanners are the only valid source of vulnerability information.

Once vulnerabilities are identified, the next phase is **prioritization**. This is where many real-world and exam scenarios focus, because not every vulnerability can or should be addressed at the same time. Prioritization is about deciding what matters most right now. Tools may label vulnerabilities as critical, high, medium, or low severity, and advisories may mention active exploitation or proof-of-concept code. These labels are helpful, but they are not the whole story. Context matters. A critical vulnerability on a publicly accessible server deserves more immediate attention than the same vulnerability on an isolated lab machine. Likewise, a medium-severity issue on a system that stores sensitive data may outrank a higher-severity issue on a non-critical device.

In practical terms, prioritization is where technicians often interact with managers, security teams, or change control processes. You might be asked to patch certain systems immediately, schedule others for the next maintenance window, and simply monitor low-risk issues. On the exam, questions that ask "what should be addressed first?" or "which system should be patched immediately?" are testing this phase of the lifecycle. The correct answer is rarely "fix everything at once," and it is almost never "ignore it." Instead, CompTIA wants you to show that you can weigh severity, exposure, and business impact when deciding what comes next.

After prioritization comes **remediation**, the phase where changes are made to reduce or eliminate the vulnerability. Most often, remediation means applying patches or updates provided by vendors. It can also involve configuration changes, such as disabling a vulnerable service, tightening firewall rules, removing unnecessary software, or changing insecure settings. In some cases, remediation includes firmware updates for hardware devices or enforcing stronger authentication requirements. For technicians, this is the most hands-on part of the cycle, and it is where operational caution matters. Applying a fix too hastily can disrupt systems just as badly as leaving a vulnerability unpatched.

There are also situations where immediate patching is not possible. A patch may not exist yet, or it may cause compatibility issues with critical applications. In those cases, remediation may involve **temporary mitigations**, such as disabling a feature, restricting access, or adding compensating controls until a proper fix is available. On the exam, this often appears as a choice between "apply the patch now" and "implement a workaround while waiting for vendor guidance." Recognizing when each is appropriate depends on understanding where you are in the lifecycle and what constraints are in play.

The final phase is **verification**, which is easy to overlook but essential. Verification is how you confirm that the remediation actually worked and that it did not introduce new problems. This might involve checking that a system shows the updated version number, reviewing patch status reports, re-running a vulnerability scan, or testing key services to ensure they still function. Verification closes the loop between action and outcome. Without it, you are assuming that risk has been reduced rather than confirming it.

Verification also has a broader role in vulnerability management. It provides feedback that informs the next cycle. If a vulnerability scan still reports the same issue after remediation, something went wrong and needs further investigation. If a patch fixes the vulnerability but causes unexpected downtime, that lesson feeds into future prioritization and testing decisions. For Security+, questions that ask "what should you do after applying the fix?" or "how do you confirm the issue is resolved?" are targeting this phase.

What makes this lifecycle especially important for the exam is that CompTIA rarely labels the steps explicitly. Instead, it describes situations and asks you to choose the most appropriate action. A scan report with no follow-up suggests you are stuck at identification. A long list of critical vulnerabilities with no order suggests prioritization has not happened. A system patched but not tested suggests verification was skipped. By mentally placing each scenario into the **identify–prioritize–remediate–verify** loop, you can often eliminate incorrect answers quickly and focus on the response that moves the process forward in a responsible way.

In real environments, this cycle never truly ends. New software is installed, new vulnerabilities are disclosed, and systems drift from their original configurations over time. Effective vulnerability management accepts that reality and focuses on keeping the cycle moving smoothly rather than chasing a mythical "perfectly secure" state.

Identifying Vulnerabilities

The vulnerability management process begins with identification, but in practice this step is broader and more nuanced than simply running a tool and reading a report. Vulnerabilities reveal themselves through many channels, some formal and automated, others informal and observational. For Security+, it is important to understand that identification is not limited to scanners or dashboards. It happens whenever you become aware that a weakness exists, whether that awareness comes from a system alert, a vendor announcement, or a user describing behavior that should not be happening.

One of the most common and straightforward ways vulnerabilities are identified is through **operating system and application updates**. When a system prompts that a "security update" or "critical patch" is available, it is effectively announcing the existence of a known vulnerability. Windows Update, macOS Software Update, Linux package managers, mobile OS update notifications, and built-in updaters for browsers and applications all serve as identification mechanisms. These messages are not just about keeping software current; they are signals that the vendor has discovered or been informed of a weakness that needs to be addressed. For exam purposes, when a scenario mentions an update notification that includes security fixes, you should recognize that as the identification phase of vulnerability management.

Beyond automated update prompts, **vendor security advisories** are another key source of vulnerability identification. Software and hardware vendors regularly publish bulletins describing newly discovered issues, affected versions, potential impact, and recommended actions. These advisories may be released on a fixed schedule or in response to urgent discoveries, especially when active exploitation is detected. In a smaller organization, these advisories may reach technicians through emails, forwarded links, or internal tickets. In larger environments, they may be integrated into centralized patch or asset management systems. On the Security+ exam, references to vendor advisories, bulletins, or notifications about newly disclosed flaws are cues that vulnerabilities have been identified and that decisions about prioritization and remediation are about to follow.

Vulnerability scanners provide a more systematic and scalable way to identify weaknesses across many systems at once. These tools examine hosts, services, and configurations, then compare what they find against databases of known vulnerabilities. A scan might flag missing patches, outdated software versions, insecure protocols, weak encryption settings, or misconfigurations such as default credentials. While entry-level technicians may not configure or tune these scanners, they are often responsible for acting on the results. A report listing "outdated browser version detected" or "unsupported operating system in use" is not an abstract security document; it is a list of identified vulnerabilities that need attention. On the exam, when a scenario includes scan results or references to vulnerability assessment tools, you are firmly in the identification stage of the lifecycle.

Identification, however, does not always begin with formal tools. Some of the most important vulnerability discoveries come from **real-world symptoms** reported by users or observed during routine support work. Unexplained pop-ups, sudden browser redirects, unauthorized software appearing on a system, or unexpected performance degradation can all indicate that a vulnerability has already been exploited or is at least present. Even if malware cleanup is required, these situations should also trigger vulnerability identification thinking. The question is not only "How do we fix this system?" but also "What weakness allowed this to happen, and where else might it exist?" CompTIA often blends incident response and vulnerability management in scenarios like this, and recognizing that both are in play is critical.

User complaints are particularly valuable sources of vulnerability information because they reflect how systems behave under real conditions. A user who reports that their browser keeps redirecting to unfamiliar sites may be unknowingly revealing that the browser was outdated or misconfigured. A report that a workstation suddenly has multiple toolbars or extensions may point to unpatched software or overly permissive installation rights. In these cases, the vulnerability may not be named explicitly, but it is still being identified through observation. For the exam, scenarios that start with "a user reports..." are often testing whether you can recognize the underlying vulnerability, not just address the symptom.

Asset inventory and configuration awareness also play a quiet role in identification. Knowing which operating systems, applications, and devices are in use allows you to quickly determine whether a newly announced vulnerability applies to your environment. If an advisory affects a specific version of a database server or a particular router model, identification involves matching that information to your asset list. CompTIA may not always spell this out, but questions that describe a vulnerability affecting a certain platform implicitly assume that you can identify whether your systems are impacted.

What ties all of these methods together is the idea that vulnerability identification is both **technical and observational**. It relies on tools, updates, and advisories, but it also depends on attention to how systems and users behave.

Treating identification as a passive, tool-only process can lead to blind spots, while treating every user complaint as a random glitch can cause you to miss patterns that reveal deeper weaknesses. Security+ rewards candidates who recognize that vulnerability identification is an ongoing awareness activity, not a single event.

Prioritizing Vulnerabilities: Severity, Exposure, and Business Impact

Once vulnerabilities have been identified, the next challenge is deciding what to address first. In real environments, resources are limited, systems are interconnected, and changes carry risk. Vulnerability management is not about fixing everything at once; it is about making informed decisions that reduce risk in the most effective way possible. For Security+, this judgment-based aspect is especially important, because many exam questions are less about knowing what a vulnerability is and more about knowing which one deserves attention right now.

Most tools and advisories begin by assigning a **severity** level to a vulnerability. You will commonly see labels such as critical, high, medium, or low, and in more detailed reports you may encounter references to **CVE** identifiers and **CVSS** scores. A CVE, or Common Vulnerabilities and Exposures identifier, is simply a standardized name for a publicly disclosed vulnerability, allowing everyone to talk about the same issue without confusion. CVSS, or Common Vulnerability Scoring System, provides a numerical estimate of severity based on factors like how the vulnerability can be exploited and what kind of impact it could have. For the Security+ exam, you do not need to calculate or memorize these scores. What matters is understanding that severity is an initial indicator of potential risk, not the final decision.

Severity alone does not determine priority. A vulnerability labeled "critical" on paper may be less urgent in practice than a lower-severity issue in a highly exposed or sensitive system. This is where **exposure** becomes a key factor. Exposure refers to how accessible the vulnerable system is to potential attackers. A service that is reachable from the internet, a system used by many users, or a device that connects to untrusted networks has higher exposure than one that is isolated or rarely accessed. The same software flaw on a public-facing server and on an offline test machine represents very different levels of risk, even if the technical severity is identical.

Business impact adds another layer to this decision-making process. Impact considers what would happen if the vulnerability were successfully exploited. Would it lead to minor inconvenience, or would it disrupt core operations, expose sensitive data, or cause financial loss? A vulnerability on a system that supports payroll, customer data, or production services carries greater impact than one on a workstation used for training or experimentation. On the exam, questions often hint at impact through phrases like "mission-critical system," "contains sensitive customer data," or "supports daily operations." These clues are there to guide your prioritization choices.

Contrasting scenarios make this clearer. Imagine a critical remote code execution vulnerability is discovered on an internal media player installed on a handful of lab machines used for occasional training. At the same time, a medium-severity authentication bypass is identified on a file server that stores shared company documents and is accessible to most employees. Even though the media player vulnerability is technically more severe, the file server issue may deserve higher priority because of its exposure and the impact of compromise. Exploiting the file server could lead to data loss or ransomware across the organization, while exploiting the media player might affect only a limited, low-risk environment.

This kind of reasoning is exactly what CompTIA tests. Many Security+ questions describe multiple vulnerabilities and ask which should be addressed first. The correct answer is rarely the one with the highest severity label alone. Instead, it is the one where severity, exposure, and impact combine to create the greatest overall risk. Recognizing that combination helps you avoid choosing answers that sound impressive but ignore real-world context.

Prioritization also requires acknowledging operational constraints. Not every vulnerability can be fixed immediately, even when it is serious. Applying a patch to a production database or point-of-sale system during business hours could cause downtime that outweighs the immediate security benefit. In these cases, prioritization does not mean ignoring the vulnerability; it means planning remediation in a controlled way. Temporary mitigations, such as restricting access, increasing monitoring, or disabling vulnerable features, may be appropriate until a full fix can be applied safely. On the exam, answers that combine urgency with control—such as scheduling an emergency patch window or implementing compensating controls—often reflect the best judgment.

It is also important to understand that prioritization is an intentional process, not negligence. Leaving a low-risk vulnerability unpatched for a short period while addressing more pressing issues is not the same as forgetting about it. Good vulnerability management includes tracking outstanding issues, revisiting priorities as conditions change, and documenting decisions. CompTIA scenarios sometimes test this distinction by presenting choices that either ignore vulnerabilities entirely or attempt to fix everything at once without planning. The best answer usually lies in between: address what matters most now and have a plan for the rest.

From a technician's perspective, prioritization often involves communication as much as technical skill. You may be asked to explain why a particular patch needs immediate attention or why another can wait until the next maintenance window. Being able to articulate how severity, exposure, and business impact interact not only helps you choose the right answer on the exam but also prepares you for real-world discussions with supervisors and security teams.

By consistently thinking in terms of these three factors, you develop a disciplined approach to vulnerability management. Instead of reacting to every alert with equal urgency, you learn to assess where the real risk lies and act accordingly.

Remediation Strategies: Patching, Configuration Changes, and Compensating Controls

Once vulnerabilities have been identified and prioritized, remediation is where security decisions turn into real changes in the environment. This is the phase where risk is actually reduced, but it is also the phase where mistakes can cause outages, data loss, or operational disruption if handled carelessly. For Security+, it is important to understand that remediation is not just about fixing vulnerabilities as fast as possible. It is about applying the **safest appropriate fix** in a way that improves security while preserving availability and stability.

The most familiar form of remediation is **patching**. Patches are updates released by vendors specifically to correct vulnerabilities in software or firmware. Operating systems, applications, network devices, and even peripherals like printers receive security patches. When a vendor releases a patch, they are acknowledging that a weakness exists and providing a supported way to close it. Applying that patch removes the vulnerability by changing the underlying code. In exam scenarios, when a vendor patch is available and does not conflict with operational constraints, applying it is often the preferred remediation choice.

However, patching is not as simple as clicking "install" everywhere, especially in professional environments. Patches can introduce new bugs, break compatibility with legacy applications, or require system reboots that interrupt users. This is why remediation must be coordinated with **change control** practices. Even when a vulnerability is serious, blindly patching a production system during peak hours can cause more harm than good. On the exam, answers that involve testing patches, scheduling maintenance windows, or following approval processes often reflect better judgment than answers that suggest immediate, unplanned changes to critical systems.

Not all remediation involves patches. Many vulnerabilities exist because of **insecure configurations**, and fixing them requires changing settings rather than updating software. Disabling unnecessary services, turning off outdated protocols, enforcing stronger encryption, tightening firewall rules, and adjusting permissions to follow **least privilege** are all forms of configuration-based remediation. For example, if a vulnerability scan reports that a legacy protocol like SMBv1 is enabled, remediation may involve disabling that protocol and verifying that dependent services continue to function using a modern alternative. These changes can significantly reduce the attack surface, but they must still be tested carefully to avoid breaking workflows.

Configuration changes are also where technicians often have the most direct control. Unlike patching, which depends on vendor releases, configuration hardening can usually be done immediately. At the same time, configuration changes can have wide-reaching effects. Blocking a port, disabling a service, or changing authentication requirements can affect multiple users or systems. For Security+, this reinforces the idea that remediation should be deliberate and proportional. The best answer is rarely the most aggressive one; it is the one that reduces risk while maintaining usability.

There are situations where immediate patching or permanent configuration changes are not possible. A vendor may not have released a patch yet, or a patch may be known to cause instability in your environment. In these cases, remediation shifts toward **compensating controls**. Compensating controls are temporary or indirect measures that reduce the likelihood or impact of exploitation without fixing the underlying vulnerability. They do not eliminate the weakness, but they make it harder to exploit or limit the damage if exploitation occurs.

Examples of compensating controls include restricting network access to a vulnerable service, disabling a specific feature known to be affected, increasing monitoring and logging, or placing additional controls like firewalls or intrusion prevention systems in front of a vulnerable system. If a web application has a known flaw and no patch is available, limiting access to trusted IP addresses or placing it behind additional authentication can reduce exposure. On the exam, when a scenario states that no patch exists yet, the correct remediation often involves implementing such controls rather than waiting passively or taking drastic actions like shutting down critical services indefinitely.

A key exam concept is recognizing when a remediation choice is **technically correct but operationally reckless**. For example, immediately rebooting a production server to apply a patch during business hours may fix the vulnerability but cause an outage that impacts customers or revenue. CompTIA often includes these tempting answers to see if candidates understand the balance between security and availability. The safer answer typically involves testing the patch, scheduling downtime, or applying temporary mitigations until the change can be made safely.

Another important aspect of remediation is scope. Fixing a vulnerability on one system should prompt you to consider whether the same issue exists elsewhere. If one workstation was vulnerable because its browser was outdated, it is likely that other workstations are affected as well. Effective remediation includes addressing the root cause across the environment, not just cleaning up a single symptom. On the exam, scenarios sometimes hint at this by describing repeated issues on multiple systems, and the best remediation choice reflects a broader fix rather than a one-off action.

Throughout remediation, documentation and communication matter. Recording what changes were made, why they were made, and when they were applied helps with troubleshooting, audits, and future decision-making. Informing users about expected downtime or behavior changes reduces confusion and resistance. While Security+ does not require deep knowledge of formal change management frameworks, it does reward answers that show awareness of coordination and accountability rather than isolated technical action.

Verification and Documentation: Proving the Risk Is Reduced

Remediation does not end when a patch is installed or a configuration is changed. Until you verify that the vulnerability is actually mitigated and that the system still functions as expected, the work is incomplete. For Security+, this follow-through step is easy to underestimate, but it is one of the most frequently tested ideas in scenario-based questions. CompTIA often presents answers that involve "applying the fix" and then asks what should happen next. The correct response almost always involves **verification**, not assumption.

Verification begins with confirming that the remediation was applied successfully. If a patch was installed, that might mean checking the system's update history, confirming the application or operating system version number, or verifying that the patch is listed as installed in the appropriate management console. If the vulnerability was identified through a scanner, verification may involve re-running that scan or waiting for the next scheduled scan to ensure the finding is no longer reported. The important idea is that you do not rely on intent or expectation. You confirm with evidence that the vulnerability is no longer present.

Verification also includes confirming that **normal functionality still works**. Security changes often affect how systems behave, and it is entirely possible to fix a vulnerability while accidentally breaking a business-critical process.

After disabling a vulnerable protocol, you need to ensure that file sharing, authentication, or application access still operates correctly. After tightening firewall rules, you need to confirm that legitimate traffic is not being blocked. On the exam, scenarios sometimes describe a system that was patched but now exhibits new problems, and the best next step is often to verify functionality or roll back a change rather than immediately applying additional fixes.

In environments that use compensating controls, verification becomes even more important. If a temporary mitigation was implemented because a patch was not available, you need to confirm that the control is actually reducing exposure. For example, if access to a vulnerable service was restricted, verification might involve testing from allowed and disallowed locations to ensure the restriction behaves as intended. If additional logging or monitoring was enabled, verification includes confirming that events are being captured and reviewed. In these cases, verification helps ensure that temporary measures are effective while you wait for a permanent solution.

Documentation is the other half of closing the loop. Recording what vulnerability was addressed, what remediation steps were taken, and when they were applied creates a trail that supports future troubleshooting and review. If an issue reappears or a similar vulnerability is discovered later, documentation helps determine whether it is a new problem or a recurrence of an old one. For technicians, documentation also protects you and your team by showing that appropriate actions were taken based on the information available at the time.

Documentation does not have to be heavy or bureaucratic to be valuable. In many environments, it may take the form of ticket updates, change records, or notes in a system management platform. What matters for Security+ is understanding why documentation exists. It provides continuity when multiple people work on the same systems, supports audits and compliance checks, and helps explain past decisions during post-incident reviews. When CompTIA includes answer choices that mention updating tickets, recording changes, or noting remediation actions, those are often signals that verification and documentation are expected next steps.

Verification also feeds directly back into the vulnerability management lifecycle. If verification shows that a vulnerability remains, the cycle returns to identification and remediation. If verification confirms the fix but reveals unintended side effects, that information informs future prioritization and change planning. In this way, verification is not just a final checkbox; it is a feedback mechanism that improves how vulnerabilities are handled over time.

Another exam-relevant aspect of verification is recognizing when **no further action is required**. If a scan is clean, systems function normally, and documentation is complete, the appropriate response may be to continue monitoring rather than making additional changes. CompTIA sometimes tests this by offering overly aggressive answers that suggest repeated patching or unnecessary configuration changes after the issue is already resolved. Understanding that verification can confirm success and allow you to move on is just as important as knowing how to fix the issue in the first place.

Vulnerability Management as Everyday IT Work

It is easy to think of vulnerability management as a specialized security function handled by scanners, dashboards, and security teams. In reality, much of vulnerability management happens quietly through everyday IT tasks, often without being labeled as "security work" at all. For entry-level technicians, this reframing is important. You are likely already doing vulnerability management whenever you install updates, adjust configurations, respond to incidents, or help users recover from problems. Security+ increasingly tests whether you recognize this connection and approach routine IT work with a security-aware mindset.

Consider something as ordinary as applying system updates. When you approve operating system patches, update a browser, or ensure that an application is running a supported version, you are reducing known vulnerabilities. Even if your motivation is to improve stability or performance, the effect is the same: closing weaknesses that attackers actively look for. Automatic updates, when appropriate for the environment, are not just a convenience feature; they are a foundational vulnerability management control. On the exam, scenarios that describe routine updates are often testing whether you see them as security actions, not just maintenance tasks.

The same is true for changing **default credentials** and tightening authentication settings. When you set a strong administrative password on a router, remove default accounts from a device, or enforce password policies for user accounts, you are addressing vulnerabilities that exist purely because of initial configurations. These weaknesses are among the first things attackers try, precisely because they are common and easy to exploit. In everyday support work, it may feel like simple setup or cleanup, but from a security perspective, it is preventive vulnerability remediation.

Configuration decisions play a similar role. Choosing to disable an unused service, restrict file permissions, or block an unnecessary port reduces the **attack surface** and removes opportunities for exploitation. These choices are often made to improve performance, reduce clutter, or simplify troubleshooting, yet they also make systems harder to attack. Security+ expects you to recognize that configuration hardening and vulnerability management are tightly linked, even when the original goal was operational efficiency.

Post-malware cleanup is another area where vulnerability management and incident response intersect. When you remove malware from a system, the job is not finished when the symptoms disappear. A security-aware technician asks what allowed the infection to occur in the first place. Was the browser outdated? Were users running with excessive privileges? Was email filtering insufficient? Identifying and addressing those underlying vulnerabilities turns a reactive incident into an opportunity for long-term risk reduction. On the exam, questions often test whether you stop at cleanup or extend your thinking to prevention.

Pattern recognition is a critical skill in this context. If one workstation is compromised because it was missing a patch, it is unlikely to be the only one. Effective vulnerability management means looking beyond the individual system in front of you and considering the broader environment. Are other machines running the same software version? Do similar configurations exist elsewhere? This mindset shift—from fixing one problem to reducing systemic risk—is subtle but powerful, and it is increasingly reflected in CompTIA's scenario-based questions.

Vulnerability management also connects naturally with **identity and access management**. Excessive privileges, shared accounts, and weak authentication practices are all vulnerabilities that technicians encounter daily. When you enforce least privilege, remove unnecessary access, or implement multi-factor authentication where appropriate, you are reducing the impact of future exploits. These actions may be framed as access control or account management tasks, but they directly influence how easily vulnerabilities can be exploited.

Monitoring and logging further reinforce this everyday connection. Reviewing logs, responding to alerts, and noticing unusual behavior are part of both operations and security. When monitoring reveals repeated failed logins, unexpected software installations, or configuration drift, it often points to underlying vulnerabilities that need to be addressed. Security+ scenarios frequently blend monitoring and vulnerability management, expecting candidates to recognize that detection and prevention are part of the same continuous effort.

What ties all of this together is mindset. Treating security as something separate from IT operations leads to missed opportunities and delayed responses. Treating vulnerability management as part of normal IT work encourages proactive thinking and continuous improvement. For the exam, this means choosing answers that reflect awareness, follow-through, and pattern recognition rather than narrow, one-off fixes.

Knowledge Check

Question 1: A security technician receives an automated report stating that several workstations are missing a recently released critical browser security patch. Which part of the vulnerability management cycle is the technician engaged in when reviewing this report and confirming which systems are affected?

A. Remediation
B. Identification
C. Verification
D. Change control

Question 2: An administrator has a scan report listing dozens of vulnerabilities, including a critical remote code execution flaw on a production file server and a medium-severity local privilege escalation on a training lab PC. According to good vulnerability management practice, what should the administrator do first?

A. Prioritize the critical file server vulnerability for rapid remediation
B. Patch the lab PC vulnerability because it is easier to fix
C. Defer both items to the next quarterly maintenance window
D. Focus only on vulnerabilities labeled medium to avoid service disruption

Question 3: A junior technician is told to disable SMBv1 on all file servers, remove default admin passwords from network printers, and tighten permissions on shared folders. These actions best describe which phase of the vulnerability management cycle?

A. Identification
B. Remediation
C. Verification
D. Risk acceptance

Question 4: A critical vulnerability is announced in a widely used web browser, but the vendor patch is not yet available. The advisory recommends disabling a specific browser feature and blocking known malicious domains at the firewall. Implementing these recommendations is an example of what?

A. Performing verification scans
B. Ignoring the vulnerability until an official fix is released
C. Lowering the CVSS score
D. Applying workarounds and compensating controls

Question 5: After applying a set of urgent security patches and configuration changes to a file server, which action best represents the verification phase of vulnerability management?

A. Confirming the patch versions, rescan, and testing key file share access
B. Documenting the changes in the ticketing system without testing
C. Immediately deploying the same changes to all servers with no further checks
D. Scheduling the next routine vulnerability scan for the following quarter

Question 6: A company discovers that a recently exploited browser vulnerability allowed malware to be installed on a user's workstation. The technician cleans the infection and then checks whether the same browser patch is missing on other systems, planning a company-wide update if needed. Which concept does this behavior best illustrate?

A. Performing a full backup before every change
B. Removing all third-party software from user systems
C. Integrating incident response with vulnerability management
D. Ignoring vendor advisories unless multiple users are affected

Question 7: A vulnerability scanner flags an old media player on a few training lab machines as having a medium-severity local privilege escalation vulnerability. The machines hold no sensitive data and are used only occasionally. The administrator decides to schedule the update for the next regular maintenance window rather than taking them offline immediately. Which risk management concept most strongly supports this decision?

A. Defense in depth
B. Default deny
C. Zero trust
D. Balancing likelihood and impact when prioritizing vulnerabilities

Question 8: A security analyst wants to quickly determine whether a specific newly published vulnerability is already known to be actively exploited and how severe it is rated across the industry. Which resource is most directly useful for this purpose?

A. Internal password policy documentation
B. Vendor or public advisories that reference CVE IDs and CVSS scores
C. The organization's asset inventory spreadsheet
D. Physical access control logs from the data center

ANSWERS

1: Correct Answer: B
Rationale: Reviewing reports of missing patches and determining which systems are affected is part of identifying and assessing vulnerabilities in the environment.

2: Correct Answer: A
Rationale: A critical remote code execution on a production file server represents higher risk and should be prioritized for rapid remediation over lower-impact, medium-severity issues.

3: Correct Answer: B
Rationale: Disabling weak protocols, changing default passwords, and tightening permissions are remediation activities that directly reduce identified vulnerabilities.

4: Correct Answer: D
Rationale: Disabling risky features and blocking malicious domains are workarounds and compensating controls used to mitigate risk until a vendor patch is available.

5: Correct Answer: D
Rationale: Verification involves confirming that patches are correctly applied, rescanning to ensure vulnerabilities are mitigated, and testing that normal services still function.

6: Correct Answer: C
Rationale: The technician is handling an incident (malware infection) while also checking for and remediating the underlying unpatched vulnerability across other systems, integrating incident response with vulnerability management.

7: Correct Answer: D
Rationale: The administrator weighs the medium severity and low business impact against operational needs, exemplifying prioritization based on the likelihood and impact of vulnerabilities.

8: Correct Answer: B
Rationale: Vendor and public advisories that include CVE identifiers and CVSS scores provide standardized information on severity and often note whether exploits are active in the wild.

4.4 Identity & Access Management

When you strip away the buzzwords, a huge part of security operations is really about people and their accounts. Every time someone logs into Windows, connects to Wi-Fi, opens a shared folder, or launches a cloud app, **identity and access management**—IAM—is silently deciding what happens next. As a support technician, you live right where users and IAM collide. You are the person they call when "my password doesn't work," "I can't open this folder anymore," or "why do I have to use this code on my phone now?" This chapter is about understanding the logic behind those decisions, so you can fix problems without undermining security.

A good way to organize your thinking is with the classic **AAA** model: **authentication**, **authorization**, and **accounting** (or auditing). Authentication is about proving who you are. Authorization is about what you're allowed to do once you're in. Accounting is about recording what you actually did. Most exam scenarios—and real help desk tickets—are some variation of "this part of AAA is broken" or "which AAA control would solve this problem?" Once you can mentally separate those pieces, IAM questions become much easier to reason through.

Identities, Accounts, and Where They Live

Start with a deceptively simple question: when a user says "my account," what are they really talking about? In technical terms, an **identity** is how a person (or sometimes a service) is represented inside an IT system, and **user accounts** are the concrete implementation of those identities. That account has a username, an internal ID, a password or other credentials, and a collection of attributes: which groups it belongs to, what its email address is, what permissions it has, and so on.

Those accounts can live in different places. On a standalone Windows PC at home, users might only have **local accounts**. These are stored on that specific machine, and they only work there. If you create a local account named "Alex" with a password, that account means nothing to any other computer. In contrast, businesses usually rely on **directory-based** or **domain accounts**, managed centrally in systems like Active Directory, Azure AD/Entra ID, or Google Workspace. Those identities live in a directory service and can be used to log into many devices and applications that trust that directory.

Understanding this distinction helps tremendously with troubleshooting. If just one computer is affected—for example, a single user can't log into one workstation but can log into others with no problem—that points toward a local account issue or a machine-specific configuration. If a problem suddenly affects a whole department across multiple systems—say everyone in Sales loses access to a particular web app at once—that suggests something changed at the directory or group policy level. Centralization makes security and administration much easier because you can enforce a policy once and have it apply everywhere, but it also means that a mistake in that centralized configuration can break access for a lot of people at the same time.

You will also encounter **service accounts**, which represent applications or services rather than human beings, and possibly guest or shared accounts. These behave like user accounts in the system's eyes, but the identity behind them is an application, a kiosk, or a generic "front desk" login. We will return to those later, because they introduce their own security complications.

Authentication: Proving Who You Are

Once an account exists, the first question any system asks is, "how do I know you are really this person?" That's the job of **authentication**. In theory, authentication should rely on something that is hard for an attacker to guess, steal, or fake. In practice, it is built from three classic categories called **authentication factors**: something you know, something you have, and something you are.

"**Something you know**" includes traditional **passwords**, PINs, and the dreaded security questions. These are easy to implement and familiar to users, which is why they are still everywhere, but they are also easy to mishandle.

People choose weak passwords, reuse them across sites, write them down, or reveal answers to "secret questions" in public social media posts. As an A+ technician, you will spend a lot of time dealing with password resets and explaining why the new password needs to be stronger or longer than the old one.

"**Something you have**" covers physical tokens and devices: a smartphone with an authenticator app, a one-time password (OTP) hardware token, a smart card, or even an SMS code sent to a mobile phone. From a security perspective, these are powerful because an attacker needs to gain control of the physical object or the phone number, which is generally harder than just guessing a password. Not all "something you have" factors are equal—SMS is better than nothing but can be intercepted or hijacked—but on the exam, any physical token or code delivered to a separate device counts in this category.

"**Something you are**" refers to **biometrics**: fingerprints, facial recognition, iris scans, and similar technologies. You see these on smartphones, in Windows Hello, and on some laptops with fingerprint readers. They are convenient because users don't have to remember anything, but they also raise privacy and reliability questions. From your perspective, the key point is recognizing that when a user logs in with a password and a fingerprint, they are using two different factor types.

That last sentence is crucial for understanding **multifactor authentication**, or MFA. True MFA combines two or more different factor types. A password plus a PIN is not MFA, because both are "something you know." A password plus a smartphone app that generates codes is MFA, because it combines something you know with something you have. Exam questions love to test this nuance. If you see a scenario describing "two passwords" or "password and security questions," that is still single-factor authentication, just using the same category twice.

You will see these concepts show up in different contexts. A Windows sign-in screen that accepts a password or PIN is basic authentication. A VPN client that prompts for a password and then sends a push notification to the user's phone is an example of MFA protecting remote network access. A web portal for Microsoft 365 that first asks for credentials and then requires a time-based one-time code is another. When a question asks how to strengthen authentication without major hardware changes, enabling MFA with a mobile authenticator app is often the best answer, because it doesn't require smart card readers or new physical tokens.

Authorization: Deciding What You Can Do

Once the system is convinced you are you, it moves on to the next decision: what are you allowed to do here? That is **authorization**. It is not enough to know that a user is legitimate; you also need to constrain their access to match their job role. This is where the **principle of least privilege** comes in: give users only the permissions they need to do their work, and nothing more.

Authorization is implemented in many different ways, but a central theme is that permissions are not usually assigned directly to individual users; instead, they are assigned to **groups** or **roles**. In a Windows domain, a user might be a member of "Domain Users," "Sales," and "Remote Desktop Users." The file server might grant the "Sales" group Read and Write access to the Sales share, while the finance share only allows access to the "Finance" group. When Alex from Sales logs in, the file server sees that Alex is a member of Sales but not Finance, and allows or denies access accordingly.

This group-based approach is an example of **role-based access control** (RBAC). Instead of individually granting every salesperson access to the CRM system and the Sales folder, you define what a "Sales" role needs, grant those permissions to the Sales group, and then add users to that group. When someone changes jobs, you modify their group membership rather than hunting for every permission they ever had. In the exam, if a scenario mentions that an organization wants to simplify managing permissions when employees move between departments, RBAC is the concept they are hinting at.

File and folder permissions are one of the most visible faces of authorization for an A+ tech. On Windows systems, **NTFS permissions** define what a user or group can do with a file or directory: read, write, modify, execute, or full control. Network **share permissions** add another layer on top. The effective permission is often the most restrictive combination of both. For example, if the NTFS permission grants Modify but the share permits only Read, the user will experience Read-only behavior when accessing the folder over the network. On Linux and macOS, you see simpler owner/group/other permission models, but the principle is similar: membership and permission bits together determine access.

When a user says "Access denied," your first mental fork in the road should be: are they being denied at login, or after login when trying to reach a specific resource? If they cannot log in at all, that is usually an authentication problem—wrong password, locked account, disabled account, or network/domain connectivity. If they can log into the system but cannot open a particular file, folder, or application, that is almost always an authorization issue: incorrect group membership, missing permissions, or a role that does not include that resource. Exam questions like to test this differentiation; the correct fix is rarely "reset the password" for an "Access denied" error on a single shared folder.

Accounting and Auditing: Who Did What, When

The third "A," **accounting** (often combined with **auditing**), is less glamorous but just as important. This is about tracking and recording activity: when users logged on and off, what resources they accessed, and whether any errors or suspicious events occurred. These records are essential when investigating incidents or disputes.

On a Windows server, for example, you might enable auditing of successful and failed logons, object access, or privilege use. The resulting events appear in the Security log of Event Viewer, where you can see that a particular user logged on interactively at a certain time, or that a series of failed logon attempts occurred from a particular workstation. In a directory service, you might find logs showing that a user was added to or removed from a security group at a specific date. Cloud services like Microsoft 365 or Google Workspace also maintain audit logs for administrative changes and user activity.

As an A+ technician, you are not expected to design a complex logging architecture, but you are expected to recognize when logs are the right tool. If a manager insists they never deleted an important file, the correct technical next step is not to reset their password—it is to check whether file auditing was enabled and, if so, review the logs to see which user account deleted it. When an exam question mentions "tracking user activity," "investigating suspicious access," or "reconstructing events," the associated actions are to **enable auditing**, **review logs**, or **configure logging** on the relevant system, not to give someone more permissions.

Password and Account Policies in Daily Operations

If there is one IAM area you will touch constantly, it is **password and account policies**. These define the rules that passwords must follow and how the system reacts to incorrect attempts. Organizations often enforce a minimum password length, and sometimes complexity requirements such as including uppercase, lowercase, numbers, and symbols. Modern best practice emphasizes longer passphrases over complicated but short strings, but the exam still expects you to recognize both length and complexity controls.

Password history prevents users from reusing the same handful of passwords over and over. Expiration policies require users to change their password periodically, though there is growing recognition that forcing frequent changes can backfire by encouraging weak patterns. When you reset a user's password, you may have the option to require them to change it at next logon, which is a good way to ensure you are not the only one who ever knows that password.

Another critical control is the **account lockout policy**. This defines how many failed login attempts are allowed before the system locks the account, and for how long. Lockouts help defend against brute-force guessing, but if thresholds are too strict, legitimate users get locked out frequently and the help desk is flooded with tickets. In a domain environment, these policies are typically set centrally and affect all users. Exam scenarios will often describe users getting locked out "every morning" or "after changing passwords," and your job is to connect that to lockout thresholds and stored credentials rather than simply turning off the lockout feature.

Accounts can also have explicit **expiration dates**, which is handy for contractors, temporary employees, or test accounts. When the expiration date is reached, the user simply cannot log in until an administrator updates or renews the account. If a question describes a contractor who suddenly cannot log in after their end date passes, even though their password is correct, account expiration is the likely cause.

From an operational perspective, you will constantly interpret symptoms and match them to the right category. A user who "can log into the computer but not open the marketing share" is having an authorization problem. A user who "gets wrong password errors, then suddenly is told their account is locked" is running into authentication controls—the lockout policy. The correct fix might involve unlocking their account, verifying their identity before resetting the password, and reminding them about Caps Lock, but it is rarely to loosen security controls across the organization.

Multifactor Authentication and Single Sign-On

As you look beyond passwords, two concepts will appear again and again: **multifactor authentication (MFA)** and **single sign-on (SSO)**. They both involve sign-ins, which makes them easy to confuse, but they solve very different problems.

MFA, as discussed earlier, strengthens a single login by requiring multiple factor types. You might see it in a corporate environment as a password plus an authenticator app on a smartphone, a smart card plus PIN for logging into a laptop, or a password plus an SMS code for a cloud application. Your role often involves helping users enroll in MFA: installing apps, scanning QR codes to bind their account, updating phone numbers when devices change, and assisting with recovery procedures if they lose their second factor. It is important not to undermine MFA in the name of convenience; for example, forwarding one-time codes over email or chat is a bad habit that can nullify its benefits.

SSO, on the other hand, is about reducing **how often** users have to authenticate and **how many** different passwords they must remember. With SSO, a user signs into a central identity provider or portal once, and that session is then used to access multiple related applications without reentering credentials. Think of logging into a corporate dashboard and then being able to open your email, intranet, and HR portal without further prompts. Behind the scenes, protocols and trust relationships make this possible, but from the user's perspective, it feels like "one login for everything."

On the exam, pay attention to the business motivation in the question. If the scenario says the organization wants to "increase login security" or "reduce the risk of credential theft," MFA is the focus. If it instead mentions "reducing password fatigue," "too many logins," or "users managing multiple sets of credentials," that is a cue for SSO or centralized authentication. In many modern environments, the two are combined: users sign in once with MFA at the start of the day, and then enjoy SSO access to the applications they are authorized to use.

Privileged, Shared, and Special-Purpose Accounts

Not all accounts are equal. Some are vastly more powerful and therefore more dangerous if misused or compromised. **Privileged accounts** include local Administrator accounts on Windows, domain administrator accounts in Active Directory, and the root account on Linux or macOS. They can install software, change system settings, manage other accounts, and in many cases access or modify any data. Best practice is to avoid using these accounts for everyday activities like browsing the web or reading email; instead, administrators should have separate standard user accounts for routine work and only elevate to admin when necessary.

On Windows, this often looks like right-clicking an application and choosing "Run as administrator," or on Linux using `sudo` to run a single command with elevated rights. This is sometimes called just-in-time or just-enough administration: you grant extra power only for the duration of a specific task. Membership in powerful groups such as "Domain Admins" should be tightly controlled and regularly reviewed. On the exam, if a user only needs to install software occasionally, it is almost never appropriate to make them a permanent local administrator just to "get rid of the error messages." That violates least privilege and greatly increases risk.

At the other end of the spectrum are **guest accounts** and **shared accounts**. Guest accounts are typically very limited built-in accounts that may be disabled by default. They are intended for temporary or anonymous access, but because they are generic and often poorly tracked, best practice is usually to keep them disabled and instead create named temporary accounts with clear owners and expiration dates when access is needed. Shared accounts—like a general "FrontDesk" or "Cashier" login—are still common in some environments, but they pose accountability problems: if something goes wrong, you cannot easily tell which human used that account at a given time. When possible, systems should identify individual users, even on shared workstations, so that accountability and auditing remain meaningful.

Service accounts deserve special mention. These are accounts used by applications, scheduled tasks, or services to run in the background. They may need access to databases, file shares, or directories, and they often have unusual logon types. Accidentally deleting or changing the password on a service account can silently break dependent services. For that reason, they should be documented, use strong, non-expiring credentials where appropriate, and be granted only the minimal permissions required to do their jobs. When you see unfamiliar accounts in permission lists, especially with names suggesting applications or services, be cautious before modifying them.

Finally, tying all of this together is your troubleshooting mindset. When you receive an IAM-related ticket, clarify the symptom: is the user unable to log in anywhere, or just to one resource? Did anything change recently—passwords, group membership, hardware, or policies? Are multiple users affected, suggesting a centralized issue, or just one? The more you practice mapping symptoms to authentication, authorization, and accounting layers, the more natural it becomes to choose solutions that both solve the problem and maintain a strong security posture.

Knowledge Check

Question 1: A user can log into their Windows domain account on multiple computers but receives "Access denied" only when trying to open a specific network folder. Which AAA component is most likely misconfigured?

A. Authentication
B. Accounting
C. Single sign-on
D. Authorization

Question 2: A company wants to reduce the number of times users must enter their credentials throughout the workday while accessing multiple internal web applications, without weakening existing password requirements. Which technology best meets this goal?

A. Multifactor authentication
B. Single sign-on
C. Account lockout policy
D. Password expiration

Question 3: A security administrator wants to improve security for remote VPN logins by requiring users to enter a password and then approve a push notification on their smartphone authenticator app. Which term BEST describes this configuration?

A. Multifactor authentication
B. Single-factor authentication
C. Role-based access control
D. Password complexity control

Question 4: A help desk technician is told to implement least privilege when granting permissions to new employees and to simplify changes when users move between departments. Which access control model should the technician primarily rely on?

A. Discretionary access control (DAC)
B. Role-based access control (RBAC)
C. Mandatory access control (MAC)
D. Rule-based access control

Question 5: Several users report they are suddenly unable to log in to the domain. The technician verifies they are entering the correct password but sees that their accounts show as "expired" in the directory. What is the MOST appropriate corrective action?

A. Disable the account lockout policy
B. Reset the users' passwords without changing account status
C. Add the users to a higher-privileged group
D. Extend or remove the account expiration dates

Question 6: An application server uses a dedicated domain account to access a database and a file share. After a password change on that account, the application stops working until the stored credentials are updated. Which type of account is this?

A. Guest account
B. Privileged administrator account
C. Service account
D. Shared user account

Question 7: A manager insists they did not delete an important file from a shared folder, but the file is missing. The environment has security logs that track successful and failed file access events. Which action BEST leverages the accounting function of AAA in this situation?

A. Review the audit logs to determine which account deleted the file
B. Add the manager to a group with full control over the share
C. Reset manager password; require change
D. Disable account lockout to prevent similar issues

Question 8: A user reports that their account gets locked every morning shortly after they change their password. The technician confirms that the user's new password meets policy and that the account is not expired. What is the MOST likely cause of these repeated lockouts?

A. Incorrect NTFS permissions on a network share
B. Stored credentials on another device or service using the old password
C. A missing group membership for the user's department
D. An expired SSL certificate on the domain controller

ANSWERS

1: Correct Answer: D
Rationale: The user authenticates successfully to the domain but is denied access to a specific resource, indicating an authorization (permissions) problem, not an authentication or accounting issue.

2: Correct Answer: B
Rationale: Single sign-on lets users authenticate once and access multiple applications, reducing repeated logins without changing password strength or other policies.

3: Correct Answer: A
Rationale: A password is something you know, and a smartphone push approval is something you have, so using both is multifactor authentication, not single-factor or an access control model.

4: Correct Answer: B
Rationale: Role-based access control assigns permissions to roles and then users to those roles, supporting least privilege and making it easy to adjust access when users change departments.

5: Correct Answer: D
Rationale: The accounts are marked as expired, so updating or removing the account expiration dates directly addresses the problem without weakening other security controls.

6: Correct Answer: C
Rationale: A dedicated account used by an application or service to access resources is a service account, distinct from guest, admin, or shared user accounts.

7: Correct Answer: A
Rationale: Accounting involves logging and auditing user actions; reviewing audit logs uses this function to identify which account deleted the file and when.

8: Correct Answer: B
Rationale: A device or service still using cached credentials with the old password will repeatedly attempt logins, causing failed attempts and triggering account lockouts.

4.5 Enterprise Security Solutions

If you think about the typical home network, the security story is fairly simple. There is usually an internet router from the ISP, maybe a Wi-Fi password, and whatever antivirus came with the laptop. That arrangement is barely acceptable for a family of four, and it completely falls apart once you scale up to a company with hundreds or thousands of devices, sensitive data, legal obligations, and users connecting from everywhere. In an enterprise environment, security becomes a layered system of specialized tools working together. As a support technician, you will live in that layered world every day, even if you never log directly into those systems. Your job is not to be the security engineer who designs all of it, but to understand what each layer is trying to do and how it shows up in the tickets and phone calls you receive.

A useful way to think about enterprise security is to imagine multiple concentric rings and focus areas. At the outer edge you have technology that controls which network traffic is even allowed to reach the organization. Deeper inside, you have tools that inspect that traffic more carefully for signs of attack, other tools that decide who and what is allowed onto the network in the first place, still others that watch the behavior of each endpoint, and finally systems that are obsessed with one thing only: making sure sensitive data does not escape where it should not go.

CompTIA wraps a lot of that world into a handful of terms you need to recognize on sight: firewalls, IDS/IPS, NAC, EDR, and DLP. Once you can map a user's symptom to the right category, enterprise security scenarios become much easier to reason about.

Firewalls: Gatekeepers of Network Traffic

The most familiar of these tools is the **firewall**, and in many offices the word "firewall" is blamed for almost any connectivity problem. In reality, a firewall does something quite specific: it allows or blocks network traffic based on rules. Those rules typically refer to IP addresses, ports, protocols, and in more advanced products, even to applications or content types. If you picture network traffic as cars moving on a highway, the firewall is the checkpoint deciding which kinds of cars may pass, on which lanes, and at what times, according to the organization's policies.

Firewalls appear in two main forms you need to distinguish. A **host-based firewall** runs on a single device. Windows Defender Firewall and the built-in firewall in macOS are good examples. Their job is to protect that one host from unwanted inbound connections, and often to control which applications on that host are allowed to initiate outbound connections. When a user installs new software that needs to accept incoming connections—say, a remote support tool or a local web service—and everyone outside the machine gets "connection timed out," it is very often the host firewall quietly blocking the relevant port. Users may see pop-up prompts asking them to "allow access" for a new application, and if they click the wrong option, you get a ticket about something suddenly not working.

A **network-based firewall**, in contrast, sits at a network boundary and protects entire segments of the environment. The classic example is the firewall at the internet edge, sitting between the organization's internal network and the public internet. Others may sit between VLANs or in front of data centers. These devices enforce policies like "block all inbound traffic from the internet unless explicitly allowed," or "only allow HTTPS from the user VLANs to the external internet," or "deny RDP from guest Wi-Fi to internal servers." When users working remotely say they cannot reach an internal web app over the VPN, or when a newly deployed server is not reachable from another site, a network firewall rule is often part of the investigation.

It helps to contrast firewalls with other security tools you already know. Antivirus focuses on files and processes: is this executable malicious? A firewall doesn't care what the file is; it cares about who is talking to whom, over which port, using which protocol. Compared to IDS/IPS, which we will come to in a moment, a firewall is primarily **policy-based**. You write explicit rules saying what to allow or deny, and those rules do not try to guess whether traffic is an attack; they simply enforce the policy. When you see words like "port," "allowed IPs," "blocked from this subnet," or "connection refused," you should be thinking in terms of firewalls somewhere along the path, either on the host or in the network.

IDS/IPS: Detecting and Preventing Intrusions

If firewalls are the bouncers checking IDs at the door based on a guest list, **intrusion detection and prevention systems** are the security team watching what people actually do once they are inside. An **IDS (Intrusion Detection System)** monitors traffic looking for suspicious patterns, such as signatures of known exploits, unusual port scans, or traffic that deviates from normal baselines. Its core job is to detect and alert; it may log events and notify the security team, but it does not necessarily block the traffic itself.

An **IPS (Intrusion Prevention System)** goes a step further. It uses similar detection techniques—signatures, rules, and sometimes behavioral analysis—but when it decides traffic matches a known attack, it can actively block or drop that traffic. In practice, many modern "next-generation firewalls" bundle firewall and IPS capabilities in one platform, but the conceptual distinction remains: firewall rules enforce explicit policy about which flows are permitted, while IPS logic tries to stop attacks within those permitted flows.

In terms of deployment, IDS/IPS usually lives at key chokepoints where a lot of important traffic passes. One sensor might monitor the link between the internal network and the internet edge. Another might sit between the user

VLANs and the server VLANs, watching for lateral movement from compromised user machines. When IPS is actively blocking, users may see odd, intermittent issues: a connection that starts fine but drops as soon as certain data is sent, or a file download that aborts halfway. From their perspective, "the network is flaky." From the IPS's perspective, it just stopped what looked like a SQL injection or shellcode exploit.

A useful mental cue is to look for patterns where basic connectivity works but specific operations seem to cause resets or failures, especially if there are corresponding alerts in security dashboards. For example, a developer might report that their new web service works fine on their local test environment but fails mysteriously when deployed to a shared QA server. Investigation reveals that certain API calls trigger IPS rules because they look similar to known attacks. In those situations, Tier 1's role is not to change IPS policies but to gather details: timestamps, URLs or endpoints involved, sample payloads if appropriate, and then escalate to the network or security team so they can tune signatures or create exceptions if the behavior is truly legitimate.

NAC: Deciding Who Can Join the Network

While firewalls and IDS/IPS focus on the traffic itself, **Network Access Control (NAC)** is concerned with who and what is allowed to join the network at all. NAC wraps around the initial connection step: when a device plugs into a wired port or connects to a corporate Wi-Fi SSID, NAC decides whether to grant full access, limited access, or no access at all. It does this by checking identity and compliance. Identity can mean the user's credentials, but also the device's identity through certificates or other attributes. Compliance means the device meets certain security requirements: current patches, approved antivirus installed, not rooted or jailbroken in strict environments, required agents running, and so on.

You will usually see NAC in action through 802.1X authentication on wired or wireless networks, sometimes combined with agent software on endpoints that reports their posture. The outcome might be completely transparent to the user—everything just works because their corporate laptop is healthy and authenticated. Or it might be very visible. A new contractor plugs into an Ethernet jack and finds they can only reach the internet but not internal file shares or web apps. From their point of view, "the cable is fine, I can browse the web." From the network's point of view, that port has placed their unmanaged device in a guest VLAN with internet-only access, precisely because NAC did not recognize it as compliant.

This is a common pattern: limited or no access right at the moment of first connection, usually affecting that one device, while others on the same port or SSID work fine. Another example is a corporate laptop that suddenly starts getting only guest access after a big OS update. Perhaps the NAC agent stopped functioning or the device certificate is missing. Basic Tier 1 checks—confirming the correct SSID, verifying the user's credentials, checking for NAC agent errors—can quickly distinguish between a general network outage and NAC blocking or quarantining that specific endpoint. Once you suspect NAC, your job is to collect practical details: MAC address, username, switch port or AP, exact time the issue occurred, and any error text like "authentication failed" or "restricted network." That information is gold for the network/security team.

EDR: Watching and Controlling Endpoint Behavior

Traditional antivirus is focused on scanning files against signatures of known malware. Modern attackers, however, rarely just drop a single obvious malicious file. They use living-off-the-land techniques, scripts, PowerShell, and chains of seemingly normal actions. This is where **Endpoint Detection and Response (EDR)** comes in. EDR tools monitor endpoint behavior at a much deeper level: which processes are running, what those processes do, which registry keys they touch, what network connections they open, and how files are modified. They then use analytics and cloud-based threat intelligence to decide whether that behavior looks malicious.

From a user's perspective, EDR shows up when things on a single machine are abruptly stopped or isolated. An application might launch and then close immediately every time, with or without a pop-up explaining that the process was blocked. An installer that worked yesterday may be silently quarantined today, leaving the user convinced "the installer is broken." In more serious cases, if the EDR agent detects ransomware-like activity or command-and-control communications, it may forcibly isolate the endpoint from the network. The machine remains powered on, the user can log in, but suddenly they cannot reach any network drives or internal systems. The local network icon might show limited connectivity, yet the switches and routers all check out fine. That is a classic EDR isolation symptom.

When you encounter strange, security-flavored behavior limited to one endpoint—processes killed, scripts blocked, sudden network isolation—it is wise to think EDR rather than network firewalls or IDS/IPS. On the A+ exam and in real life, disabling or uninstalling the EDR agent should not be your first thought. Instead, check whether the EDR client is showing alerts, whether there are system tray notifications, or whether corporate documentation describes known conflicts. Capture the exact time of the incident and what the user was doing, and include that in your escalation. Security teams rely heavily on EDR telemetry during incident response, and your careful observations can help them quickly distinguish malicious activity from a false positive that is blocking business-critical software.

DLP: Keeping Sensitive Data from Walking Out

The last major tool in this group, **Data Loss (or Leakage) Prevention (DLP)**, is less concerned with who is on the network or what processes are running, and much more concerned with what happens to sensitive data. DLP solutions monitor and sometimes control how information moves: through email, web uploads, cloud storage, printing, copying to USB drives, and even screenshots or clipboard access in advanced deployments. Underneath, DLP systems use patterns, keywords, document classifications, and other techniques to recognize content such as credit card numbers, Social Security numbers, protected health information, or files labeled "Confidential."

DLP becomes visible when users try to move data in ways that violate company policy. Imagine a salesperson trying to email a customer list spreadsheet to their personal Gmail account so they can "finish it at home." Outlook sends the message, but almost immediately the user receives a notification that the email was blocked due to a policy violation. Or perhaps their message is delayed and then they receive a warning from an automated compliance system. In another case, a user plugs in a USB flash drive, copies a folder of HR documents onto it, and gets a vague error message about the operation not being permitted. The same drive works fine on their home PC, but on the corporate laptop it refuses to hold certain files. In both cases, DLP is quietly enforcing rules that say "this kind of data must not leave through that channel."

From Tier 1's perspective, DLP issues often look like selective blocking tied to the content itself, not to basic connectivity. Users may report that "some emails go out but others don't," or "I can copy some files to USB but not this spreadsheet," or "I can upload photos to this website but not this PDF with customer information." Recognizing that pattern—particular data types and destinations being blocked by policy—is key. Your role is to confirm the exact error text, ask what kind of information is in the file or email, and then explain, within policy, that corporate and regulatory requirements might forbid that transfer. Instead of trying to bypass the restriction, you help direct the user to approved methods, such as secure internal file sharing, a company-approved cloud service, or remote access to work systems from home.

Putting the Pieces Together in Real Scenarios

Once you see these tools as different specialists rather than a single vague idea of "security," it becomes much easier to diagnose which one is likely involved in a scenario. Start by thinking about scope and symptom. If a problem affects many users or an entire office and is framed in terms of "can't reach this site" or "this port seems closed," your thoughts should drift toward network firewalls or IPS rules. If the impact appears the moment a device tries to join the network and only that device is affected—such as a personal phone that cannot join corporate Wi-Fi while company laptops work fine—NAC is a strong candidate. If one computer is having its processes terminated, installers quarantined, or is abruptly isolated from the network while the rest of the office is normal, EDR is near the top of the list. And if the complaint is specifically about certain files or messages being blocked when sent externally or copied to certain media, especially with references to "policy" in the error messages, DLP is most likely the cause.

In everyday support work, the most important skill here is not reconfiguring these enterprise tools; it is quickly recognizing their fingerprints, avoiding unsafe workarounds, and gathering the right evidence. Instead of telling a user, "The network is just weird today," you can say, "It looks like our DLP system is blocking that data from being emailed externally; let's look at our approved sharing options," or "Your laptop appears to be on a guest network, which is probably NAC; I'll collect your device details and escalate this to the network team." Security teams appreciate technicians who can speak this language, and exam writers reward candidates who can map descriptions like "guest network," "connection dropped when sending certain data," or "file transfer blocked by policy" to the right layer of enterprise defense.

Knowledge Check

Question 1: A user reports that they can browse the internet but cannot access an internal web application over a VPN. Other remote users can access it without issues. Which enterprise security control is the most likely cause of this specific connectivity problem?

- **A.** Host-based antivirus
- **B.** Network Access Control (NAC)
- **C.** Data Loss Prevention (DLP)
- **D.** Network-based firewall

Question 2: A security appliance is monitoring traffic between the user VLANs and server VLANs. It allows most traffic but occasionally drops specific packets when they resemble known exploit patterns, causing certain file transfers to fail midway. Which type of solution is this?

- **A.** Network Access Control (NAC)
- **B.** Endpoint Detection and Response (EDR)
- **C.** Intrusion Prevention System (IPS)
- **D.** Data Loss Prevention (DLP)

Question 3: A contractor connects a laptop to a corporate Ethernet port and can access the internet but not internal file shares or web applications. Corporate laptops on the same switch work normally. Which control is most likely enforcing this behavior?

- **A.** Host-based firewall on the contractor's laptop
- **B.** Data Loss Prevention on the file servers
- **C.** Endpoint Detection and Response on the contractor's laptop
- **D.** Network Access Control (NAC)

Question 4: A user reports that an application launches and then immediately closes on a single corporate laptop. Other users can run the same application without problems. The security team confirms that the behavior-based agent on that laptop is terminating the process. Which solution is most likely responsible?

- **A.** Endpoint Detection and Response (EDR)
- **B.** Intrusion Detection System (IDS)
- **C.** Network Access Control (NAC)
- **D.** Data Loss Prevention (DLP)

Question 5: An employee attempts to email a spreadsheet containing hundreds of customer Social Security numbers to their personal email account. The message appears to send but is quickly returned with an automated notice stating it was blocked due to a policy violation. Which security control is most likely responsible?

A. Intrusion Prevention System (IPS)
B. Data Loss Prevention (DLP)
C. Network Access Control (NAC)
D. Host-based firewall

Question 6: A help desk technician needs to distinguish between a host-based firewall and a network-based firewall. Which scenario best illustrates a host-based firewall issue?

A. A newly installed remote support tool on one laptop is unreachable from other systems until the user allows it through a Windows firewall prompt
B. All users on a specific VLAN cannot browse to external HTTPS sites after a new rule is applied at the edge device
C. Remote VPN users intermittently lose access to all internal resources after an IPS signature update
D. Multiple offices lose connectivity to a shared data center because of a misconfigured router ACL

Question 7: A user says, "My laptop shows 'limited connectivity' and I suddenly can't reach any internal systems, but the rest of the office is fine." The security team later confirms the device was automatically isolated after detecting ransomware-like activity. Which technology most likely performed this isolation?

A. Network Access Control (NAC)
B. Endpoint Detection and Response (EDR)
C. Data Loss Prevention (DLP)
D. Intrusion Detection System (IDS)

Question 8: Several users complain that they can copy regular documents to USB drives, but when they try to copy HR files marked "Confidential," they receive an error and the copy fails. The same USB drives work at home. Which enterprise security solution is most likely enforcing this restriction?

A. Intrusion Prevention System (IPS)
B. Network Access Control (NAC)
C. Data Loss Prevention (DLP)
D. Endpoint Detection and Response (EDR)

ANSWERS

1: Correct Answer: D
Rationale: The problem affects access to an internal app over a VPN and is likely due to a rule controlling traffic between networks, which is handled by a network-based firewall. The other controls do not typically block only a specific internal web app over VPN.

2: Correct Answer: C
Rationale: The device inspects traffic for exploit signatures and actively drops matching packets, which is the behavior of an Intrusion Prevention System. NAC, EDR, and DLP do not selectively drop packets based on exploit patterns in transit.

3: Correct Answer: D
Rationale: Network Access Control can place unknown or noncompliant devices into a restricted or guest VLAN, allowing only internet access while blocking internal resources. The other options act on the endpoint or data, not on network access segmentation.

4: Correct Answer: A
Rationale: Endpoint Detection and Response agents monitor process behavior on a single endpoint and can terminate applications they classify as suspicious. IDS, NAC, and DLP do not directly kill local processes on one laptop.

5: Correct Answer: B
Rationale: Data Loss Prevention inspects outbound content and blocks messages containing sensitive data such as SSNs, returning a policy-violation notice. IPS, NAC, and host-based firewalls focus on traffic or access, not content-aware email blocking.

6: Correct Answer: A
Rationale: Only one laptop is affected, and the issue is resolved by allowing the app through the local OS firewall, which indicates a host-based firewall. The other scenarios describe network-wide issues typical of network-based controls.

7: Correct Answer: B
Rationale: Endpoint Detection and Response can detect ransomware-like behavior and automatically isolate the endpoint from the network. NAC usually controls initial access, DLP protects data movement, and IDS only alerts without isolating hosts.

8: Correct Answer: C
Rationale: Data Loss Prevention enforces policies on sensitive files and can block copying "Confidential" data to removable media. IPS inspects network traffic, NAC manages network access, and EDR focuses on threat detection rather than content-based copy control.

CHAPTER 5
Security Operations II

5.1 Security Monitoring & Logging

If you ask experienced security professionals where they spend a surprising amount of their time, many will give you a slightly tired smile and say, "In the logs." Modern systems quietly record almost everything they do, from routine service startups to failed login attempts and blocked network traffic. Those records are your eyes and ears after the fact. When a user says "something weird happened" or an automated tool sends an alert at 2 a.m., your ability to find, read, and make sense of logs is what turns vague stories into concrete facts. In this chapter, we stay firmly in that detection space: how systems and tools tell you what is happening, and how you, as a front-line technician, can use that information to troubleshoot and to spot possible security problems before they become major incidents.

Why Monitoring and Logging Exist: Detection Before Damage

Before you worry about where logs are stored or how to filter them, it is critical to understand *why* monitoring and logging exist in the first place. In security, technology is often described in terms of three broad functions: **prevention**, **detection**, and **response**. Prevention is everything you do to stop bad things from happening in the first place—patching systems, configuring firewalls, enforcing authentication controls, and hardening configurations. Response is what you do after something has clearly gone wrong—containing an incident, removing malware, restoring systems, and learning from what happened. Monitoring and logging live squarely in the middle. They are the primary mechanisms of **detection**, the bridge between hoping nothing is wrong and knowing that something is.

Logs exist because systems cannot explain themselves verbally. Every operating system, application, and security device continuously makes decisions: allowing or denying access, starting or stopping services, accepting or rejecting network connections. Logging is how those decisions are recorded. A log is not an opinion or an interpretation; it is a **historical record** of what a system claims it did at a specific moment in time. When a security professional says, "If it's not logged, it didn't happen," they do not mean the event literally never occurred. They mean that without a record, you cannot prove it happened, analyze it reliably, or defend your conclusions to others.

Monitoring builds on that idea by adding **near-real-time awareness**. While logs are often reviewed after the fact, monitoring tools continuously observe systems as they operate. They track metrics, patterns, and events as they occur and compare them against expected behavior. When something deviates far enough from normal—too many failed logins, a service stopping unexpectedly, network traffic spiking beyond a baseline—monitoring systems raise alerts. Those alerts are not conclusions; they are signals that deserve attention. Logs are what you turn to next to confirm whether the signal represents a real problem or harmless noise.

This distinction is subtle but important for the exam. **Logs tell you what happened. Monitoring tells you that something might be happening right now.** Together, they form the foundation of detection. Without logs, monitoring alerts are little more than warnings with no context. Without monitoring, logs are silent archives that may only be discovered long after damage is done.

Security incidents, in particular, cannot be investigated or reconstructed without logs. When an account is suspected of being compromised, logs are how you determine whether login attempts succeeded or failed, where they came from, and over what time period they occurred. When malware is discovered on a system, logs help establish when it first appeared, what processes were involved, and whether other systems showed similar activity. When a data breach is alleged, logs are often the only evidence available to answer basic questions: what data was accessed, by whom, and when. From a legal, compliance, and organizational standpoint, logs are the difference between informed response and speculation.

This is why monitoring and logging are not optional "nice-to-have" features in secure environments. They are prerequisites for accountability. Without logs, you cannot distinguish between a user who mistyped a password and an attacker attempting a brute-force login. Without logs, you cannot tell whether a firewall blocked malicious traffic or whether that traffic was never seen at all. Without logs, you cannot demonstrate that security controls worked as designed. CompTIA frequently tests this idea by framing scenarios where something suspicious occurred and asking what evidence you would rely on. The correct answer almost always involves reviewing logs, not guessing or immediately reconfiguring systems.

Another important concept is that logs represent **after-the-fact truth**, while monitoring represents **ongoing observation**. Logs are written regardless of whether anyone is watching them at the moment. Monitoring tools watch those logs, metrics, and events and decide when to notify humans. This means that even if no alert was triggered, logs may still contain valuable information. On the exam, you may see scenarios where no alert fired, but investigation is still possible because the relevant events were logged and can be reviewed.

Understanding the purpose of monitoring and logging also changes how you approach everyday IT work. Logs are not just for diagnosing crashes or explaining why a service failed to start. They are the raw material of security awareness. Monitoring is not just about uptime dashboards; it is about recognizing early warning signs before small problems turn into incidents. When you view logs and monitoring through this lens, you stop treating them as passive records and start treating them as active security controls.

What Logs Actually Are and How to Read Them

At first glance, logs can feel overwhelming. Open a system log for the first time and you are often met with hundreds or thousands of lines of text, numbers, timestamps, and cryptic messages scrolling past. The key to working with logs—both on the exam and in real environments—is understanding that they are not random output. Each log entry is a structured record of a specific event, and when you learn how to read that structure, the noise starts to resolve into a clear story.

A **log entry** is a single recorded event generated by a system, application, or device. While the exact format varies by platform, most entries share the same core components. There is almost always a **timestamp**, which tells you precisely when the event occurred. There is a **source**, identifying which process, service, or component generated the entry. Many logs include an **event type or event ID**, which categorizes what kind of action took place. A **severity level** often indicates how important or abnormal the event is, and finally there is a **message** or description that provides human-readable context about what happened. Once you recognize these elements, a log entry stops being a wall of text and becomes a sentence in a timeline.

The timestamp is your anchor. Nearly every log investigation starts with time. Users rarely describe problems in technical terms; they describe them in moments. "It stopped working around 10:15," or "I tried to log in just before lunch," or "It happened overnight." Your first task when reading logs is to align those statements with recorded events. By narrowing your view to the relevant time window, you immediately reduce noise and increase relevance. On the exam, this skill shows up in scenarios where multiple log entries are presented and only one matches the timeframe described in the question.

Once you have the time window, the next step is to look at the **source** of each entry. The source tells you which part of the system is speaking. A message from an authentication service means something very different from a message generated by a printer driver or a backup agent. Understanding the source helps you decide whether an entry is related to the symptom you are investigating or just background activity. Many incorrect exam answers rely on ignoring the source and focusing only on alarming wording in a message.

Severity levels add another layer of meaning, but they must be interpreted carefully. Logs often classify events using terms like informational, warning, error, or critical. An **informational** entry usually records normal activity, such as a service starting successfully. A **warning** suggests something unexpected but not necessarily fatal, like a temporary resource shortage. An **error** indicates that something failed to occur as intended, and a **critical** event often signals a serious problem that requires immediate attention. For Security+ and Network+, you do not need to memorize exact severity scales or numeric values. What matters is understanding that higher severity entries deserve closer inspection, especially when they cluster around the time a problem occurred. At the same time, not every error is a crisis, and not every critical message is security-related. Context always matters.

The most important mental shift when reading logs is learning to see them as a **timeline** rather than isolated messages. A single entry rarely tells the whole story. Instead, patterns emerge when you look at sequences. A failed login attempt followed by several more from the same source, ending in an account lockout, tells a very different story than one failed attempt followed by a successful login. A service crash followed by repeated restart attempts and configuration errors points to a systemic problem, not a one-time glitch. On the exam, CompTIA often presents multiple log entries and asks which one explains the issue. The correct choice is frequently the one that fits into a sequence that matches the described behavior.

Correlation is what turns logs into explanations. Correlating timestamps with user reports, system behavior, and other logs allows you to move from "something happened" to "this is why it happened." If a user reports losing network access at 14:30, and you see a firewall rule update logged at 14:29 followed by denied connection entries at 14:30, the cause-and-effect relationship becomes clear. If an application crashes at the same moment a disk fills up or a service stops, the timeline tells you which event triggered the failure. CompTIA tests this skill by embedding subtle timing clues into questions and expecting you to connect them logically.

Another useful habit is distinguishing between **normal background noise** and meaningful deviations. Systems generate logs constantly: scheduled tasks run, health checks execute, connections are opened and closed. When you first start reading logs, it is tempting to treat every unfamiliar message as suspicious. Over time, you learn what "normal" looks like for a given system. On the exam, you simulate this by focusing on what changed around the reported issue rather than on everything that exists in the log. The correct answer usually involves the new, repeated, or time-aligned entry, not the static background messages that appear all day long.

Finally, remember that logs do not interpret themselves. They do not tell you what to think; they tell you what happened. Your role is to apply context, timing, and system knowledge to interpret them correctly. This is why CompTIA emphasizes log interpretation rather than memorization. A candidate who understands how to read logs as a coherent narrative can answer a wide range of questions, even when the exact platform or log format is unfamiliar.

Monitoring vs Logging: Metrics, Alerts, and Thresholds

Although monitoring and logging are closely related, they serve different purposes and operate in different ways. Confusing the two is a common mistake, both in real environments and on the exam. Logging is about **recording events** after they occur. Monitoring is about **observing behavior over time** and noticing when that behavior changes. Understanding how these two work together—and where their responsibilities begin and end—is essential for interpreting alerts correctly and responding appropriately.

Logging is fundamentally passive. Systems generate log entries whenever something happens: a user logs in, a service starts, a connection is blocked, or a configuration changes. These events are written to logs regardless of whether anyone is watching. Logs are comprehensive but quiet. They do not demand attention; they wait to be read. Their strength lies in detail and accuracy. If you want to know exactly what happened at a specific time, logs are your source of truth.

Monitoring, by contrast, is active and continuous. Monitoring tools constantly collect **metrics**, which are numerical measurements of system behavior. These might include CPU usage, memory consumption, disk space, network throughput, session counts, or authentication failure rates. Metrics are not individual events; they are ongoing measurements sampled repeatedly over time. By themselves, metrics do not tell you whether something is wrong. Their value comes from comparison.

That comparison relies on **baselines** and **thresholds**. A baseline represents what "normal" looks like for a system under typical conditions. For example, a server might normally run at 30% CPU usage during the day and spike to 60% during backups at night. A threshold is a predefined limit that, when crossed, indicates abnormal behavior. Monitoring systems use thresholds to decide when to raise alerts. CPU usage above 85% for more than ten minutes, disk space below 10%, or more than a certain number of failed logins within a short time window are all examples of threshold-based conditions.

An **alert** is generated when monitoring detects that a metric has crossed a threshold or that a pattern deviates significantly from the baseline. Alerts are designed to draw attention, not to explain. They tell you that something deserves investigation, not that an incident has definitely occurred. This distinction is critical for the exam. CompTIA often presents alerts as the starting point of a scenario and asks what you should do next. The correct answer is rarely "assume the worst and take drastic action." Instead, the next step is usually to **verify the alert using logs**.

For example, a monitoring system might generate an alert for excessive failed login attempts. That alert indicates a pattern that could be benign or malicious. A user might be repeatedly mistyping a password, or a background service might be using outdated credentials. Alternatively, it could be a brute-force attack. The alert alone does not tell you which is true. Logs are what allow you to confirm the cause. By reviewing authentication logs, you can see the source of the attempts, the usernames involved, the timing, and whether any attempts succeeded. Monitoring raised the question; logging provides the answer.

This relationship between monitoring and logging is one of confirmation and context. Monitoring is optimized for speed and visibility. It sacrifices detail in favor of rapid detection. Logging is optimized for completeness and accuracy. It sacrifices immediacy in favor of forensic value. Together, they form a feedback loop. Monitoring surfaces potential problems quickly. Logging validates, explains, and documents what actually happened.

Another exam-relevant concept is that alerts are based on **patterns**, not single events. One failed login is normal. One dropped packet is routine. One brief spike in CPU usage is expected. Alerts are usually triggered by repeated events, sustained conditions, or combinations of signals that cross defined thresholds. When CompTIA describes an alert, pay attention to the pattern it implies. Is it about frequency, duration, or deviation from normal behavior? Understanding this helps you interpret what the alert is actually telling you.

It is also important to recognize that alerts can be noisy or misleading if thresholds are poorly tuned. A threshold that is too low can generate constant alerts, leading to alert fatigue. A threshold that is too high can allow real problems to go unnoticed. While entry-level technicians may not be responsible for designing thresholds, they are responsible for responding to alerts intelligently. On the exam, answers that involve validating alerts before acting reflect good operational judgment.

In practice, this means resisting the temptation to treat alerts as conclusions. A "critical" alert does not automatically mean a security breach has occurred. It means the system has detected behavior that exceeds normal expectations. Your role is to investigate, correlate, and decide what action is appropriate. CompTIA frequently tests this by offering answer choices that jump straight to containment or escalation without verification. The better choice usually involves reviewing relevant logs or metrics first.

From Logs to Action: Operational Issues vs Security Incidents

Logs by themselves do not tell you what to do. They provide facts, timestamps, and patterns, but turning that information into the right action requires judgment. This is where many Security+ questions focus, because real security work is rarely about recognizing a single log entry. It is about deciding whether what you are seeing represents a routine operational issue, a potential security incident, or something that needs immediate escalation. CompTIA is not testing whether you can spot an error message; it is testing whether you know what comes next.

Many symptoms look the same on the surface. A system running slowly, a user locked out of an account, or a connection failing to a remote service can all have innocent explanations or serious security implications. The difference lies in the **patterns** you see in the logs. A single failed login followed by a successful one from the same user is usually an operational issue: a mistyped password. Dozens of failed logins across multiple systems from the same external address over a short time window point to something very different. The symptom is the same—failed authentication—but the pattern changes the meaning entirely.

Consider account lockouts. Logs might show that an account was locked after exceeding the failed login threshold. If the failures come from the user's workstation at the start of the workday, the likely cause is cached credentials or a password change that was not updated everywhere. That is an operational problem, and the appropriate response is troubleshooting: resetting credentials, updating saved passwords, and verifying the user can log in normally. If the failures come from unfamiliar IP addresses or from systems the user does not normally access, especially outside business hours, the same lockout event becomes a possible security incident. In that case, the next step is not just unlocking the account, but considering containment and escalation.

This distinction is critical for the exam. CompTIA often frames questions where the first instinct is to "fix" the problem immediately, such as unlocking an account or restarting a service. While that may resolve the symptom, it may also erase evidence or allow an attacker to continue. The better answer usually involves **verifying intent and scope** before taking corrective action. Logs are what allow you to make that determination.

Performance issues follow a similar pattern. Logs and monitoring data might show high CPU usage, memory exhaustion, or disk saturation. If those conditions align with scheduled tasks like backups, updates, or batch jobs, the issue is likely operational. The response is to adjust schedules, allocate resources, or tune configurations. If the same resource exhaustion coincides with unfamiliar processes starting, repeated failures, or connections to unknown external hosts, the context shifts. What looks like a routine performance issue may be the result of malware, cryptomining, or unauthorized activity. On the exam, recognizing this difference depends on reading logs for context, not just reacting to metrics.

Failed connections and access denials are another area where judgment matters. Firewall logs showing blocked traffic can simply reflect normal security policy doing its job. A user complaining that they cannot reach a partner site may just need a rule adjustment or DNS fix. However, repeated denied connections to unusual ports, especially from internal systems, may indicate misconfiguration at best or compromised hosts probing the network at worst. The technician's role is to determine whether the behavior fits expected use or represents a deviation that should be investigated further.

Knowing when to escalate is just as important as knowing how to troubleshoot. **Technician boundaries** exist for a reason. Entry-level technicians are not expected to conduct forensic investigations or make unilateral decisions about containment that could disrupt business operations. When logs suggest possible compromise—successful logins from unexpected locations, privilege changes without authorization, malware detections across multiple systems—the correct action is often to document what you observed and escalate to the security or incident response team. CompTIA tests this explicitly by offering choices that involve doing too much on your own versus handing off appropriately.

Escalation does not mean panic. It means recognizing that the situation has crossed from routine support into security response. Proper escalation includes preserving evidence, avoiding unnecessary changes, and following established procedures. On the exam, answers that mention documenting log findings, notifying the appropriate team, or following incident response processes usually reflect good judgment when security is involved.

At the same time, not every unusual log entry is a crisis. Over-escalating normal behavior wastes time and resources. This is why pattern recognition and baseline awareness are so important. Understanding what is normal for your environment allows you to distinguish between harmless anomalies and meaningful signals. CompTIA scenarios often include subtle clues—time of day, source addresses, repetition—that guide you toward the correct level of response.

Centralized Logging and SIEM: Seeing the Bigger Picture

As environments grow beyond a handful of systems, relying on individual devices to tell their own stories quickly becomes impractical. Logs still exist on each server, workstation, firewall, and application, but the truth they contain is fragmented. One system might show failed logins, another might show network blocks, and a third might show a service crash—all related to the same underlying activity. **Centralized logging** and **SIEM** platforms exist to bring those fragments together so patterns become visible that would otherwise remain hidden.

Centralized logging is the practice of collecting logs from many different sources and storing them in a single location. Instead of checking a Windows Security log on one server, a firewall log on another device, and an application log somewhere else, events are forwarded to a central system. This immediately reduces blind spots. If an attacker touches multiple systems, their activity is no longer scattered across isolated logs that no one thinks to correlate. From an operational standpoint, centralized logging also improves reliability. Local logs can be overwritten, lost during crashes, or deleted when disks fill up. Central collection ensures that even if a system fails, its recent activity is preserved elsewhere.

A **SIEM**, or Security Information and Event Management system, builds on centralized logging by adding structure and intelligence. One of the first challenges in aggregating logs is that different systems describe similar events in very different ways. A failed login on Windows, a failed SSH attempt on Linux, and a rejected VPN authentication all look different in raw form. A SIEM performs **normalization**, translating these diverse log formats into a common structure so that similar events can be analyzed together. This is a foundational concept for the exam: SIEMs do not just store logs; they make them comparable.

Once events are normalized, the real value of a SIEM comes from **correlation**. Correlation is the process of linking related events across systems and over time. A single failed login is noise. A single firewall deny is noise. But multiple failed logins across different servers from the same external IP address, followed by a successful login on a privileged account, form a pattern that deserves attention. Individually, none of those events may trigger alarm. Together, they suggest an attack in progress. This ability to connect low-level events into meaningful narratives is what transforms logs from historical records into active detection tools.

SIEMs are especially effective at **pattern detection**. They apply rules and analytics that look for sequences, frequencies, and combinations of events that match known attack behaviors or deviate sharply from normal baselines. For example, a SIEM might detect that a user account logged in from two geographically distant locations within minutes, something that is physically implausible. It might notice a sudden spike in authentication failures across multiple services, or a workstation communicating with an external host immediately after malware was detected locally. These patterns are difficult, if not impossible, to recognize when reviewing logs one system at a time.

For Security+ and Network+, it is important to understand that SIEM alerts are **not magic truths**. Just like alerts generated by monitoring systems, SIEM alerts are indicators that something merits investigation. They reduce noise by filtering and correlating events, but they do not replace human judgment. The exam often tests this nuance by presenting SIEM alerts as the starting point of a scenario and asking what you should do next. The correct response usually involves reviewing the underlying events, confirming the pattern, and deciding whether escalation or containment is required, rather than assuming a breach has already occurred.

Another key reason SIEMs matter is visibility across domains. Modern attacks rarely stay confined to a single layer. An attacker might begin with a phishing email, move laterally through network services, escalate privileges on a server, and exfiltrate data through a cloud application. Each step may be logged by a different system. Without centralized logging and correlation, these steps appear unrelated. With a SIEM, they can be linked into a single timeline that shows how the incident unfolded. This holistic view is what people mean when they say a SIEM provides a "single pane of glass."

From an exam perspective, it is also important to recognize what SIEMs are **not** primarily about. They are not configuration tools, and they are not just storage repositories. CompTIA questions rarely care about how to set up log forwarding, tune correlation rules, or design dashboards. Instead, they focus on purpose. When a question asks why an organization uses a SIEM, the correct answer usually involves improved detection, reduced blind spots, faster investigation, or correlation across multiple log sources. Answers that focus on patching, encryption, or access control are almost always incorrect in that context.

Centralized logging and SIEMs also support accountability and investigation after incidents. When an organization needs to reconstruct what happened during a suspected breach, a SIEM provides the data needed to build that narrative. Timelines, correlated events, and preserved logs allow teams to understand scope and impact, support audits, and refine future defenses. While entry-level technicians may not manage SIEM platforms directly, they are often users of the information those systems produce, relying on alerts and dashboards to guide their actions.

Logs as Evidence: Retention, Documentation, and Caution

As soon as you move beyond basic troubleshooting, logs stop being just diagnostic text and start becoming **evidence**. They are records of what happened, when it happened, and which systems or accounts were involved. In security work, evidence is what allows you to prove that an event occurred, reconstruct its sequence, and explain its impact to others who were not present at the time. This is why logs carry weight not only in technical investigations, but also in audits, compliance reviews, and post-incident analysis. For an entry-level technician, understanding that logs may later be treated as evidence fundamentally changes how you interact with them.

One of the most important implications of logs as evidence is **retention**. Systems do not keep logs forever by default. Local logs on workstations and servers are often configured to retain only a limited amount of data before older entries are overwritten. On a busy system, that window might be days or even hours. Centralized logging platforms and SIEMs typically extend retention significantly, storing logs for months or years depending on policy, storage capacity, and regulatory requirements. From a practical standpoint, this means two things. First, when investigating an issue, you should be aware that older events may no longer exist on the local system and may need to be retrieved from a centralized log store. Second, delays in recognizing and escalating potential security incidents can result in lost evidence simply because the logs aged out.

Retention is not just about keeping data longer; it is also about keeping the **right data**. Organizations define which systems must log which events and how long those logs must be preserved. Authentication logs, access control changes, firewall decisions, and administrative actions are typically retained longer than routine informational messages because of their security relevance. For the exam, it is enough to recognize that log retention policies exist for both operational and legal reasons, and that deleting or failing to retain logs can leave an organization unable to demonstrate compliance or investigate incidents properly.

Because logs may later be examined by people outside the immediate technical team, **documentation** becomes critical. When you investigate an issue and find relevant log entries, it is not sufficient to say "I saw some errors in the log." Effective documentation captures the specific details that matter: timestamps, event identifiers, source systems, usernames, IP addresses, and brief descriptions of what the entries indicate. This practice serves several purposes. It allows another technician or security analyst to retrace your steps without repeating the entire investigation. It preserves context if the logs themselves are rotated or archived later. It also creates a written record that supports audits and incident reviews.

Good documentation is especially important when dealing with time-sensitive events. Many security questions hinge on **when** something happened. Did the failed login attempts occur before or after a password reset? Did the firewall block traffic before the service outage or as a response to it? Timestamps in logs provide that ordering, but only if they are recorded accurately and consistently. When you document findings, noting both the timestamp and the time zone helps avoid confusion later, particularly in environments that span multiple regions or rely on centralized logging systems that standardize on UTC.

Treating logs as evidence also requires **caution** in how you handle them. One of the most common mistakes made by well-meaning technicians is clearing logs or reinstalling systems too quickly. From a troubleshooting perspective, wiping a system and starting fresh can seem efficient. From an investigative perspective, it can destroy the only record of how a compromise occurred. This is why incident response procedures often emphasize preservation of evidence. Even at an entry level, you should recognize that if there is any possibility of a security incident, you should avoid actions that alter or delete logs until you have checked policy or escalated appropriately.

This caution extends to access and modification. Logs should be protected against unauthorized changes because altered logs undermine trust. Many systems restrict who can view or clear security logs for exactly this reason. On the exam, scenarios may hint at improper handling by mentioning that logs were cleared before an investigation or that no records exist to confirm an event. In those cases, the underlying issue is not just a missing file, but a breakdown in evidence handling and forensic readiness.

The idea of **chain of custody**, while more commonly associated with formal forensic investigations, applies conceptually even in everyday IT work. Chain of custody refers to the documented handling of evidence to show that it has not been tampered with. At your level, this does not mean filling out legal forms, but it does mean understanding boundaries. If you identify suspicious log activity, your role is typically to preserve what you see, document it, and escalate, not to copy logs to personal devices, email them around, or attempt deep forensic analysis on your own. Following established procedures protects both the organization and you as a technician.

Retention and documentation also support learning and improvement. After an incident is resolved, logs are often reviewed to understand what was missed and how detection can be improved. If logs were incomplete or poorly documented, those lessons are harder to extract. Conversely, clear records allow teams to refine alert thresholds, improve monitoring coverage, and update response playbooks. In this way, logs as evidence contribute not only to accountability, but to stronger security over time.

Monitoring and Logging as Everyday IT Work

For many technicians, monitoring and logging feel like "security topics" that live somewhere outside normal support duties. In reality, you interact with logs and monitoring data constantly, even if you do not label the activity that way. Every time you open Event Viewer to understand why a service failed, check authentication logs to unlock an account, or glance at a dashboard to see whether a server is overloaded, you are already doing security monitoring. The difference this section asks you to internalize is not about learning new tools, but about recognizing the broader meaning of work you already perform.

Most IT problems begin with symptoms, not diagnoses. A user reports that their system is slow, an application crashes repeatedly, or their account is locked again for the third time this week. Your first instinct is usually to look for evidence, and that evidence lives in logs and monitoring data. Performance metrics tell you whether a system is starved for CPU, memory, disk, or network resources. System and application logs tell you whether a process is failing, restarting, or encountering errors. Security logs tell you whether authentication is failing because of user error, misconfiguration, or repeated attempts from an unfamiliar source. These are not abstract security exercises; they are the everyday mechanics of effective troubleshooting.

What changes as you develop a security mindset is how you interpret those same signals. A locked account might be a user repeatedly mistyping a password, or it might be part of a credential-stuffing attempt using leaked passwords from another breach. A slow system might be struggling under legitimate workload, or it might be running a hidden crypto-mining process installed through an unpatched vulnerability. Logs and monitoring do not tell you which interpretation is correct by themselves; they give you the context needed to ask the right follow-up questions. This is where monitoring and logging naturally bridge into **incident response**. You are not just fixing what is broken, you are deciding whether what you see fits normal behavior or something that needs escalation.

The same bridge exists between monitoring and **vulnerability management**. When you notice repeated application crashes tied to a specific module, or strange browser behavior on multiple systems, logs often reveal that the affected machines share the same outdated software version or insecure configuration. At that point, the problem is no longer a one-off ticket. It becomes a pattern that suggests an underlying vulnerability. Monitoring helps you see that pattern forming, and logs help you confirm its scope. Acting on that insight—by updating software across systems, adjusting configurations, or notifying a security team—is vulnerability management in practice, even if no one uses that phrase in the ticket system.

Monitoring and logging also support **automation**, which is increasingly present even in small environments. Automated systems rely on data to decide when to act. A script that disables an account after repeated failed logins, a monitoring tool that restarts a failed service, or an alert that opens a ticket when disk space runs low are all examples of automation driven by logs and metrics. Understanding what those systems watch for, and how they decide that something is "wrong," helps you trust them appropriately. It also helps you recognize when automation has acted on incomplete information and needs human review. On the exam, this understanding often shows up in questions where automation generates an alert or takes an action, and you are asked what the technician should do next.

Seeing monitoring and logging as everyday work also clarifies professional boundaries. You are not expected to be a full forensic analyst or a SIEM engineer. Your role is to recognize when normal operational issues cross into potential security incidents, preserve relevant information, and escalate according to policy. Logs and monitoring data give you the confidence to make that judgment. They let you explain not just that "something seems wrong," but why it seems wrong, using concrete observations rather than intuition.

For CompTIA exams, this integrated mindset is critical. Questions rarely isolate monitoring, logging, incident response, or vulnerability management into neat boxes. Instead, they describe realistic situations where these areas overlap. A user complaint leads to a log review, which reveals a suspicious pattern, which suggests a vulnerability or attack, which triggers escalation. Students who treat each topic as separate often struggle to see the flow. Students who understand monitoring and logging as the connective tissue of IT operations can follow that flow naturally.

Knowledge Check

Question 1: A technician needs to investigate repeated blue screen crashes on a Windows server. Which log in Event Viewer is the most appropriate starting point?

- **A.** System log
- **B.** Security log
- **C.** Application log
- **D.** Setup log

Question 2: A support technician is asked to determine whether a user's account was locked out due to multiple failed login attempts. Which log source on a Windows domain controller is the most relevant for this task?

- **A.** System log
- **B.** Application log
- **C.** Setup log
- **D.** Security log

Question 3: A Linux administrator wants to review authentication-related activity, such as SSH logins and sudo usage. Which log file is the best place to start?

- **A.** /var/log/kern.log
- **B.** /var/log/dmesg
- **C.** /var/log/auth.log
- **D.** /var/log/httpd/access.log

Question 4: A monitoring system generates a notification when a web server's CPU usage stays above 95% for more than 30 minutes. This notification is best described as which of the following?

A. Baseline
B. Log entry
C. Alert
D. Raw metric

Question 5: Which statement best describes the primary purpose of a SIEM in a security operations environment?

A. It centralizes and correlates logs from multiple systems to support detection and investigation.
B. It replaces all endpoint antivirus tools with a unified agent.
C. It automatically patches operating systems and applications.
D. It acts as a perimeter firewall to block unwanted network traffic.

Question 6: A network firewall is blocking outbound connections to a partner site, and users are unable to connect. Where should the technician look to confirm that the firewall is responsible?

A. Windows Application log on the user's workstation
B. Firewall logs on the network device
C. /var/log/messages on the partner's server
D. Email server logs

Question 7: Which scenario best illustrates the value of SIEM correlation rules?

A. A single failed login attempt on a workstation is logged locally.
B. A scheduled backup job reports completion in the application log.
C. A router logs a single dropped packet due to a transient error.
D. Multiple failed logins on several servers from the same IP, followed by one successful admin login, trigger a single high-priority alert.

Question 8: A help desk technician receives an alert: "High: Excessive failed logins for user Bob." According to the chapter, what is the technician's most appropriate next step?

A. Verify alert via logs, troubleshoot, escalate if needed.
B. Immediately clear all logs on the affected system to free disk space.
C. Disable logging on the system to prevent additional alerts.
D. Change Bob's password without any further investigation.

ANSWERS

1: Correct Answer: A
Rationale: The System log records low-level OS events such as driver problems, hardware errors, and crashes (e.g., blue screens), making it the correct starting point.

2: Correct Answer: D
Rationale: Authentication and authorization events, including logon failures and account lockouts, are recorded in the Windows Security log.

3: Correct Answer: C
Rationale: On many Linux systems, /var/log/auth.log (or /var/log/secure on some distros) stores authentication-related messages such as SSH logins and sudo usage.

4: Correct Answer: C
Rationale: An alert is a notification generated when a defined threshold condition is met, such as CPU usage staying above a set level for a period of time.

5: Correct Answer: A
Rationale: A SIEM's core role is to collect, centralize, normalize, and correlate logs from many sources to support detection, investigation, and monitoring.

6: Correct Answer: B
Rationale: Firewalls log allowed and denied connections; reviewing the firewall's own logs confirms whether it is blocking outbound traffic to the partner site.

7: Correct Answer: D
Rationale: Correlation rules combine multiple low-level events (e.g., many failed logins across systems followed by a successful admin login) into a single, higher-priority alert indicating a possible attack.

8: Correct Answer: A
Rationale: The technician should validate the alert via logs, perform initial troubleshooting, and decide whether to escalate as a potential security incident, rather than clearing logs or making changes blindly.

5.2 Security Automation & Orchestration

If you think back to the previous section on security monitoring and logging, you might remember how quickly the data starts to pile up. Every workstation, server, firewall, router, and application is constantly generating events: logons, logoffs, configuration changes, alerts, errors, traffic flows, and more. In a small lab with a handful of systems, you can scroll through logs by hand and spot patterns. In even a modest business environment, that approach falls apart almost immediately. There are simply too many events and too many routine security tasks for humans to handle one by one. This is where **security automation** and **orchestration** move from "nice to have" to "the only way this is possible."

At its core, automation in security operations is just software doing something on its own so you don't have to click a button each time. That "something" might be simple, like running a nightly antivirus scan or pushing out a patch at 2:00 a.m. every Wednesday. Or it might be slightly more involved, like checking disk space across all servers every hour and emailing the team if any of them drop below a threshold. Orchestration goes a step further. It is about coordinating multiple automated and manual steps across different tools so that an alert in one place can trigger actions in several others in a controlled way. Think of automation as one robot doing one repetitive job, and orchestration as the factory system that coordinates all the robots, the conveyor belts, and the human workers so the entire workflow runs smoothly.

From an entry-level IT perspective, you probably will not be the one designing complex orchestration or building enterprise platforms from scratch, but you will be living inside these workflows. Remote monitoring and management (RMM) agents on endpoints, EDR and antivirus consoles, centralized patching tools, and ticketing systems already depend heavily on automation. When a user's account locks after too many failed logins, when a suspicious file on a laptop gets quarantined immediately, or when a patch deployment happens overnight without user intervention, you are seeing automation in action. Part of your job is recognizing which tasks are good candidates for automation, understanding which tools participate in those automated flows, and knowing where human review and approval still need to come into the picture.

Automation, Orchestration, and SOAR

It helps to clearly separate three terms that tend to get mixed together: **automation**, **orchestration**, and **SOAR**. While they are related, the exam will expect you to recognize the difference from the context of a scenario.

Automation is the simplest of the three. It is a single task or small set of tasks performed automatically, usually based on a trigger or a schedule. A classic example is a scheduled antivirus scan. The administrator or security team configures the endpoint protection client to run a quick scan every day at noon and a full scan once a week. After that, no human has to remember to initiate the scans; the software simply does it. The same is true for automatic system updates on workstations, nightly backup jobs that fire at 1:00 a.m., or a script that checks for low disk space and sends an alert email if a server's storage drops below 10 percent. There is a trigger, an action, and usually a notification, all without someone manually starting the process each time.

Orchestration has a broader, more "big-picture" flavor. It is about linking multiple automated pieces and sometimes human tasks into a repeatable **workflow**, especially when multiple tools are involved. Imagine an intrusion detection system (IDS) that flags unusual outbound traffic from a particular workstation. On its own, that is just an alert. In an orchestrated environment, that alert is forwarded to a SIEM, which correlates it with other events and determines that it is high severity. The SIEM then uses an integration to automatically create a ticket in the help desk system. At the same time, the endpoint detection and response (EDR) solution may automatically place that workstation into a restricted mode that limits its network connectivity. A technician is paged, opens the ticket, runs through a checklist to verify what is happening, and then either confirms the threat and escalates or determines it is a false alarm and restores normal access. That end-to-end chain—from the original alert all the way through containment and human review—is a simple example of orchestration.

SOAR, or **Security Orchestration, Automation, and Response**, is a category of platforms that formalize this kind of coordination for security use cases. At the A+ level, you can think of a SOAR platform as a central "brain" for security operations. It ingests alerts and events from systems like SIEM, firewalls, IDS/IPS, EDR, email security gateways, and cloud services. It then runs those events through **playbooks**, which are standardized sets of steps for handling common situations. For instance, if an email is reported as phishing, a playbook might have the SOAR tool automatically collect the email headers, compare the sender against threat intelligence feeds, search for similar messages in other mailboxes, quarantine those messages if they are suspicious, and create a ticket for a human analyst to verify the findings. In this sense, SOAR is orchestration plus built-in security-focused automation and response logic.

One subtle point the exam can test is that not everything involving a SIEM or logs is SOAR. Sending logs from a firewall to a SIEM is just centralized logging. Having the SIEM raise an alert is still mostly monitoring. When you add the piece that says, "When we see this pattern, automatically do X, Y, and Z across multiple systems according to a defined playbook," that is when it starts to look like SOAR or orchestration. In short, automation is about doing tasks automatically; orchestration and SOAR are about making many tasks and tools work together as part of a planned, repeatable process.

Everyday Security Automation in A+ Roles

All of this can sound abstract until you look at your daily workload as a junior technician. Many of the problems you encounter on a help desk or support team are repetitive and time-sensitive, which makes them perfect candidates for automation.

Patching is a good example. Manually updating one workstation is easy: open the settings, check for updates, click install, and reboot. Doing that for two hundred or two thousand machines, across different time zones and business units, is not realistic. Organizations rely instead on automated patch management, using tools such as WSUS, SCCM, RMM platforms, or mobile device management (MDM) systems. These tools enforce policies like "install approved security patches every Sunday at 3:00 a.m." or "defer feature updates for 30 days but apply critical fixes immediately." The role of the technician often becomes confirming that agents are installed, troubleshooting endpoints that are not checking in, and answering user questions when they come in Monday morning after an update. On the exam, when a scenario describes a need to keep many systems up to date without depending on users to act, the best answer almost always involves automated patch deployment rather than manual installs.

Endpoint protection is another rich area for automation. Modern antivirus and EDR tools almost always rely on scheduled scans, automatic signature updates, and predefined responses when certain kinds of threats are detected. For instance, a suspicious executable might be quarantined automatically, or a device might be placed in a "network quarantine" VLAN where it has access only to remediation servers until the issue is resolved. These tools then notify the SIEM or send emails, which can generate tickets or trigger follow-up actions. From your perspective, you may be the person who gets the ticket that says, "Host ABC has been isolated due to suspected malware," and your next steps are dictated by the organization's incident response procedures.

Monitoring and alerting, while conceptually part of logging, also lean heavily on automation. Performance monitoring tools may continuously watch CPU, memory, disk utilization, or network bandwidth. When thresholds are crossed, they send alerts via email, SMS, chat, or ticketing systems. You do not manually log into each server every hour to check its health; automation does that for you and only bothers you when something is wrong. The same mindset applies to security-relevant events: multiple failed logon attempts within a short time, unusual account lockout patterns, or sign-ins from impossible locations (for example, logging in from New York and then five minutes later from Europe) can all trigger automated alerts and sometimes automatic defensive actions.

User account and access operations showcase a subtler form of automation that still has major security impact. Account lockout policies, for example, automatically disable accounts temporarily after a certain number of failed logon attempts. That is automation enforcing a security policy without a human being watching each login. In many organizations, account lifecycle tasks are also partially automated. When HR marks an employee as terminated in their system, an integration may automatically disable the user's account in Active Directory, remove their licenses from cloud applications, and schedule their mailbox for archiving. Scripts may run periodically to find inactive accounts—such as accounts that have not logged in for ninety days—and export a list for an administrator to review and disable. Automation ensures that least privilege principles are enforced consistently, instead of relying on someone to remember to clean up accounts.

Even backup and recovery routines, which are often thought of as operational rather than security-focused, are important pieces of security automation. Nightly backups of critical systems, automated replication of data to off-site locations, and automated verification of backup integrity all support the availability side of the security triad. When ransomware hits or a server fails, those automated processes determine whether you have clean, recent data to restore. As a junior technician, you might be asked to verify that backup jobs completed successfully, restore a file on request, or troubleshoot failed jobs, but the actual backup schedule and execution are almost always automated.

How SOAR Glues Tools Together

Although you may not work directly with a branded SOAR product in an entry-level role, understanding how SOAR-style workflows operate will make sense of what you see in ticket queues and consoles. Think about the tools you have already heard about: SIEM for centralized logging and correlation, IDS/IPS and firewalls for network security, EDR and antivirus for endpoint protection, email gateways for anti-phishing, and cloud services with their own security alerts. Each of these produces events, often in large volumes. A SOAR platform sits in the middle and listens to all of them.

When a new event arrives—for example, an email marked as suspicious by the spam filter—the SOAR system asks, "Do I have a playbook that matches this?" If it does, the playbook defines a set of steps. The first steps might be information gathering: pull the email headers, extract any URLs, check the sender domain against blocklists, search for similar emails in other users' inboxes, and query threat intelligence services. The next steps might involve action: quarantine matching emails from other mailboxes, add the sender's domain to a block list, or create a help desk ticket with detailed context for a technician to follow up with affected users. In more severe cases, a SOAR playbook for "suspected credential theft" might disable certain accounts or force a password reset before passing the case to a human analyst.

In many organizations that do not have a formal SOAR product, scripts, webhooks, and integrations between tools accomplish a similar effect. For instance, a SIEM alert could trigger a webhook that calls an RMM platform's API to run a remediation script on a specific endpoint. Or the ticketing system could be configured so that when a ticket of a certain type is opened, it automatically runs a data-collection script on the affected device before a technician even looks at it. Whether or not it is labeled "SOAR," the idea is the same: coordinated responses using multiple tools, partially automated, partially human-driven, following consistent patterns.

Scripting as the Engine of Automation

Underneath a lot of this automation is **scripting**. For an A+ candidate, you are not expected to write complex programs, but you do need to understand what scripts are doing in this context and why they are so valuable to security operations.

A script is simply a small program, usually written in a language that is interpreted on the fly, such as PowerShell on Windows or Bash on Linux and macOS. Python is also common in security environments because of its readability and broad library support. These scripts are often only a few lines to a few dozen lines long, and their purpose is usually to automate a specific, repetitive task. For security and operations teams, that might include collecting specific log files from many machines and copying them to a central share, checking each endpoint for certain missing patches, querying all servers in a particular group to verify that a specific registry key or configuration setting is in place, or gathering system information and running process lists from a machine involved in an incident.

The value of scripting becomes obvious when you compare it to manual work. Suppose you are investigating a potential malware infection that might have spread to ten devices. A senior analyst might hand you a PowerShell script that collects running processes, installed applications, recent logon events, and certain registry keys, then zips everything into a single archive and uploads it to a secure share. Running that script on each affected workstation might take a minute per machine. Trying to gather the same information manually, step by step, would be tedious and error-prone, and you would almost certainly forget something on at least one system. With a script, the same set of steps is followed exactly on every device, which is crucial for consistent incident response and, later, for digital forensics.

In many organizations, junior technicians are not writing these scripts from scratch, but they are running them, tweaking simple parameters, and interpreting the results. You might receive instructions like, "Run the approved patch assessment script on this group of machines and attach the output to the ticket," or "Use this collection script on the user's laptop before you re-image it." It is important to understand the basics of what the script does in plain language, to test new or updated scripts on a non-critical system first, and to follow change-control policies before deploying anything widely. Scripts and automated tasks themselves become powerful tools that must be handled carefully, because mistakes can scale very quickly when they are automated.

Benefits and Risks of Security Automation

Security automation offers clear advantages, which is why it is so pervasive. It improves speed by responding to events immediately instead of waiting for someone to notice and act. When an EDR tool isolates a compromised endpoint within seconds of detecting malware, the damage is usually far less than if that response took hours. It improves consistency because the same steps are taken every time under the same conditions, following playbooks or policies rather than relying on each individual's memory. It allows teams to scale, enabling a handful of administrators and analysts to manage and protect hundreds or thousands of endpoints without drowning in manual work. And it reduces routine human error; automation does not get tired and "forget" to disable an account when HR says an employee has left.

However, the exam will also expect you to recognize that automation is not risk-free. Misconfigured or poorly tested automation can cause widespread problems very quickly. A faulty patch deployment script that reboots servers outside of maintenance windows can bring down critical business services in the middle of the workday. An overly aggressive email filtering rule driven by automated threat intelligence might quarantine large volumes of legitimate email, disrupting business communication. Account lockout policies that are set too strict can result in users being locked out constantly, generating a flood of support calls and potentially pushing users to adopt insecure workarounds.

There is also the danger of over-automation, where teams place too much trust in tools and not enough in human judgment. Automatically deleting all emails that "look like phishing" without human review might remove real threats, but it also risks losing legitimate messages. Automatically disabling user accounts based on suspicious behavior without a sanity check can interrupt work for high-value employees, such as traveling executives, who often generate unusual login patterns. False positives are a fact of life in security, and automation that reacts too aggressively to them can cause as many problems as it solves.

Finally, the automation systems themselves must be secured. Scripts, management consoles, and service accounts often have elevated privileges because they need to make changes across many systems. If an attacker compromises these, they gain powerful tools to deploy malware, alter configurations, or disable protections at scale. For that reason, organizations apply strict access controls, logging, and change management around their automation systems, and they expect technicians at every level to respect those controls.

In an A+ role, best practice usually means using automation where it makes sense, but always within a framework of testing, approvals, documentation, and monitoring. You might start with automation on a small group of pilot systems, observe the effects, and only then roll it out more broadly. You document what a scheduled task or script does, when it runs, and which systems it affects. You monitor the results, watching tickets and user feedback after new automation is introduced. And when automation misbehaves or causes unexpected side effects, you escalate appropriately and provide clear, user-friendly explanations to those impacted, bridging the gap between complex security operations and the everyday experience of your coworkers.

Knowledge Check

Question 1: A security team wants a nightly antivirus scan to run on all endpoints without a technician manually starting it each time. Which concept BEST describes this configuration?

A. Security automation
B. Security orchestration
C. SOAR platform
D. Centralized logging

Question 2: An IDS flags unusual outbound traffic. The alert is sent to a SIEM, which creates a ticket, triggers the EDR to restrict the host, and notifies a technician to review and approve next steps. Which term BEST describes this end-to-end process?

A. Simple automation
B. Centralized monitoring
C. Orchestration
D. Log aggregation

Question 3: A junior technician is told to identify tasks that should be automated. Which of the following is the BEST candidate for basic security automation?

A. Deploying approved security patches to all workstations every Sunday at 3:00 a.m.
B. Manually reviewing every firewall log entry at the end of each day
C. Conducting in-person security awareness training with each new hire
D. Writing custom EDR detection rules for zero-day threats every week

Question 4: A company deploys a SOAR platform that receives phishing alerts from an email gateway, automatically pulls message headers, checks URLs against threat intelligence, quarantines similar emails, and then opens a ticket for an analyst to verify. In this scenario, which role is the SOAR platform primarily playing?

A. Replacing the SIEM by storing all logs
B. Acting as a central "brain" that executes playbooks across multiple tools
C. Serving only as a standalone antivirus replacement
D. Providing manual-only workflows with no automation

Question 5: A security analyst wants to distinguish between SIEM usage and SOAR functionality. Which scenario MOST clearly represents SOAR rather than just SIEM monitoring?

A. Forwarding firewall logs to a SIEM for centralized storage
B. Having the SIEM generate a high-severity alert when it detects a pattern
C. Using the SIEM solely to generate compliance reports at month-end
D. Automatically disable user, quarantine endpoint, open ticket

Question 6: A help desk team uses a script that, when a specific ticket type is opened, automatically runs on the affected endpoint to collect logs and system info, then attaches the results to the ticket. This approach is MOST closely aligned with which concept?

A. Manual incident response
B. Basic log aggregation
C. SOAR-style workflow using scripting and integrations
D. Non-technical user training

Question 7: Which of the following BEST explains why scripting is so valuable for security operations and incident response?

A. It allows teams to run consistent, repeatable tasks across many systems quickly and with fewer manual errors.
B. It completely removes the need for any human review of automated actions.
C. It guarantees that no false positives will occur in automated alerts.
D. It replaces the need for dedicated security tools such as SIEM or EDR.

Question 8: Which of the following scenarios BEST illustrates a potential RISK of security automation?

A. Automatically deploying critical patches only during approved maintenance windows
B. Misconfigured script reboots critical servers in the middle of the business day
C. Using automation to generate tickets when disk space falls below 10%
D. Running a tested backup job on a daily schedule to protect critical data

ANSWERS

1: Correct Answer: A
Rationale: A scheduled antivirus scan that runs without manual intervention is a single, repeatable task triggered automatically, which is classic security automation.

2: Correct Answer: C
Rationale: Orchestration coordinates multiple automated and human steps across several tools (IDS, SIEM, EDR, ticketing, technician review) in a defined workflow.

3: Correct Answer: A
Rationale: Large-scale, recurring patch deployment is a textbook use case for automation, especially when many endpoints must be updated consistently without user action.

4: Correct Answer: B
Rationale: A SOAR platform acts as a central "brain" that runs playbooks, tying together multiple tools (email gateway, threat intel, ticketing) to automate and coordinate responses.

5: Correct Answer: D
Rationale: Automatically executing multiple actions across systems based on a pattern (disable accounts, quarantine endpoints, open tickets) is indicative of SOAR/orchestration, not just SIEM monitoring.

6: Correct Answer: C
Rationale: Automatically triggering scripts and attaching results to tickets via tool integrations reflects a SOAR-style orchestrated workflow using automation and scripting.

7: Correct Answer: A
Rationale: Scripting lets teams automate repetitive tasks consistently across many systems, saving time and reducing human error—critical benefits in security operations.

8: Correct Answer: B
Rationale: Poorly tested or misconfigured automation can cause widespread outages, such as rebooting critical servers during business hours, illustrating a key risk of automation.

5.3 Incident Response Process

When something goes wrong in IT, it rarely announces itself with a neat label that says "security incident." More often, it shows up as a confused user saying their screen looks weird, an automated ticket from the antivirus platform, or a sudden spike in CPU usage that doesn't make sense. For a front-line support technician, this is where **incident response** begins. Your job is not only to fix things but to react in a way that protects systems and data, supports the organization's policies, and doesn't accidentally make a small problem much worse.

In an A+-level environment, the word "incident" has a specific meaning. A security incident is any event that threatens the confidentiality, integrity, or availability of systems or data. That might be the obvious case of ransomware locking a user's files, but it also includes a lost laptop with sensitive information, an account that appears to be used from another country, a malware alert on a file server, or even a misdirected email containing customer data. Not every strange behavior or alert is truly an incident; sometimes monitoring tools generate false positives, and sometimes users misinterpret benign messages. However, when something looks suspicious, you do not treat it like a random glitch. You follow a structured, repeatable process.

Organizations formalize this process in an **incident response plan**, sometimes broken down into detailed playbooks for specific scenarios such as "suspected phishing," "lost mobile device," or "malware on endpoint." These documents exist because "I just tried stuff until it seemed fixed" is not a strategy. Improvised responses can destroy evidence, violate legal or regulatory requirements, or unintentionally notify the wrong people at the wrong time. As a support technician, you might not write the plan, but you are often the first person to see the problem, and the way you respond sets the tone for the entire incident. On the CompTIA A+ exam, questions that ask "What should the technician do first?" are usually testing whether you recognize that you must plug yourself into this formal process instead of jumping straight into solo troubleshooting.

The Incident Response Lifecycle

The industry has converged on a fairly standard set of phases for handling security incidents. Different organizations might tweak the wording, but the logic is consistent. You prepare before anything happens. You detect and analyze suspicious activity. You contain the damage to keep it from spreading. You eradicate the root cause. You recover normal operations in a safe way. Finally, you review what happened and learn from it. The exam expresses these as six core phases: **preparation; detection and analysis; containment; eradication; recovery; and lessons learned**.

A simple way to keep them straight is to think of the flow as "stop, confirm, contain, clean, restore, reflect." Preparation is everything you do so you are ready to stop and respond. Detection and analysis are about confirming that something truly is an incident and understanding its scope. Containment is the immediate "stop the bleeding" phase. Eradication is cleaning out the infection or threat. Recovery is restoring service so users can get back to work without re-introducing the risk. Lessons learned is your chance to reflect and improve. In practice, these phases overlap somewhat, and you may loop back to earlier activities as new information comes in, but the order matters, especially in exam scenarios where you are asked for the best next step.

Preparation: Getting Ready Before Things Break

The most effective incident response work happens long before anyone reports that "something weird" is happening. Preparation is partly technical—having the right tools and monitoring in place—but at the A+ level it is largely procedural and awareness-based. You need to know what your organization considers a security incident, how incidents are classified, and what your role is when one occurs. Many organizations define categories such as "informational event," "suspicious activity," and "confirmed incident," with associated priorities and escalation paths. If a user forgets their password, that's a routine support issue. If a user reports that someone else is sending messages from their account, that crosses into security territory.

Being prepared means being familiar with the assets and environments you support, so that you can recognize when something is out of place. If you regularly work with certain endpoints, servers, or cloud applications, you start to develop a sense of what normal performance and behavior look like. That makes it easier to notice when a workstation is constantly making outbound connections it never made before, or when a shared folder has been modified in unusual ways. It also means making sure basic tools are ready: your ticketing system, your ability to view logs, your remote access utilities, and the consoles for antivirus, EDR, or MDM platforms you are authorized to use.

Organizations that take security seriously often run tabletop exercises or drills. In those sessions, a simulated incident is described—maybe a ransomware outbreak or suspicious access to HR data—and the team walks through who would do what, in what order, and through which communication channels. As a technician, participation in these exercises is part of your preparation. It gives you a safe environment to ask questions like "At what point do I call the incident commander?" or "Who is authorized to approve taking this server offline?" The A+ exam reflects this mindset: in many questions, the right first step is not "run a virus scan," but "follow the organization's incident response procedures."

Detection and Analysis: Recognizing When You Really Have a Problem

In the real world, detection almost never starts with a flashing red "breach" alarm. Instead, incidents are discovered in a mix of ways. A user might call the help desk and say, "I can't open any of my documents and my filenames all have a strange extension" or "I keep getting MFA prompts I didn't initiate." An automated system might create a ticket because it saw multiple failed login attempts from an unfamiliar country, or your antivirus might generate a high-severity alert on a sensitive server. User complaints about slow performance or strange pop-ups can also be symptoms of infection. These initial signals are detection: something unusual has been noticed.

Analysis is the process of turning that initial signal into an assessment: is this likely a security incident, and if so, how serious is it? At the technician level, analysis is mostly about structured information gathering rather than deep forensic work. When a user reports an issue, you ask focused questions: what exactly did you see on the screen, at what time did it first happen, what were you doing right before it occurred, did you open any attachments, click any links, or install anything new? The way you ask matters. Vague questions like "Did you do anything weird?" are less helpful than "Did you receive any emails with attachments today and open them?"

You can then correlate what the user tells you with what the system shows. Within the limits of your permissions and policy, you might check for active security alerts in the antivirus or EDR console, look at basic event logs, or view running processes and network connections. The key is to collect facts without altering or destroying potential evidence. It is usually inappropriate at this stage to start uninstalling software, clearing logs, or reimaging the system. If your policy emphasizes evidence preservation, you might even be instructed to stop certain troubleshooting steps and hand over the case once you've collected core details such as hostname, IP address, logged-in user, observed symptoms, screenshots, and any error messages.

You are not expected to decide on your own whether a specific pattern of log entries proves a sophisticated intrusion. That responsibility typically sits with a security analyst or incident handler. Your responsibility is to recognize that something is likely wrong, gather information cleanly and carefully, and escalate according to the incident response plan. If you are in doubt, plan guidance usually favors caution: treat it as a potential incident and escalate, rather than dismissing it.

Containment: Stopping the Bleeding

Once an incident is confirmed or strongly suspected, the next priority is containment. At a human level, this is where you try to make sure the problem does not get worse while the organization figures out exactly what happened. Applied to systems, containment is about limiting spread, limiting access, and limiting damage. The contained system may still be compromised, but you are trying to keep that compromise from affecting other systems or additional data.

For a workstation infected with malware, short-term containment might involve isolating it from the network. Depending on policy and available tools, you might disconnect the Ethernet cable, disable Wi-Fi, move the device to a quarantined VLAN, or trigger an isolation feature in your EDR platform. A crucial detail here is power: many organizations want potentially compromised systems left powered on, because volatile data in memory can be valuable for later forensic analysis. Unless policy specifically instructs you to shut down, you should avoid powering off a system just because "that's what I normally do when Windows is acting up." That standard troubleshooting instinct can work against evidence preservation during an incident.

In account-based incidents, containment often means limiting access. If there are signs that a user's credentials have been stolen or abused, the response might include disabling the account temporarily or forcing an immediate password reset, along with reviewing or resetting multi-factor authentication methods. In network-centric incidents, containment might mean blocking specific IP addresses, domains, or URLs at the firewall, DNS filter, or secure web gateway. As a technician, you might not configure those devices directly, but you could be the person who opens an urgent ticket to the network team with accurate details of the malicious destination that needs blocking.

It is also useful to distinguish between short-term containment, which can be disruptive but must happen quickly, and longer-term containment, which balances security with business continuity. Short-term containment might mean pulling the plug on a handful of systems to stop an infection wave. Longer-term containment might involve temporarily segmenting part of the network, applying emergency group policies, or restricting access to certain applications while a deeper investigation continues. In exam questions, if you see malware actively spreading or suspicious logins still happening, the correct next step is usually a containment action, not jumping ahead to full cleanup and reimage.

Eradication: Removing the Root Cause

Only after the situation is stable—meaning the threat is no longer spreading or actively exploiting systems—does eradication become the focus. Eradication is about removing the underlying cause of the incident: the malicious software, the misconfiguration, the backdoor account, or the vulnerable component that was exploited. At the A+ level, this usually looks like following defined remediation steps rather than inventing your own.

In a malware incident, eradication might involve running full antivirus or EDR scans with approved tools and allowing them to quarantine or delete detected threats. It can also include removing malicious scripts, killing unauthorized processes, cleaning up scheduled tasks that were created by the malware, or uninstalling unauthorized applications and browser extensions. In some cases, eradication requires applying patches to close vulnerabilities that allowed the intrusion in the first place, such as an unpatched operating system or a long-neglected application.

Account-based incidents might require revoking API keys or tokens that were exposed, resetting compromised passwords, and checking for unauthorized changes made while the account was in someone else's control. Throughout eradication, documentation is crucial: what tools were run, what they found, what was removed, and at what times. This information not only supports the later lessons-learned phase, it can also be important if the incident turns out to have legal or regulatory impact and a formal investigation is launched.

Technicians must be careful not to skip straight from detection to eradication in their thinking. On the exam, a classic trap answer is "reimage the system immediately" when the scenario describes an incident that has not yet been contained. Reimaging might well be part of eradication, but if you do it before isolating the system or preserving necessary evidence, you may destroy information that the organization needs to understand the attack.

Recovery: Returning to Normal without Repeating the Past

With the active threat removed, the goal shifts to bringing systems and users back to normal operation, but in a way that does not re-introduce the same problem. Recovery often feels familiar to technicians, because it uses the same skills you apply in everyday support work: restoring from backups, rebuilding machines, verifying functionality, and communicating with users about downtime and changes.

If data was corrupted, encrypted, or deleted, you may need to assist in restoring from **known-good backups**, those that were taken before the incident began and are confirmed clean. If the malware was particularly persistent or policy dictates it, systems may be completely reimaged to a clean baseline instead of trying to surgically clean them. After restoration or rebuild, you verify that required applications are installed, configuration is correct, and the user can perform their tasks. At the same time, you confirm that security controls—such as antivirus software, host firewalls, and EDR agents—are installed, up to date, and reporting correctly.

A careful recovery includes a period of heightened monitoring. Even after you think the issue is resolved, the organization might choose to watch the affected systems, accounts, or network segments more closely for a defined window. As a technician, this might translate to keeping an eye on specific dashboards, being more alert to follow-up alerts, or checking in with users to see if any recurrence of symptoms appears. Recovery also involves clear communication: users and stakeholders should be informed about what to expect in terms of downtime, data availability, and any changes to processes they need to follow going forward.

Lessons Learned: Turning Incidents into Improvements

Once the dust has settled and systems are stable, a mature organization does not just move on and forget. The **lessons learned** phase is where the team reflects on what happened, how effective the response was, and what needs to change to reduce the chance or impact of a similar event in the future. This might be a formal meeting with an incident report, or it might be a shorter debrief, but in either case the information you captured as a technician is essential.

During this review, technicians contribute by providing a clear, factual timeline: when the first symptoms were observed, when the incident was reported, what containment actions were taken, which tools were run, what eradication steps were completed, and how recovery proceeded. The group might identify gaps, such as users not recognizing phishing emails, patches not being applied in a timely way, or monitoring missing key signals. Outcomes of lessons learned often include updates to training materials, adjustments to patch management schedules, new or refined security controls, or changes to the documented incident response procedures themselves.

This phase is also where cultural improvement happens. If technicians felt unsure whom to call, or if communication channels were confusing or slow, those issues should be recognized and addressed. Over time, an organization that takes lessons learned seriously becomes more resilient, because each incident leads to more refined processes and better-prepared people. The A+ exam alludes to this by including scenario answers that mention updating documentation, revising procedures, or providing additional user training after an incident has been resolved.

Documentation, Communication, and Boundaries Throughout

Threaded through every phase of incident response is the discipline of documentation and controlled communication. From the moment you suspect an incident, you should be recording key facts in the ticketing system or designated incident tracking tool: times, symptoms, commands you ran, and changes you made. This record supports later forensic work, legal inquiries, audits, and internal reviews. It also protects you and your team from misremembered sequences or accusations of inappropriate action.

Communication must follow a need-to-know principle. You share incident details with authorized stakeholders—your supervisor, the security team, the incident commander—but you avoid casually discussing specifics with coworkers who are not involved, and you certainly do not post about incidents on social media or external forums. To users, you provide calm, accurate information about impact and next steps, but you avoid speculation such as "I think your data is stolen" unless that has been confirmed and cleared to communicate. Decisions about notifying customers, regulators, or law enforcement are far above the A+ technician's pay grade; those are handled by management and legal teams.

Just as important are the boundaries of your technical actions. Without explicit guidance, you should not attempt "forensics" by experimenting, copying data to personal devices, or poking around areas you are not authorized to access. You should not clear logs, disable logging, or wipe systems to make your life easier during an incident, because those actions can destroy evidence that the next chapter—on digital forensics and investigations—relies on. In many cases, your incident response plan will tell you whether to disconnect a system, leave it running, or perform specific evidence-preserving steps. Your role is to follow that plan carefully, document what you do, and hand over clean, accurate information to the teams that will carry the investigation further.

Knowledge check

Question 1: A help desk technician receives an antivirus alert for malware on a user's workstation. According to incident response best practices for the preparation and detection phases, what should the technician do first?

A. Follow the organization's incident response procedures and begin documenting the incident
B. Immediately reimage the system to restore normal operation
C. Power off the computer to stop the malware from running
D. Tell the user to continue working while monitoring the system informally

Question 2: A user reports suspicious pop-ups and sluggish performance on their workstation. During the detection and analysis phase, what is the technician's primary responsibility?

A. Disable all user accounts on the network until the cause is found
B. Immediately uninstall any recently installed software and clear system logs
C. Declare the situation a confirmed breach and notify law enforcement
D. Collect details while avoiding changes that could destroy evidence

Question 3: An organization runs a tabletop exercise simulating a ransomware outbreak. Technicians walk through who to contact, what tools to use, and which systems to prioritize. Which incident response phase does this activity BEST represent?

A. Preparation
B. Detection and analysis
C. Recovery
D. Lessons learned

Question 4: A workstation is confirmed to be infected with malware that is attempting to spread laterally over the network. Which of the following actions BEST represents the containment phase?

A. Running a full antivirus scan and deleting all detected threats
B. Restoring the workstation from a known-good backup
C. Isolating the workstation from the network while leaving it powered on
D. Conducting a post-incident review to update documentation and training

Question 5: After a credential theft incident, the security team has contained the threat. The technician is now instructed to remove the attacker's access and fix the underlying issue. Which of the following is the BEST example of an eradication activity in this scenario?

A. Notifying affected users about expected downtime during cleanup
B. Restoring user data from backups taken before the compromise
C. Increasing log retention to improve future investigations
D. Resetting compromised passwords and revoking unauthorized tokens or API keys

Question 6: A server was impacted by malware, but the infection has been contained and eradicated. The technician is now tasked with returning the system to normal operation while minimizing the chance of reinfection. Which action is MOST appropriate in the recovery phase?

A. Shut down the server and store it for potential future legal review
B. Recover from known-good backup and verify security tools
C. Disable all network access to the server permanently to prevent future attacks
D. Immediately resume full production use without any validation or monitoring

Question 7: After a phishing-related incident has been fully resolved and normal operations restored, the organization holds a debrief meeting to review the timeline, identify gaps in user awareness, and update procedures. Which incident response phase does this meeting BEST represent?

A. Containment
B. Eradication
C. Recovery
D. Lessons learned

Question 8: While supporting an ongoing incident, a technician carefully records timestamps of user reports, actions taken, tools used, and any changes made to affected systems. Why is this level of documentation especially important throughout the incident response lifecycle?

A. It allows the technician to troubleshoot more quickly by clearing old logs
B. It preserves an accurate record that can support forensics, audits, and post-incident review
C. It enables the technician to share detailed incident data on external forums for advice
D. It eliminates the need for a formal incident response plan or playbooks

ANSWERS

1: Correct Answer: A
Rationale: Incident response begins by following the documented plan and starting formal documentation. Powering off or reimaging may destroy evidence and bypass the process, and informal monitoring is not aligned with best practices.

2: Correct Answer: D
Rationale: In detection and analysis, the focus is on gathering detailed, structured information while preserving evidence. Clearing logs, uninstalling software, or making drastic decisions like calling law enforcement or disabling all accounts are premature.

3: Correct Answer: A
Rationale: Tabletop exercises are a preparation activity used to validate people, processes, and tools before an actual incident. Detection, recovery, and lessons learned occur during or after real incidents.

4: Correct Answer: C
Rationale: Containment aims to limit spread and damage while preserving evidence, so isolating the host from the network but keeping it powered on is appropriate. Scanning, restoring, or post-incident reviews are eradication, recovery, or lessons-learned activities.

5: Correct Answer: D
Rationale: Eradication removes the attacker's foothold and root cause. For credential theft, this means resetting compromised credentials and revoking unauthorized tokens or keys. The other options are communication, recovery, or future-focused improvements.

6: Correct Answer: B
Rationale: Recovery focuses on safely restoring normal operations, typically from known-good backups, and ensuring security controls are active and effective. Shutting down, permanently disabling access, or resuming without validation do not meet recovery goals.

7: Correct Answer: D
Rationale: A debrief that reviews the incident, identifies gaps, and updates procedures is a lessons-learned activity. Containment, eradication, and recovery occur earlier, while the incident is still being handled.

8: Correct Answer: B
Rationale: Detailed documentation creates a reliable record that supports forensic analysis, regulatory or legal inquiries, audits, and the lessons-learned review. Clearing logs, sharing externally, or replacing formal plans are not appropriate purposes.

5.4 Digital Forensics & Investigations

When you hear "digital forensics," it might conjure images of crime dramas, dark rooms full of monitors, and experts pulling incriminating files from a shattered hard drive. In reality, digital forensics in an IT support environment is much more modest—but no less important. At your level, you are not expected to be the person carving deleted data from disk images or testifying in court as an expert witness. Instead, your role sits at the front edge of the process: recognizing when something might later become evidence, preserving it as intact as possible, and then handing it off correctly to the people whose job is to investigate.

It helps to think of **digital forensics** as the disciplined process of identifying, preserving, analyzing, and presenting digital evidence to answer questions like "What happened?", "Who did it?", and "How did they do it?" An **investigation** might be internal, such as HR reviewing whether an employee misused company systems, or external, such as law enforcement collecting evidence of fraud, harassment, or data theft. Even if law enforcement never gets involved, your organization's legal team and executives treat many of these cases just as seriously. From your perspective, what changes is not so much the technology you touch, but your mindset. Once you realize a situation could have legal, regulatory, or HR implications, your priority shifts from "fix it fast" to "preserve and report."

This is where digital forensics intersects with the incident response process you saw in the previous section. In a normal outage or misconfiguration, you might reboot systems freely, clear logs to make them readable, or reinstall software without a second thought. In a potential investigation, those same actions can destroy crucial information. The same skills—reading logs, understanding alerts, documenting your work—are still in play, but now they have an extra dimension: your actions may be reviewed months later by security specialists, HR, or lawyers, and they will care not just whether you fixed the symptom, but whether you protected the **evidence**.

When Routine Support Becomes a Potential Investigation

Most investigations do not announce themselves with a flashing red warning that says "Important legal matter—handle carefully." They start as ordinary tickets. A user complains that "all my files are gone." An antivirus alert pops up on someone's laptop. You notice repeated failed logins in a system log while you are troubleshooting a different issue. Individually, each of these could have a mundane explanation. The challenge is recognizing the moment when you should stop treating the situation as pure break/fix and start treating it as potentially evidentiary.

Imagine a user opening a ticket because their documents from the last week have disappeared from a shared design workstation. If you have worked in IT for a while, your first instinct is probably to restore from backup or the recycle bin and move on. But now suppose you also spot that another user account logged in to that machine late last night, well outside normal working hours. That extra detail changes the story. Maybe nothing malicious happened—but it could also indicate unauthorized access or even deliberate deletion. At that point you should pause and consider that someone, later, may need to reconstruct exactly who accessed what, and when.

The same mental shift applies when you see a high-severity malware alert, especially for something like a remote access Trojan. Clicking "Remove" might make the alert go away, but it may also erase traces that investigators need to figure out where the malware came from, whether data was stolen, and whether other systems are compromised. Or consider a manager quietly asking you to "check what this employee has been browsing." That request itself is a red flag that HR or legal issues may be in play. You are no longer just trying to get a website to load; you are dealing with a situation that could affect someone's job and your organization's liability.

In all these situations, cues like suspicious timing, unusual access to sensitive systems, explicit HR or legal involvement, or possible data theft should trigger what you can think of as an investigative mindset. From that moment, unnecessary changes become dangerous. You avoid clearing logs, avoid reinstalling the operating system, and avoid "tidying up" files. Instead, you notify the appropriate contacts—your security team, your supervisor, or whatever your incident response plan specifies—and proceed carefully.

Evidence, Volatility, and the "Do No Harm" Principle

To operate in that investigative mindset, you need a working sense of what counts as **evidence**. In a digital context, evidence is any data or object that might help reconstruct what happened: log entries, email messages, files on disk, USB drives, browser history, configuration settings, screenshots, even the physical laptop or phone itself. Some of this evidence is easy to preserve, while some is fragile and disappears quickly. The difference is captured in two terms: **volatile data** and **nonvolatile data**.

Volatile data is information that exists only while the system is powered on and can be lost when the system shuts down, reboots, or simply continues operating. Think of the contents of RAM, running processes, active network connections, and in-memory encryption keys. At an A+ level, you are not expected to capture full memory images, but you should appreciate why powering off or restarting a system in the middle of a suspicious incident can destroy information that a forensics team would love to see.

Nonvolatile data is information that persists across power cycles. That includes files stored on a hard drive or SSD, many types of logs, email stored on a server, and cloud account histories. This data is more durable, but it is not permanent. Logs rotate and are overwritten. Users delete files. Systems apply updates that change configurations. Attackers may even try to cover their tracks by clearing logs or wiping activity histories.

Because of this fragility, a simple principle guides your actions when you suspect something may be evidentiary: **do no harm**. You do not run system cleaners, you do not empty the recycle bin, you do not uninstall applications or "just wipe the system" unless that course of action is clearly authorized by your security or incident response team. You also avoid changing log settings or clearing logs "to make them easier to read." If your normal troubleshooting habits involve frequent reboots "just to see if it fixes it," you now pause and ask whether rebooting might be discarding volatile information that someone else will need.

This does not mean you never disconnect or shut down a system in an incident. If ransomware is actively encrypting files on a file server, you might be instructed to pull the network cable or even cut power to stop the damage. In that case, containment takes priority and your actions should follow your incident response plan. The key is that you are acting intentionally, with an awareness of the impact on evidence and under the guidance of policy, not just out of habit.

Chain of Custody: Tracking Who Had What, When, and Where

Once you start treating data or devices as evidence, another concept becomes central: **chain of custody**. Chain of custody is the documented history of who had control of the evidence, when they had it, and what was done with it. It answers questions like, "Who collected this laptop?", "Where was it stored?", and "Who accessed the log export before it reached the security team?" The goal is to be able to show, later, that the evidence was not tampered with, lost, or mixed up with something else.

A typical chain of custody record will identify the item in enough detail that it is clearly distinguishable: for example, "Dell Latitude laptop, asset tag ACME-L-1037, 512 GB SSD, user assigned: j.smith." It will include unique identifiers like serial numbers or asset tags, the date and time the item was collected, where it was collected from, and by whom. Each time the item changes hands—from you to a security analyst, from the analyst to an external forensics firm—there should be a documented transfer, with names, dates, times, and usually signatures or electronic acknowledgments. If the item is placed in secure storage, the location and conditions of storage are recorded as well.

As a frontline technician, you may be the person who first takes possession of a laptop, a USB drive, or an external disk that might be evidence. You might also be the one exporting application logs or downloading an email archive at HR's request. Your responsibility is to plug yourself into the chain of custody process your organization has defined. That usually means filling out a form or updating a case record with what you collected, when, and from where, then making sure any handoff to security, HR, or management is recorded. Dropping a laptop on someone's desk with "Here, this might be important" and walking away is exactly what you want to avoid. A good way to think about it is package tracking for evidence: if there are gaps in the tracking history, the integrity of the evidence can be questioned.

Handling Devices and Data as Evidence

Evidence does not just live in logs or cloud dashboards; very often it is the device itself. When you are told that a workstation, laptop, phone, or removable drive is part of an investigation, you treat it differently from a normal support asset. The first step is usually to stop normal use. You do not let the user "just finish this document" or plug in another USB stick to copy their personal files off. Every action taken on that device changes its state, potentially overwriting deleted data or modifying timestamps that investigators rely on.

Depending on your organization's procedures, you may be instructed to disconnect the device from the network to prevent remote tampering or wiping, especially for mobile devices and laptops. When possible, this is often done logically—turning off Wi-Fi, unplugging Ethernet, disabling network ports—rather than simply powering off the machine, because of the volatile data considerations already discussed. In some cases, though, policy will explicitly say to power the machine down. The important point for the exam and for real life is that you follow the policy, not your impulse, and you document whatever action you take.

Once the device is under your control and stabilized, you label it clearly with identifying information and the relevant incident or ticket number. It should then be placed in a secure location—such as a locked cabinet or an evidence locker—until the appropriate team can collect and image it. You do not continue using it as a loaner machine, and you do not casually browse the user's documents "to see what's going on." More advanced teams will sometimes use tools such as write blockers, which allow them to read from storage devices without modifying any data on them. You are not expected to configure or operate those tools, but you should recognize that they exist and that one reason you are asked not to work on a suspect drive is to preserve it for that kind of specialized handling.

Often, the evidence you deal with will not require seizing an entire device. You might be asked to capture screenshots of an unusual error message, an offensive email, or a suspicious browser window. You might export logs from Event Viewer, from a firewall, or from a cloud service like a file-sharing platform. In those cases, you are still handling evidence; you just do it in the form of data.

With screenshots, it is important to capture the relevant information completely and in context. That usually means including the full window showing the message, any visible usernames, URLs, or timestamps, and the system clock if practical. Saving these images to a secure, access-controlled location, and naming or tagging them so that they tie back to the case, helps later reviewers understand what they are seeing. With logs, the main rule is that you export rather than alter. You might save events to a file, generate a report, or provide read-only access to a security analyst. You avoid changing log retention settings, turning logging off, or clearing old entries "to make room," especially once an incident is suspected.

Cloud and SaaS applications add another layer. Many of them track login history, IP addresses for sign-ins, file access, and administrative changes. These are rich sources of evidence in investigations about unauthorized access or data leakage. As an A+-level technician, you may be asked to locate and export those logs or grant appropriate people access to them. The same pattern applies: you preserve, you document, you do not modify more than is necessary to fulfill the request. Time matters here because many services only retain detailed activity logs for a limited number of days or weeks, so if you see hints of suspicious behavior, escalating promptly can make the difference between having a useful record and discovering that the trail has been overwritten by routine activity.

Common Evidence Sources and Your Role

By this point in the book, you have already encountered different kinds of logs and artifacts in the context of monitoring and troubleshooting. In a forensic context, those same sources tell the story of who did what, from where, and when. Operating system logs record logons, logoffs, service failures, and system changes. Security logs track things like failed authentication attempts, account lockouts, and malware detections. Applications—whether a web server, a database, or a line-of-business tool—often keep their own logs of user actions, errors, and configuration changes.

At the network level, firewalls and routers maintain records of connections, blocked and allowed traffic, and sometimes URLs visited or categories of content accessed. VPN concentrators log remote connections and the IP addresses associated with them. DHCP servers track which device had which IP address at a given time, which can be invaluable when an incident starts from a suspicious IP log. Packet captures, created by network or security teams, provide even more detail by recording actual traffic; you are unlikely to capture those yourself, but you might be asked to help identify which systems were communicating at the time.

On individual endpoints, evidence can include user documents, downloads, browser history, cached files, and temporary folders. There is a strong temptation to start clicking around here to satisfy curiosity or to try to "prove" that a user did or did not do something. Professionally, you need to resist that urge unless you are explicitly authorized and trained for that role. Simply understanding that these artifacts are important and should not be altered is enough at your level. Finally, cloud and account histories—login records, file access logs, email messages and their metadata, deleted items folders—round out the picture, especially in organizations that rely heavily on cloud productivity suites.

In all of these areas, your job is not to interpret the evidence in a legal sense. You are not deciding guilt or innocence, or even necessarily determining root cause. You are preserving and enabling access. You may recognize that multiple failed logins from an overseas IP look suspicious, or that an employee appears to have downloaded large numbers of customer records. But rather than confronting the user or drawing conclusions in your documentation, you focus on capturing the relevant data, maintaining its integrity through proper chain of custody, and escalating through the appropriate channels.

This is also where your documentation habits become part of the evidentiary picture. The notes you enter into a ticketing system are often the first written record of an incident. They should be factual and neutral: what you saw, what you did, and when you did it. "Observed twelve failed login attempts to account 'j.smith' from IP 203.0.113.10 between 09:15 and 09:17. Notified security team at 09:20. Per instruction from security, disconnected workstation from network at 09:22." That kind of writing is far more valuable than "User is probably being hacked" or "This seems fishy," which adds opinion but no clarity. Months later, if HR or legal reviews the case, those clear, time-stamped notes may carry more weight than anyone's memory.

Overlaying all of this are legal, privacy, and policy boundaries that you are expected to respect. Many organizations have acceptable use policies that inform employees that their activity may be monitored, but that does not give you personal license to browse through their photos or private emails. Especially in environments with bring-your-own-device (BYOD) policies, corporate and personal data coexist awkwardly on the same hardware. You follow your organization's process: if HR or legal authorizes a search, they will specify what is to be collected and by whom. If law enforcement becomes involved, instructions typically flow through management or legal; you do not generally hand devices directly to officers or answer investigative questions on your own initiative without guidance.

In practical terms, digital forensics and investigations sit right next to incident response in the larger security lifecycle. An alert or a user report leads to detection. Initial response focuses on containment and stabilizing the situation. Evidence preservation—what you have been reading about in this section—ensures that data from that period is available to support a full investigation, which is usually driven by security, HR, or external specialists. Later, the organization analyzes what happened, learns from it, and adjusts controls and training. Your contribution at the beginning, though mostly invisible if you do it well, can make the difference between "We think something bad happened, but we have no proof" and "Here is a clear, well-documented sequence of events backed by reliable evidence."

Knowledge Check

Question 1: A help desk technician discovers suspicious after-hours logins on a user's workstation while investigating missing files. Which action best reflects the "do no harm" principle in this situation?

A. Immediately reinstall the operating system to remove any potential malware
B. Clear the event logs so only new, relevant entries are visible
C. Allow the user to keep working while silently collecting more information
D. Stop normal troubleshooting, avoid altering logs, and escalate per the incident response plan

Question 2: Which of the following best describes the primary purpose of maintaining a chain of custody for digital evidence?

A. To prove that evidence has not been tampered with by documenting who handled it and when
B. To ensure evidence is always encrypted while in transit
C. To allow technicians to reuse devices quickly after an investigation
D. To guarantee that an internal investigation will not involve law enforcement

Question 3: A technician collects a laptop that may be involved in an HR investigation. What is the technician's most appropriate responsibility at this stage?

A. Review the user's documents and browser history to summarize findings for HR
B. Preserve device and document chain of custody
C. Perform a full malware scan and remove any detected threats
D. Back up the user's personal data to a USB drive before turning in the laptop

Question 4: Which of the following is the best example of volatile data in a forensic context?

A. Web server access logs stored on an SSD
B. Email archives stored in a cloud service
C. Files saved on a removable USB drive
D. Active network connections and running processes in system memory

Question 5: A technician is asked to provide evidence from a SaaS file-sharing platform related to suspected data theft. Which action is most appropriate?

A. Increase log retention by deleting older entries to free space
B. Disable logging to prevent further changes while investigating
C. Export relevant activity logs or grant read-only access, without altering existing records
D. Edit the logs to highlight only entries that appear suspicious

Question 6: While investigating a high-severity malware alert, the technician is tempted to click "Remove" in the antivirus console. What is the best action if the situation might lead to a formal investigation?

A. Pause, make no changes, and escalate to the security team
B. Reboot the system several times to verify the malware persists
C. Disable all logging so logs do not fill the disk during the incident
D. Immediately run multiple antimalware tools to ensure full cleanup

Question 7: A technician needs to capture a screenshot of an offensive email as evidence. Which practice best supports later forensic review?

A. Cropping the screenshot to only show the offensive sentence
B. Capture usernames, timestamps, and context; store securely
C. Forwarding the email to their personal account for safekeeping
D. Printing the email and deleting it from the server to prevent further access

Question 8: Which of the following ticket notes best aligns with recommended documentation practices for potential investigations?

A. "User is likely lying about missing files; seems suspicious."
B. "Pretty sure this is just user error, restored from backup."
C. "User's activity looks shady; this might be an HR issue."
D. "Observed multiple failed logins to 'j.smith' from IP 203.0.113.10 between 09:15–09:17; notified security at 09:20 per procedure."

ANSWERS

1: Correct Answer: D
Rationale: When activity may be related to an incident, the technician should stop routine troubleshooting, avoid altering potential evidence such as logs, and escalate according to the incident response plan, reflecting the "do no harm" principle.

2: Correct Answer: A
Rationale: Chain of custody is the documented tracking of who handled evidence, when, and how, to show it has not been altered and to preserve evidentiary integrity.

3: Correct Answer: B
Rationale: The technician should preserve the device, record collection details, and transfer it via the defined chain of custody, not analyze user data or modify the system.

4: Correct Answer: D
Rationale: Active network connections and running processes reside in RAM and are lost on shutdown, making them volatile data, unlike data stored on persistent media.

5: Correct Answer: C
Rationale: The technician should export or provide read-only access to relevant logs while avoiding any modification or deletion that could affect the integrity of the evidence.

6: Correct Answer: A
Rationale: If a formal investigation is possible, the technician should avoid actions that might destroy or change evidence and instead escalate to the security or incident response team for direction.

7: Correct Answer: B
Rationale: Capturing full context (usernames, timestamps, and relevant screen details) and storing the screenshot securely preserves evidentiary value and supports later forensic review.

8: Correct Answer: D
Rationale: Documentation should be factual, time-stamped, and objective, describing observed events and actions taken without speculation or subjective judgments.

CHAPTER 6

Security Program Management & Oversight

6.1 Security Governance & Documentation

If you talk to people who have been in IT for a while, you'll hear stories that all start the same way: "Technically, I could have done it—but policy wouldn't let me." That tension between what you can do and what you are allowed to do is exactly where security governance lives. On paper, governance sounds like something handled in boardrooms and legal meetings, far away from the help desk. In reality, you experience governance every time you say, "I need your manager's approval for that," or "I can't reset that password without verifying your identity," or "We're required to log this as a security incident." The whole purpose of this chapter is to make that invisible structure visible, so you can work confidently inside it and recognize what CompTIA is really testing when they ask governance-style questions.

At a high level, **security governance** is simply how an organization directs and controls its security efforts. Management decides what risks the business is willing to take, what must be protected, and what rules everyone has to follow. Those decisions are not left in people's heads; they are written down and turned into documents, approval paths, and daily routines. As an entry-level technician, you are not expected to design this system, but you are expected to recognize it, use it, and respect it. On the Security+ exam, the "right" answer is often not the clever technical fix, but the action that lines up with the company's documented rules.

The Security Documentation "Stack"

Organizations don't write a single mega-document that covers every detail from "Protect customer data" down to "Click this button and then that button." Instead, they use a layered set of documents, each with a specific purpose and level of detail. Understanding how these layers relate to each other is crucial, because exam questions will often describe one type but call it another, and you'll have to classify it based on what it does, not what it's called in the scenario.

At the top of the stack is the **policy**. A policy is a high-level statement of what is required or prohibited and why it matters. It is approved by senior management and applies broadly across the organization. A policy might declare that all company laptops must be encrypted, or that business communication must use corporate email accounts, or that users are responsible for protecting their passwords. Policies don't usually spell out which brand of encryption tool to use or the exact steps to configure it; they draw the boundaries and set the expectations. When you tell a user, "The company doesn't allow that," you are almost always referring—directly or indirectly—to a policy.

Supporting each policy are one or more **standards**. Where a policy says "we will use encryption," a standard answers the question "which encryption, and how strong does it have to be?" Think of standards as the minimum technical requirements that make policies real. A password-related standard, for instance, might specify that passwords must be at least 12 characters, must include a mix of character types, cannot be reused within the last 10 passwords, and must be changed every 90 days. An encryption standard might require a particular algorithm, key length, and approved tools. From your perspective, standards show up in the settings you configure on domain controllers, VPN appliances, mobile device management systems, and similar tools. If a question describes specific technical minimums—like "the organization requires 12-character passwords with complexity" or "WPA3 must be used on all wireless networks"—you're looking at something that belongs in a standard, not a high-level policy or a procedural checklist.

Further down the stack are **procedures**. While policies speak in terms of "must" and standards talk about "how strong" or "which option," procedures answer a different question: "Exactly how do I do this task?" A procedure is a step-by-step document that someone can follow to get a consistent, repeatable result. For a help desk technician, procedures are the documents you probably touch the most. There might be a procedure for onboarding a new employee—create the account in the directory service, add the correct group memberships, set up the mailbox, record the actions in the ticketing system. Another procedure might cover wiping and decommissioning a workstation—boot from a specific tool, run a multi-pass wipe, verify, apply an asset tag change, and update the inventory database. Incident response procedures tell you what to do when you suspect malware: disconnect the machine from the network, preserve logs, notify the security team, and so on. On the exam, whenever a scenario describes a numbered list of steps or a detailed workflow, that's a procedure, even if the distractor answer choice tries to label it as a policy.

Finally, there are **guidelines**, which are best-practice recommendations rather than hard requirements. A guideline might suggest that system reboots be scheduled outside of core business hours when possible, or that administrators notify affected teams before making major configuration changes. Guidelines help optimize security, usability, and operations, but they usually use softer language like "should" or "recommended," in contrast to the "must" and "required" tone found in policies and standards. In test questions, this difference in wording is often your only clue. If the text says the organization "recommends" using a particular hardening checklist but does not mandate it, that belongs in a guideline, not a standard.

All four types work together. Imagine an email environment. An **Email Security Policy** might declare that company email is for business use, that confidential data must be protected in transit, and that malicious attachments must be blocked. A supporting standard could state that all email must be scanned by a specific gateway using particular filtering rules, that TLS is required for external connections when supported, and that executable attachments are automatically quarantined. A procedure would then spell out how to configure the gateway, update the filters, handle quarantined messages, and investigate potential phishing messages. A guideline might suggest that administrators send a notification before tightening filters significantly, to manage user expectations. If an exam question asks you to identify the type of document involved, focus less on the title and more on whether it's setting broad rules, technical minimums, detailed steps, or recommendations.

Common Security Policies You Will See

Once you understand the structure, it helps to look at specific policy types that frequently affect daily IT support work. The first one you'll encounter almost anywhere is the **Acceptable Use Policy**, often abbreviated AUP. This is the set of rules that governs how users may use company devices, networks, and internet access. It typically addresses whether limited personal use is allowed, what kinds of websites are off-limits, whether users may install their own software, how removable storage can be used, and what kind of monitoring the company performs. When a user asks you to install a peer-to-peer file sharing client, or you see evidence of streaming movies on a production server, the AUP is the authority you rely on when you say "no" or when you open a ticket to report a violation. On the exam, any scenario where a user misuses computer or network resources—torrenting at work, visiting inappropriate sites, running cryptocurrency miners—points directly back to the acceptable use policy.

Closely related are **password and authentication policies**. These policies and their related standards document how users must choose, handle, and protect their credentials. At the policy level, management might state that all accounts must be protected by strong authentication, that passwords are confidential and must not be shared, and that multi-factor authentication is required for remote access or privileged roles. Supporting standards then translate those decisions into technical settings: minimum password length, required complexity, expiration period, lockout thresholds, and MFA methods. Procedures back this up by describing how to reset a password, how to verify a user's identity before doing so, and how to onboard someone into an MFA system. From your perspective, when a user calls locked out of their account, you are applying all three layers: you follow a reset procedure that enforces the organization's password standards, in order to uphold the overarching policy about strong authentication.

Another category that often gets less attention but matters greatly in security is the group of **clean desk and data handling policies**. These policies address how sensitive information should be stored, displayed, and disposed of, both in digital and physical form. A clean desk policy might require that users lock their screens whenever they step away, that printed documents with sensitive data not be left out in the open, and that laptops not be left unattended in public places. Data handling rules add expectations about encryption for data at rest and in transit, how long certain records are retained, and how paper documents must be shredded rather than tossed into the trash. IT staff both follow these policies and help enforce them. You might configure automatic screen lock timers or secure printing features that require users to authenticate at the printer before jobs are released, all in support of these compliance requirements.

As you move into security operations, you will encounter **incident response and reporting policies**. These documents define what counts as a security incident, who must be notified when an incident is suspected, and what kinds of actions are authorized. An incident might be a confirmed malware infection, a suspected data breach, repeated failed login attempts, or a lost device. The policy itself sets expectations like "all suspected incidents must be reported to the security team immediately" and "logs relevant to an incident must be preserved." Procedures then explain what you, as a frontline technician, should actually do: isolate the affected device without wiping it, collect basic information, create or update an incident ticket, and escalate to the appropriate team. On the exam, if you see a scenario where a technician discovers something suspicious, the tested behavior is usually to follow the incident response procedure and escalate, not to quietly delete logs, reinstall Windows, or ignore the issue.

Remote work and mobile computing bring in their own set of expectations, formalized in **remote access** and **mobile/BYOD policies**. A remote access policy specifies how employees may connect from outside the office: perhaps only via a corporate VPN, maybe with strict MFA, and only from systems that meet certain security requirements. If a user wants to install a third-party remote control tool they found on the internet, or bypass the VPN because it "slows things down," you refer back to this policy. A mobile or Bring Your Own Device (BYOD) policy explains what users must accept when they use personal phones or tablets for work email and apps. That might include installing a mobile device management (MDM) agent, allowing remote wipe if the device is lost, or agreeing to certain screen lock and encryption settings. You might be the person who helps set up that MDM profile or who explains why a lost phone must be reported immediately.

Finally, nearly every mature IT environment is governed by a **change management policy**. This policy addresses how planned changes to systems are proposed, reviewed, approved, tested, and scheduled. The goal is to reduce outages and security incidents caused by ad-hoc, undocumented changes. From your point of view, this often means you cannot simply modify firewall rules, upgrade a production server, or push out a new version of an application because a single user requested it. Instead, you open a change request, document the reason, identify the potential impact, and wait for the change advisory process to approve and schedule it. Security+ questions often test this indirectly: a technician wants to make a configuration change in production to fix an issue, and the answer that respects governance is the one that mentions following the change management process, not the one that bypasses it for speed.

People Behind the Policies: Roles and Responsibilities

Documents do not enforce themselves; people do. Governance always ties back to specific roles, and understanding who is responsible for what helps you decide when to act and when to escalate. At the widest level are **end users**. Every employee who touches company systems—sales staff, nurses, engineers, accountants—is responsible for following policies, protecting their passwords, reporting suspicious activity, and using systems appropriately. They are not expected to understand every technical detail, but they are expected to act within the rules.

As an **IT support or help desk technician**, your role is more specialized. You are both a user of the governance system and a front-line enforcer of it. You follow all applicable policies, standards, and procedures in your own work. You verify identity before making account changes or sharing information, because the password reset procedure requires it. You refuse to perform actions that would violate policy, even when a user pushes hard, and you explain calmly that you are bound by those rules. You document your actions in tickets, including when you had to deviate because of an authorized exception, and you escalate tickets that look like security incidents or serious policy violations. Technicians are often the first to notice patterns—multiple users reporting the same phishing email, or repeated failed login attempts from an unusual location—and your responsibility is to route that information through the proper channels.

Above you, **supervisors and managers** play a dual role. They help interpret policy, approve certain access requests, and participate in the escalation chain for both operational and security issues. When a user insists on an exception—"My team really needs local admin rights" or "We can't wait for the normal change process"—you should know that this is a management-level decision, not something you approve on your own. Managers may also be data owners or have the authority to speak for data owners when access decisions are made.

Most organizations also have a **security officer or security team**. Titles vary—Information Security Officer, Chief Information Security Officer (CISO), security analyst—but the functions are similar. These individuals help design and maintain policies and standards, coordinate incident response, run security awareness training, and review logs and alerts from security systems. While they may occasionally interact directly with end users, their main relationship with you is through documentation and escalations. When you notice suspicious behavior or a possible breach, you follow the incident response procedure, which usually leads to a handoff to the security team. Your role is not to perform forensics or make final decisions about whether something is a reportable breach; instead, you collect and pass on accurate information.

A final pair of roles you should know conceptually are **data owners** and **data custodians**. A data owner is a person or group with business responsibility for a particular set of information. For example, the head of Human Resources may be the data owner for employee records, while the finance director owns financial reporting data. Data owners decide who should have access and what level of protection is appropriate. Data custodians, often IT administrators, manage the systems that store and process that data. They apply permissions, backups, and technical controls according to the owner's decisions. When a user requests access to a shared folder, the correct process is often for IT to ask, "Do we have approval from the data owner?" not just "Does the requester's manager say it's okay?" As an entry-level tech, you implement changes once the documented approvals are in place.

Working Inside Governance Day to Day

In practical terms, operating within governance means pausing before you act. When a ticket comes in, you first understand what is being asked. A user wants a password reset, access to a new shared drive, an unapproved application installed, or a firewall port opened. Next, you mentally align that request with the relevant security documents. Password resets trigger the password and authentication policy, along with the reset procedure. Access requests involve data ownership and access control procedures. Software installation invokes the acceptable use policy and any approved software list. Network changes must respect the change management policy and security standards.

Once you know what applies, you act by following the documented steps and obtaining any required approvals, rather than relying solely on your own judgment. If the procedure says you must verify the caller using specific methods before resetting a password, you do exactly that, even if the caller is in a hurry or identifies themselves as an executive. If an installation request involves software that isn't on the approved list, you do not quietly install it; you explain that it's not authorized and, if appropriate, help the user submit a formal request for review. Afterward, you update the ticket or records to reflect what was done, who approved it, and any deviations from standard practice.

Sometimes this will put you in conflict with frustrated users. Someone will say, "Just do it; I don't care about policy." In those moments, your professionalism is measured by how you hold the line. You can empathize with their urgency while still explaining that policies aren't optional and that they protect not only the company but also the user. If your governance structure allows, you can offer to escalate to a manager or security representative who has authority to consider exceptions. What you should not do—on the exam or in real life—is bypass controls because someone sounds important or impatient.

All of this can feel like bureaucracy until you see how it plays out after an incident. When something goes wrong—a data leak, a compromised account, a system outage—investigations look back through tickets, logs, and documentation to reconstruct what happened. If your records show that you followed the written procedure, obtained the required approvals, and documented your actions, that becomes evidence that the organization's governance worked as designed. If, on the other hand, there is no record, or the record shows you made an off-the-books change, then you personally and the organization generally are in a much weaker position. Governance and documentation are not extra layers piled on top of "real work"; they are part of doing the work correctly, defensibly, and in a way that scales beyond a single person's memory or judgment.

Knowledge Check

Question 1: A help desk technician receives a request from a user's manager to grant the user access to a finance share. The technician replies, "I need approval from the folder's data owner before I can make that change." This behavior BEST demonstrates which aspect of security governance?

A. Implementing technical controls without management involvement
B. Following documented roles and responsibilities for access decisions
C. Applying incident response procedures
D. Enforcing acceptable use of personal devices

Question 2: An organization publishes a document stating that "all company laptops must be encrypted to protect customer data" but does not specify which encryption algorithm or key length to use. Which type of document does this MOST likely represent?

A. Procedure
B. Standard
C. Policy
D. Guideline

Question 3: A document states that all VPN connections must use AES-256 encryption, TLS 1.2 or higher, and approved corporate VPN clients only. Which type of security documentation is this MOST likely describing?

A. Policy
B. Procedure
C. Guideline
D. Standard

Question 4: A step-by-step document walks a technician through resetting a user's password, including how to verify the user's identity, where to log the request, and how to notify the user of the change. What type of document is this?

A. Policy
B. Standard
C. Guideline
D. Procedure

Question 5: A company has a document that states: "Administrators should notify affected users before making major configuration changes when possible, and should schedule non-urgent reboots outside of business hours." The language is explicitly described as recommended, not mandatory. What type of document is this?

A. Policy
B. Standard
C. Guideline
D. Procedure

Question 6: A user insists that the help desk install a peer-to-peer file sharing program on their company laptop so they can "share large files faster." The technician refuses, citing the document that governs how employees may use company devices, networks, and internet access. Which policy is the technician MOST likely referring to?

A. Acceptable use policy
B. Change management policy
C. Incident response policy
D. Remote access policy

Question 7: A technician receives a ticket requesting that a firewall port be opened immediately to resolve a minor application issue in production. According to security governance best practices, what should the technician do FIRST?

- **A.** Open the port immediately, then document the change afterward
- **B.** Submit or update a formal change request and wait for the required approvals
- **C.** Escalate directly to the security officer to bypass normal approvals
- **D.** Deny the request without taking any further action

Question 8: A front-line technician discovers malware on a workstation. According to the organization's governance, the incident response policy requires that all suspected incidents be reported to the security team and that relevant logs be preserved. Which action BEST aligns with this policy?

- **A.** Immediately wipe and reimage the workstation to get the user working again
- **B.** Disconnect the workstation and delete all logs to protect user privacy
- **C.** Ignore the issue because the malware was blocked by antivirus
- **D.** Isolate the workstation from the network, preserve logs, and escalate to the security team

ANSWERS

1: Correct Answer: B
Rationale: The technician is deferring to the data owner for access approval, which reflects adherence to documented roles and responsibilities in access control governance.

2: Correct Answer: C
Rationale: This is a high-level, mandatory statement of intent ("must be encrypted") without technical specifics, which is characteristic of a policy rather than a standard, procedure, or guideline.

3: Correct Answer: D
Rationale: It specifies required technical details (cipher, protocol version, approved clients), which is the purpose of a standard, not a broad policy, optional guideline, or step-by-step procedure.

4: Correct Answer: D
Rationale: A detailed, ordered "how-to" for performing a task is a procedure, not a high-level policy, technical standard, or optional guideline.

5: Correct Answer: C
Rationale: The use of "should" and "recommended" indicates non-mandatory guidance, which defines a guideline rather than an enforceable policy, standard, or procedure.

6: Correct Answer: A
Rationale: An acceptable use policy defines what users may and may not do with company devices and network resources, including installing unauthorized software.

7: Correct Answer: B
Rationale: Change management requires production changes to follow a formal request and approval process; the technician should initiate or update the change request and wait for approvals before opening the port.

8: Correct Answer: D
Rationale: Isolating the system, preserving logs as evidence, and escalating to the security team follows incident response policy requirements for reporting and containment, unlike the other options.

6.2 Risk Management & Business Impact

If you work on a help desk for more than a few days, you quickly realize that many of the "simple" questions you get are really about something bigger than just fixing a glitch. A user might ask you to "just turn off that annoying security pop-up," or "install this tool my friend recommended," or "let me use my personal laptop; it's faster." On the surface those are technical requests. Underneath, they are **risk** decisions. The organization has already tried to think through what could go wrong, how bad it would be, and what it is willing to live with. Policies, standards, and procedures—the documents you saw in the previous section—are simply those risk decisions written down.

Risk management is about more than worst-case scenarios and scary hacking stories. It is the everyday process of deciding what could harm the business, how likely it is, and what to do about it. As an entry-level technician, you are not expected to design a corporate risk management program. However, you are expected to operate inside it. When you follow or ignore policy, when you choose what to escalate, when you prioritize which system to restore first after an outage, you are either supporting or undermining the organization's approach to risk. This chapter gives you enough of the language and concepts to see how your day-to-day work connects to that bigger picture.

Understanding What "Risk" Really Means

Risk starts with assets. An **asset** is anything of value to the organization: not just servers and laptops, but also data, services, and even reputation. The payroll system, the customer database, the Wi-Fi network that keeps a retail store processing credit cards, and the CEO's laptop full of strategic plans are all assets. When we talk about protecting IT, we are really talking about protecting these assets so the business can function, stay compliant, and maintain trust with customers and partners.

Against those assets stand **threats**. A threat is anything that can cause harm. Some threats are intentional, like an attacker trying to steal customer data or deploy ransomware. Others are accidental, like an employee clicking a phishing link or deleting a shared folder. Still others come from the environment: a fire in the server room, a flood in the basement, a power surge that fries a switch. Threats by themselves are possibilities—they are "bad things that could happen," not things that have already happened.

Threats become much more dangerous when they find a **vulnerability**. A vulnerability is a weakness that a threat can exploit. Think of an unpatched operating system with known security flaws, a weak password on an administrator account, an unlocked network closet, or a critical server with no backup. None of these problems guarantees damage by itself, but each one is like a door left unlocked. If a threat comes along at the right moment, the vulnerability provides the path in.

When a threat successfully exploits a vulnerability and affects an asset, the result is an **impact**. Impact is the harm that actually occurs: servers down, data lost, sensitive information exposed, employees unable to work, or customers unable to place orders. Impact always has at least two dimensions. There is the technical impact—systems offline, corrupted databases, locked accounts—and there is the business impact, which shows up as lost revenue, regulatory penalties, overtime costs, and damage to reputation. A three-day outage on an internal print server may be annoying but survivable. A three-day outage of an online order processing system might cost the company hundreds of thousands in lost sales and angry customers.

To talk about risk, we also care about **likelihood**. Likelihood is simply how probable it is that a particular threat event will occur. A major earthquake might be very low likelihood for a small office in a geologically stable area, while phishing emails trying to trick users into entering their passwords might be daily occurrences. You can think of **risk** itself as the combination of likelihood and impact: the potential for loss or damage when a threat acts on a vulnerability and harms an asset. In simple terms, if something is very likely to happen and would cause serious damage, it is a high risk. If it is unlikely and would cause only minor inconvenience, it is a low risk.

Putting this together, you can trace a cause-and-effect chain. Imagine a file server in a small business running an old, unsupported operating system that has not received security updates in years. That old OS is a vulnerability. The server is directly connected to the internet and employees regularly receive email attachments containing malware; those are threats. One day, a user opens a malicious attachment, the malware reaches the vulnerable server, and ransomware encrypts its data. The encryption of business files is the incident; the three days of downtime while the company struggles to restore from incomplete backups is the technical impact; the lost sales, delayed customer projects, and angry phone calls are the business impact. When management reviews the incident, they are likely to classify the overall risk of "old, unpatched internet-facing servers" as high and invest in upgrades or stricter patching processes. On the exam and in real life, keep the order straight: the vulnerability is the weakness, the threat is the potential danger, the incident or attack is the event, and the impact is the damage that results.

How Organizations Evaluate Risk

Because organizations cannot eliminate all risk, they need a way to compare different risks and decide what to address first. Should they spend their limited budget on better backups, on a second internet connection, or on more security awareness training? To answer those kinds of questions, they perform **risk assessments**, which can be done in two broad ways: qualitative and quantitative.

A **qualitative risk assessment** uses descriptive categories instead of precise numbers. You will see words like "low," "medium," or "high" to describe both likelihood and impact, sometimes color-coded as green, yellow, or red. These assessments rely heavily on expert judgment, experience, discussion, and sometimes checklists. In a small medical clinic, for example, the IT manager, office manager, and doctor-owner might sit down and talk through various scenarios. Allowing personal USB drives for staff might be rated as high impact and medium likelihood, given the sensitivity of patient data and past malware incidents, and so the overall risk is treated as high. On that basis they might decide to block personal USB storage entirely. As a technician, you might later see a rule in the endpoint management console labeled as "High-risk use case – USB storage blocked by policy." That label comes from a qualitative risk assessment. When change requests are marked "high risk" or "low risk," this same qualitative thinking is usually behind the scenes.

A **quantitative risk assessment** tries instead to express risk in numbers, often in terms of money. Here, instead of saying "high impact," the organization estimates cost: "If this server goes down, we lose about $5,000 per hour in missed sales and employee downtime." Instead of "medium likelihood," they might say, "Historically we see an outage of this type about once every five years, so about a 20 percent chance per year." Even without complex formulas, you can see how this helps. If a particular kind of ransomware incident is estimated to cost $50,000 on average and has a 10 percent chance of happening each year, the expected annual loss is around $5,000. If a better backup solution costs $2,000 per year and would greatly reduce the impact, that looks like a smart investment.

At the A+ level, you do not need to memorize detailed formulas, but you should recognize the difference in style. When you see scenarios using labels like low, medium, high, or red/yellow/green, that is qualitative. When you see references to dollar amounts, probabilities per year, or "expected loss," that is quantitative. Both methods have the same goal: to make risk visible so management can make defensible decisions about where to put time, money, and attention.

What Organizations Do With Risk

Once a risk is identified and evaluated, the next step is to decide what to do about it. Organizations have four basic choices, often called risk treatment options, and almost every policy or control you encounter fits into one of these.

Sometimes, a business chooses **risk acceptance**. This is a conscious decision to live with a particular risk because it is low, or because the cost of addressing it is higher than the potential loss. A small local shop might accept the risk of its only printer failing rather than buying a second printer that will rarely be used. Similarly, a department might keep using an older internal application with a known bug because replacing it would be far more expensive than occasionally dealing with the glitch. As a technician, you may see notes in documentation such as "Application X is end-of-life; risk accepted until replacement next year." That does not mean you can ignore security controls around it, but it does mean someone higher up has decided that the remaining risk is tolerable for now.

Other times, the choice is **risk avoidance**. Here, the organization eliminates the risk by refusing to do the risky activity at all. If a company decides that allowing employees to store company data on personal smartphones is too hard to secure, it may simply ban that practice and require all work email to be accessed through managed, corporate devices. When a user asks you to install unapproved remote-control software on their home PC so they can access the office file server, and policy clearly says that personal devices cannot store corporate data, the organization is avoiding that entire category of risk. Your role is to enforce and explain that choice, not to find a clever workaround that contradicts the policy.

The third option is **risk transfer**, where some of the financial or operational impact of a risk is shifted to a third party. Cyber insurance is a classic example: the organization pays a premium so that if a covered incident occurs, the insurer bears part of the financial loss. Using a cloud backup provider or outsourcing email to a cloud platform with a strong uptime guarantee are also forms of risk transfer. The business is saying, "If your service fails, you bear part of the cost and responsibility under our contract." Notice that transfer does not magically remove the risk; it changes who is on the hook when something goes wrong. Later, when you read about service-level agreements and vendor risk in the next section, you will see how this ties directly into third-party and supply chain considerations.

Finally, there is **risk mitigation**, which is the one you touch most often in everyday work. Mitigation means reducing the likelihood that an incident will happen, reducing the impact if it does, or both. Regular patching reduces vulnerabilities and lowers the chance of successful exploits. Strong passwords and multi-factor authentication reduce the probability that an attacker can compromise an account. Backups reduce the impact of data loss because you can restore. Network segmentation can limit how far malware can spread. When you apply updates, configure access permissions carefully, test backups, or remind a user not to share their password, you are actively implementing risk mitigation.

In practice, these approaches are often combined. For a given threat, an organization might mitigate some risk with technical controls, transfer some through insurance or contracts, avoid certain particularly risky behaviors entirely, and accept whatever remains as the cost of doing business. When you understand these categories, it becomes easier to read between the lines of policies and decisions you see: "We will no longer permit X" is avoidance; "We will buy a new control to reduce Y" is mitigation; "We have purchased coverage in case Z happens" is transfer; and "We acknowledge this risk but will continue as is" is acceptance.

Business Impact and BIA in Everyday Terms

Risk management is not an abstract exercise; it is tightly connected to how much damage outages and incidents cause to the business. This is where **business impact analysis**, or BIA, comes in. A BIA is a structured way for an organization to figure out which business functions are most critical, which IT systems support them, what happens if those systems go down, and how quickly they must be restored. It is the bridge between "this server is offline" and "payroll cannot be processed, which will violate labor laws and upset employees."

At a practical level, BIA results show up in decisions you see all the time. Systems are labeled as "critical," "important," or "non-critical." Some services get more frequent backups than others. Certain changes are only allowed during scheduled maintenance windows, while others can be done during the workday. Disaster recovery and incident response plans often explicitly say which systems to bring back online first after a major outage. All of that flows from the impact information gathered in a BIA.

A **critical system** is any system whose failure significantly affects the organization's ability to operate, stay compliant, or keep people safe. For a hospital, electronic medical records and medication dispensing systems are critical; downtime directly affects patient care and safety. For an online retailer, the e-commerce site and payment processing systems are critical, because every minute they are down means lost sales. In a ten-person consulting firm, the shared file server that holds client contracts and work products, and the internet connection used to access cloud tools, may be the critical pieces. Understanding which systems fall into this category helps you prioritize. You do not treat a minor update to a test lab system the same way you treat a firmware upgrade on the core router that all offices use for connectivity.

To make these priorities concrete, organizations often define two key metrics. A **Recovery Time Objective (RTO)** is the target maximum amount of time a system or service can be down before the impact becomes unacceptable. If the BIA determines that the email system can be offline for up to four hours without serious harm, its RTO might be four hours. A **Recovery Point Objective (RPO)** focuses instead on data loss, specifying the maximum acceptable amount of data that can be lost, measured in time. If the business decides it cannot afford to lose more than one hour of order data, its RPO for the order database is one hour, meaning backups or replication must capture data at least that frequently.

These numbers drive technical choices. If a system has a very short RTO, you may need redundant hardware, clustering, or high-availability configurations so failover is quick. If the RPO is five minutes, nightly backups to tape will not be enough; you need frequent snapshots or continuous replication. From your point of view on the help desk, you might not design these solutions, but you do need to respect them. If documentation says a particular database has an RPO of one hour and is backed up hourly, you cannot quietly change that schedule to "once a day to save space" without dramatically increasing the risk of unacceptable data loss.

BIA also guides decisions during incidents. Imagine a power problem causes two servers to fail: one hosts the accounting file shares used for payroll and invoicing, and the other hosts a training portal with HR onboarding videos. Both the sales manager and the HR manager call insisting that their system is "top priority." If you rely only on who is yelling the loudest, you will make inconsistent, and often wrong, choices. Instead, you consult your documentation and see that the accounting server is classified as a Tier 1 critical system with a one-hour RTO, while the training portal is Tier 3 with a 24-hour RTO. Even though the HR manager may be more vocal in the moment, the business impact analysis has already decided: getting accounting back online must come first to protect cash flow and legal obligations. Your job is to follow that prioritization and communicate it professionally.

Bringing Risk and Impact Thinking into Daily Support Work

Where this really matters for you is in the seemingly small decisions you make during a normal day. Consider the tempting "quick fix" of disabling antivirus or endpoint protection so you can install an application that is being blocked. If you turn it off temporarily in a controlled way, follow policy, complete the installation, and immediately re-enable and verify protection, you may still be within acceptable risk. But if you simply disable it "for a while" and forget to turn it back on, you have increased the vulnerability of that system dramatically. The convenience of a fast install has to be weighed against the increased likelihood and potential impact of malware infection. Thinking like a professional means pausing to consider those factors instead of blindly doing whatever seems fastest.

The same mindset applies to change management. Formal change control processes, which you learn about elsewhere in this book, exist because changes are one of the biggest sources of outages. When you fill out a change request, describe what you will do, note which systems are affected, and outline a rollback plan, you are helping others evaluate the risk of that change. Will it affect critical systems identified in the BIA? Could it increase vulnerabilities or disrupt service during business hours? That review is not just bureaucracy; it is a structured way to keep risk at an acceptable level.

Finally, understanding risk and business impact helps you know when to escalate. Requests to disable multi-factor authentication "just for today," to share admin passwords, or to create accounts that bypass normal onboarding should immediately raise red flags. Those are not routine IT favors; they are high-risk security decisions that belong in the hands of management and security staff. Likewise, when you see unusual behavior, such as many machines suddenly showing ransomware pop-ups, that is not a random collection of isolated tickets—it is likely a high-impact incident that requires immediate activation of the incident response plan. Recognizing when the likelihood and potential impact are high, based on what you have learned here, tells you when to stop treating an issue as a simple support call and start treating it as a risk event that must be handled through proper channels.

Knowledge Check

Question 1: A technician discovers a legacy file server directly exposed to the internet, running an unsupported OS with no recent patches. Which term best describes this weakness in the environment?

A. Asset
B. Threat
C. Impact
D. Vulnerability

Question 2: A security team classifies various incidents as "low," "medium," or "high" risk using color-coded charts, based mainly on expert judgment and discussion rather than exact dollar amounts. Which type of risk assessment are they performing?

A. Qualitative
B. Quantitative
C. Predictive
D. Statistical

Question 3: Management wants to calculate the expected annual financial loss from a specific type of ransomware incident, using historical frequency and estimated recovery cost. Which type of assessment are they using?

A. Qualitative, because it labels incidents with categories like "critical"
B. Quantitative, because it uses money and probabilities
C. Qualitative, because it relies on expert interviews
D. Quantitative, because it relies only on color-coded risk matrices

Question 4: A company decides that allowing users to store corporate data on personal smartphones is too risky and bans the practice entirely, requiring all work to be done on managed corporate devices. Which risk treatment option does this decision represent?

A. Risk acceptance
B. Risk avoidance
C. Risk mitigation
D. Risk transfer

Question 5: A small business knows that if its only office printer fails, it will need to rush out and buy a replacement, causing minor inconvenience and cost. Management decides not to purchase a backup printer because the risk and impact seem low. Which risk treatment option is the business using?

A. Risk acceptance
B. Risk mitigation
C. Risk avoidance
D. Risk transfer

Question 6: An organization purchases cyber insurance and signs a contract with a cloud backup provider that includes financial penalties if the provider fails to meet uptime guarantees. What is the primary risk treatment strategy involved in these actions?

A. Risk avoidance
B. Risk acceptance
C. Risk transfer
D. Risk mitigation

Question 7: A hospital identifies its electronic medical records (EMR) system as a critical service. The BIA states that EMR downtime beyond 30 minutes would create unacceptable patient safety and regulatory risks. Which metric is the "30 minutes" value describing?

A. Mean time to repair (MTTR)
B. Maximum tolerable outage (MTO)
C. Recovery Point Objective (RPO)
D. Recovery Time Objective (RTO)

Question 8: A company decides it cannot afford to lose more than 15 minutes of new order data if its order-processing database fails. Backups are configured to run every 15 minutes to meet this requirement. Which metric is the "15 minutes" value describing?

A. Recovery Point Objective (RPO)
B. Recovery Time Objective (RTO)
C. Mean time between failures (MTBF)
D. Maximum tolerable downtime (MTD)

ANSWERS

1: Correct Answer: D
Rationale: A vulnerability is a weakness that a threat can exploit; an old, unpatched, internet-facing server is a clear vulnerability.

2: Correct Answer: A
Rationale: Qualitative risk assessment uses descriptive scales (low/medium/high) and expert judgment instead of precise numeric values.

3: Correct Answer: B
Rationale: Quantitative risk assessment expresses risk with numeric values such as dollar loss and event frequency to estimate expected loss.

4: Correct Answer: B
Rationale: Risk avoidance removes the risky activity altogether, such as prohibiting corporate data on personal smartphones.

5: Correct Answer: A
Rationale: Risk acceptance is choosing to tolerate a risk when its likelihood or impact is low or mitigation is not cost-effective.

6: Correct Answer: C
Rationale: Risk transfer shifts some financial impact to a third party through mechanisms like insurance and contractual penalties.

7: Correct Answer: D
Rationale: Recovery Time Objective (RTO) is the maximum acceptable downtime for a system before the consequences become unacceptable.

8: Correct Answer: A
Rationale: Recovery Point Objective (RPO) is the maximum acceptable amount of data loss measured in time, such as 15 minutes of new orders.

6.3 Third-Party & Supply Chain Risk

When you think about risk in IT, it is tempting to picture only the things you can directly touch: the endpoints you support, the switches you reboot, the operating systems you patch. In reality, a huge portion of your organization's technology stack is built on systems and services you do not own and cannot fully control. Cloud email, customer management systems, payroll platforms, remote monitoring tools, even the firmware running on the switches in the closet—all of these involve other companies somewhere along the line. The risk that comes from depending on those outsiders is what we mean by **third-party** and **supply chain** risk, and it shows up constantly in the day-to-day life of an IT support technician.

It helps to separate the two terms, even though they overlap. **Third-party risk** is about the ongoing relationships your organization has with outside providers: your ISP, your cloud email host, your SaaS CRM, your managed service provider, and contractors who need access to your systems. **Supply chain risk** focuses more on where your hardware and software come from and what has happened to them before they reach you: how they were manufactured, shipped, distributed, and updated. From an executive or legal perspective, these are big, strategic concerns. From your perspective on the help desk, they are hands-on issues that affect how you troubleshoot, which websites you trust for drivers, what you say "yes" or "no" to when a vendor asks for access, and when you realize, "this is not a local PC issue anymore; the problem is out there."

In a typical small or medium business, you see the same pattern repeat over and over: a small set of in-house systems supported by a surprisingly large web of external services. Email might run in Microsoft 365 or Google Workspace. File sharing might use a cloud-based storage provider. The sales team lives in a SaaS CRM. The backups might go off-site to a cloud backup service. Your internet connectivity is handled by an ISP. You might have an MSP that handles things like patching and monitoring, and you may also see temporary workers or contractors who need accounts for a few weeks or months. None of these things is unusual; in fact, this is the normal way businesses operate now. But every one of those connections is another place where confidentiality, integrity, or availability can be affected by something you cannot directly fix.

Consider how this changes troubleshooting. If one user cannot open Outlook, you might look at that user's profile, network connectivity, or local machine. If half the office suddenly cannot send or receive email, and you confirm their internet connections are fine, your thinking should shift to "Is there a problem with our cloud email provider?" In that moment you are not just fixing a PC; you are managing third-party risk operationally by checking the provider's status page, opening a ticket with the vendor, and communicating their service-level expectations to your users. Recognizing that you are dealing with a third-party dependency is often the difference between wasting an hour on fruitless local fixes and taking the correct next step within a minute.

Different types of third parties bring different kinds of risk into the environment, and recognizing those patterns will help you make better decisions. Cloud and SaaS providers are the most obvious. When your CRM or ticketing system is hosted in the cloud, your users' productivity depends on that external platform being online and secured. Outages at the provider mean downtime for your users even if your own infrastructure is perfectly healthy. Misconfigurations in sharing permissions can accidentally expose files to the wrong people, and changes in how the cloud service authenticates might suddenly affect your users' ability to log in. From the technician's point of view, these show up as login failures across many users, unexpected "service unavailable" messages, or support tickets complaining that "my shared document is visible to people it shouldn't be." Those symptoms look like typical IT problems, but the root cause may be a third-party change or outage rather than anything you can fix locally.

Managed service providers and outsourced IT present another scenario. An **MSP** may use remote management tools that have deep access to your network: agents on workstations, remote access to servers, and administrative control over configurations. That access is necessary for them to deliver their service, but it is also powerful. If the MSP's tools are misconfigured, or if their own accounts are compromised, an attacker could use those high-privilege channels against you. As a frontline tech, you may be asked to install agents, create accounts, or enable remote access for the MSP. Your task is to follow documented procedures carefully, avoid improvising "shortcut" accounts like a generic "vendor_admin," and make sure that access is granted in controlled, auditable ways, not by sharing your own administrator credentials.

Hardware vendors and distributors bring risk in a more physical form. When you unpack a brand-new laptop or router, you usually trust that it is what it says on the box. But the global nature of manufacturing and distribution means there is a real possibility of **counterfeit** or tampered equipment, especially if it comes from gray market channels or suspiciously cheap online sellers. Counterfeit power supplies might be unsafe; network equipment with altered firmware could include hidden backdoors. For you, this translates into habits: verify that purchases go through approved channels, confirm model and serial numbers match what was ordered, and be especially cautious when someone suggests "we can save money by buying these from an auction site." When a device behaves in unexpectedly strange ways right out of the box, you do not just treat it as a defective unit—you consider the possibility that there is a supply chain issue and escalate appropriately.

On the software side, third-party developers and vendors supply line-of-business applications, browser plugins, mobile apps, and utilities. Here, supply chain risk shows up as untrusted installers, bundled adware, or malicious "driver update" tools masquerading as helpful software. An entry-level tech may be the one who chooses where to download a driver or which "PDF converter" to install for a user. In those decisions, the safest practice is to stay with official vendor sites, trusted app stores, or internally approved repositories, and to avoid random download sites that aggregate "free drivers" and "updates." The source of the software is part of its supply chain; downloading from a shady site is equivalent to buying hardware from an unknown street vendor.

A category that often gets overlooked is external people: contractors, temp staff, and short-term consultants who need access to systems. These individuals are third parties in a very direct sense. From a risk perspective, the main issues involve **onboarding** and **offboarding**, and how well you enforce least privilege. A contractor who only needs access to one project share should not receive broad access across the entire file server. A temp who leaves after two weeks should not still have an active account three months later. Shared generic accounts like "TempUser" multiply the problem because you cannot trace actions back to a specific person. As a technician, you are usually the one who actually creates and disables these accounts, so your adherence to policy is what makes the difference between good control and lingering risk.

Underneath all of these examples are a few core principles that guide how you, at the operational level, manage vendor risk. The first is **least privilege**. Just because a vendor asks for a high-privilege account does not mean they should get it. When a payroll software vendor says, "Please create a domain administrator account so we can troubleshoot," alarm bells should go off in your head. Domain admin is an extremely powerful role that typically far exceeds what is needed to troubleshoot one application. A safer pattern would be to provide a time-limited account scoped only to the application server they need, or to arrange a supervised remote session where you retain control of the environment. If you are not authorized to make that kind of exception—and in most organizations, you are not—you document the request and escalate it to your supervisor or security team rather than trying to solve it alone.

Another principle is using approved channels and documented procedures whenever you deal with external providers. If the ISP needs to run tests, you work with them through your organization's defined support channel and within your normal remote access process. You do not, for instance, give an ISP technician VPN access into your internal network so they can "take a quick look," unless that is explicitly authorized and controlled. If a vendor claims to be calling you, you verify their identity by calling back through a known-good number from the official website or from your internal documentation, not from contact information in a random email. Verification is a simple but powerful defense against social engineering that exploits vendor relationships.

Data handling is another area where third-party risk plays out in ordinary tasks. **Data minimization** is the idea that you only share the smallest amount of information necessary for a given purpose. When a vendor requests logs, configuration files, or sample data to reproduce a bug, your job is to check whether those artifacts contain sensitive information and follow policy on how, or whether, they can be shared. A request for an entire customer database "so we can test in our environment" should stop you in your tracks. Even if the vendor is legitimate, you generally are not authorized to export sensitive data at that scale. This is a classic case where you document what was requested and escalate to someone who can make a policy decision.

Contracts and **Service Level Agreements (SLAs)** form the formal backbone of these relationships, even though you will rarely see the full legal documents. You do not need to negotiate terms, but you should know that the SLA usually defines uptime guarantees, response time targets, support channels, and sometimes data protection obligations. When a cloud provider's SLA promises that critical incidents receive a response within one hour, that timing informs how you manage user expectations during an outage. If a payroll system is down right before payday, and you see in the SLA that the vendor targets a four-hour resolution window for such incidents, you can convey that context to management and track progress appropriately. The same SLA might specify that tickets must be opened through a secure web portal, not by emailing random employees, which tells you the right way to seek help.

Supply chain thinking extends into how you handle updates and patches. When users see a pop-up offering a "new driver update" or a download for a video codec, it is tempting to click through and "just get it working." But those pop-ups are a favorite delivery mechanism for malware. A more trustworthy pattern is to rely on the device's built-in update mechanisms, the official vendor portal, or an authorized update repository. From your perspective, this is part of controlling the digital supply chain: you are choosing to pull software only from sources that your organization has reason to trust. If a vendor issues a security advisory and an urgent patch, it is the same supply chain in action—you receive the notification, validate it, and then help implement the update through controlled channels rather than ad hoc downloads.

In day-to-day operations, "monitoring" third parties does not mean you are personally auditing their data centers. It mostly means staying alert to patterns that suggest a vendor or supply chain issue instead of a purely local failure. If users across multiple departments all report that the same cloud CRM is throwing the same error, and those users are on different networks or sites, that convergence is a strong clue that the issue lies with the service, not with individual machines. Your correct response is not to reinstall the CRM plugin ten times; it is to check the vendor's status page, open a support ticket following the SLA, record the incident number, and update your internal tickets with whatever ETA the vendor provides.

Security advisories and product warnings are another signal. Vendors sometimes email customer admins about breaches, vulnerabilities, or upcoming changes. While management or security staff may formally evaluate these, you might be the one who actually implements the technical response: updating an agent, changing a configuration, or temporarily disabling a vulnerable feature. Knowing that "this is a vendor-originated risk" helps you avoid improvising technical fixes that conflict with the vendor's remediation guidance or your internal policies.

A crucial skill here is recognizing red flags in vendor interactions and knowing when to stop and escalate. Requests for excessive data, such as asking for full, unmasked payment information or entire databases, are an obvious example. Requests for permanent high-privilege credentials, especially sent through insecure channels like personal email, are another. If you discover that someone purchased a batch of critical equipment from an unknown online seller and you see unusual behavior on those devices—unexpected management interfaces, unknown software pre-installed—you treat that as a potential supply chain concern rather than quietly ignoring it. Even vendor patches can be part of the picture: if a new firmware or software update immediately causes widespread instability, you document the timing, correlate it with vendor release notes, and escalate rather than randomly rolling devices back without coordination.

Everything you have seen in this chapter comes together in how you reason through scenarios. When you see a problem, you ask not only "What is broken?" but also "Who else is involved in this service, and how might they be affecting it?" You distinguish between a single-user configuration issue and a multi-user outage that points toward a cloud provider. You apply least privilege when creating accounts or granting access to external technicians. You treat official vendor sites and channels as your default for software, drivers, and updates, and you are suspicious of anything that deviates from that pattern. And whenever a third party asks for access or data that feels outside the norm, you pause, document exactly what they requested, and bring it to someone with the authority to decide what happens next.

Knowledge Check

Question 1: A help desk technician notices that users in multiple departments, across different sites, all report that the cloud-based CRM is returning the same error, while local network connectivity checks out fine. What is the MOST appropriate next step from a third-party risk perspective?

A. Check the CRM provider's status page and open a support ticket with the vendor according to the SLA
B. Reinstall the CRM client or browser plugin on several affected users' machines
C. Escalate to facilities to check the building power and HVAC systems
D. Instruct users to reboot and wait 24 hours before further troubleshooting

Question 2: A payroll software vendor asks you to create a domain administrator account for them so they can "troubleshoot performance issues." Which principle should guide your response?

A. Ensuring the vendor has continuous, unrestricted access for faster support
B. Enforcing least privilege and escalating the request to appropriate management or security
C. Providing your own administrator credentials instead so the vendor doesn't need a new account
D. Creating a shared "vendor_admin" account and emailing the password to the vendor contact

Question 3: A contractor will be working for three weeks and needs access only to a single project share. Which account management approach BEST minimizes third-party risk?

A. Giving the contractor access to the entire file server to avoid permission issues
B. Creating an individual, time-limited account with access only to the required project share
C. Providing the credentials to a generic "TempUser" account that already has broad access
D. Allowing the contractor to use a full-time employee's account during the engagement

Question 4: You receive an email that appears to be from your cloud backup provider asking you to "urgently confirm your admin password" via a link to avoid account suspension. What is the MOST appropriate action?

A. Click the link and change the password immediately to avoid downtime
B. Forward the email to all IT staff so they can update their passwords too
C. Verify via known-good contact before taking any action
D. Reply to the email with the requested password details over an encrypted channel

Question 5: A user asks you to install a "free driver update utility" they found on a random website so their webcam will work. From a supply chain risk perspective, what is the BEST response?

A. Install the tool but create a system restore point first in case it causes problems
B. Allow the user to install the tool under their own account so it has fewer privileges
C. Approve the tool temporarily and monitor it with endpoint antivirus
D. Decline and obtain the correct driver only from the hardware vendor's official site or internal repository

Question 6: A recently purchased batch of network switches from an unfamiliar online auction site is behaving strangely right out of the box. What should you do FIRST from a supply chain risk standpoint?

A. Treat the devices as a potential counterfeit/tampering issue and escalate through proper channels
B. Assume they are just defective units and attempt to repair them locally
C. Place them into production but monitor closely for a few weeks
D. Immediately discard the devices without documenting the incident

Question 7: A vendor requests log files to diagnose an application issue. The logs appear to contain customer names and partial payment information. What is the MOST appropriate action?

A. Refuse to share any logs under any circumstances
B. Send the full logs immediately because the vendor is trusted and under contract
C. Minimize data, redact per policy, and escalate if needed before sending anything
D. Upload the logs to a public file-sharing site and send the vendor the link for convenience

Question 8: While troubleshooting, an ISP technician you are on the phone with asks for VPN credentials to "log in and quickly check your internal network devices." How should you respond?

A. Provide a shared administrative VPN account but change the password afterward
B. Create a permanent low-privilege VPN account and email the credentials
C. Allow them to remote-control your workstation using consumer remote-access software
D. Decline, explain that such access is not permitted outside approved processes, and follow your organization's documented support and remote-access procedures

ANSWERS

1: Correct Answer: A
Rationale: A centralized error across sites with local connectivity intact indicates a provider-side issue. Checking the vendor's status page and opening a ticket per the SLA is the proper third-party escalation. The other options delay or misdirect troubleshooting.

2: Correct Answer: B
Rationale: Security+ emphasizes least privilege and proper approval for elevated access, especially for vendors. Granting domain admin or sharing credentials violates policy and increases risk; the request should be constrained and escalated.

3: Correct Answer: B
Rationale: An individual, time-bound, least-privilege account limits access to only what is needed and supports auditing. Broad access, shared accounts, or using an employee's account create excessive and non-attributable risk.

4: Correct Answer: C
Rationale: This is likely a phishing attempt abusing a third-party relationship. You should independently verify via known-good contact methods before acting. Clicking links or sending passwords, even encrypted, violates basic security practices.

5: Correct Answer: D
Rationale: Unverified "free utilities" from random sites are classic supply chain malware vectors. Drivers and updates should come only from trusted vendor sources or approved repositories, not from unknown third parties.

6: Correct Answer: A
Rationale: Strange behavior from hardware bought via an untrusted channel is a supply chain red flag for counterfeit or tampered devices. Treat it as a potential security incident and escalate; using, repairing, or discarding without review is inappropriate.

7: Correct Answer: C
Rationale: Logs with customer and payment data must be handled under data minimization and privacy policies: review, redact, limit, and escalate as needed before sharing. Sending full logs, refusing all sharing, or using public sites is improper.

8: Correct Answer: D
Rationale: Third parties must not receive direct VPN or internal access outside formal, approved processes. Declining and following documented remote-access and support procedures aligns with least privilege and vendor risk management.

6.4 Compliance & Regulatory Requirements

By this point in the book you have seen a lot of "how": how to secure accounts, how to protect devices, how to respond to incidents. Compliance is where the "why" becomes very real. Organizations do not secure systems just because security professionals like complicated passwords and locked server rooms. They do it because they are operating inside a web of laws, regulations, contracts, industry expectations, and internal rules. As an entry-level security or IT professional, you live inside that web every day, whether you think about it explicitly or not. This chapter is about making those invisible boundaries visible so you can recognize when they matter, both on the exam and in your job.

At the highest level, **compliance** simply means "playing by the rules you are obligated to follow." Some of those rules come from governments, some from industry groups or business partners, and some from your own organization's leadership. They all share a common purpose: protecting people and organizations from harm. In the security context, that usually means protecting data from unauthorized access or misuse, protecting systems from being abused, and protecting the organization from legal and financial consequences when something goes wrong. When you see security controls that feel inconvenient—multi-factor authentication, strict password reset procedures, logging requirements—it is almost always because someone, somewhere, is trying to make sure the organization stays compliant with these external and internal obligations.

From an organizational perspective, non-compliance is a risk just as real as a hardware failure or a malware infection. If a company mishandles personal data, ignores sector-specific privacy rules, or lets employees bypass policies, the consequences can include government fines, lawsuits, loss of business licenses, cancelled contracts, and severe reputational damage. At the individual level, ignoring compliance can cost people their jobs or even expose them to personal liability if they knowingly violate laws or policies. That is why, for a technician, compliance is not an abstract legal issue to leave to the lawyers. It shapes how you open tickets, what you put in emails, how you run remote support sessions, and when you say "no" to a user request—even if that request would technically solve their problem faster.

A helpful way to think about this space is to imagine three layers of requirements stacked on top of each other. At the top are **laws and regulations**. These are government-mandated rules that organizations must follow if they fall within a particular scope. The scope might be based on geography, on the type of data they handle, or on the sector they work in. For example, many countries have privacy laws that govern how personal data can be collected, used, and shared. Other rules focus on financial reporting, healthcare information, or the protection of children's data. You are not expected at Security+ level to memorize legal codes, but you should recognize that when a law applies, it is not optional. The organization cannot simply decide it prefers a different approach; instead, it has to interpret those legal requirements and build them into its security program.

Sitting between that legal layer and your day-to-day work are **industry standards and frameworks**. These could be standards from payment card brands, security frameworks published by recognized bodies, or specific control requirements written into contracts by large customers or cloud providers. Unlike laws, they are not created by governments, but they can be just as binding in practice because they are tied to business relationships. A company that processes payment cards, for example, will be required by its payment processors to implement specific protections around cardholder data. Failing to meet those standards might not put someone in jail, but it can result in the organization losing the ability to accept payments or failing audits that key customers demand.

The bottom layer, and the one you interact with constantly, is **internal policy and procedure**. This is where those high-level requirements get translated into concrete rules and step-by-step instructions. If a privacy regulation says personal data must only be accessed on a need-to-know basis, your organization might implement that through an access control policy, role-based permissions, and a help desk procedure that requires identity verification before any account changes. If an industry standard requires detailed logging, your logging policy might specify what systems must log, how long logs are retained, and who is allowed to view them. From an exam and job perspective, this is crucial: the question you should always be asking yourself is, "What does policy require me to do here?" Even if you know a faster or more convenient technical workaround, in a compliant organization your responsibility is to follow the documented procedure unless you are explicitly authorized to deviate.

Across different laws, standards, and policies, certain themes show up again and again. One of the most important is **privacy and personal data protection**. Personal data includes obvious items like names, addresses, phone numbers, and national ID numbers, but it can also cover account details, IP addresses, device identifiers, and combinations of fields that together can identify a person. In some environments, even seemingly mundane information, like classroom rosters or HR attendance records, can be considered sensitive. The recurring idea is that personal data should only be collected for legitimate purposes, only accessed by those who genuinely need it for their role, and only kept as long as necessary. As a technician, that means you should never browse through user files or databases out of curiosity, and you should not leave personal data scattered across unprotected notes, screenshots, or local folders.

A related theme is **financial and payment data**. Anything tied to bank accounts, credit or debit cards, payroll records, or detailed billing information is subject to heightened protection. In practice, that might mean the data is encrypted at rest and in transit, access is tightly controlled and logged, and there are very specific rules for how it can appear in reports or logs. For you, it means you do not casually write down card numbers on sticky notes, you do not paste full account details into trouble tickets, and you follow any masking rules your organization has put in place. If the ticketing system or chat tool you use is not approved for sensitive data, you find another way, or you escalate the issue instead of inventing your own workaround.

In healthcare or benefits environments, **health-related data** is treated as especially sensitive. Regulations in many jurisdictions strictly limit who can see patient information, why they can access it, and how it must be protected. The fact that you are able to open a patient record does not mean you are allowed to. If your job is to fix login errors in a hospital's electronic health record system, your need-to-know may extend to confirming that a user can open a test patient record, but not to browsing actual patient histories. The safest mindset is to assume that health data is off limits unless you have a clear work task and procedure telling you otherwise.

Educational environments introduce another specialized category: **children's or student data**. Schools, universities, and training organizations often hold detailed records on minors or young adults, and there are frequently extra legal protections around how that information is used and shared. Even something as simple as printing a list of student names with grades for a class can have restrictions; leaving that list on a shared printer would be a serious violation in many institutions. When you support systems in these environments, treat any identifiable student data as if it were highly confidential: only access it under clear instructions, do not copy it into tickets unless the policy explicitly allows for a secure field, and never use it in training materials without proper anonymization and approval.

Another recurring element of compliance is **monitoring and logging**. Many laws and standards require organizations to track who accesses which systems and data, and when. That is part of how they prove, during an audit or investigation, that they controlled access and can reconstruct events surrounding an incident. From your perspective, this has two important implications. First, you may be responsible for keeping logging enabled, ensuring log storage is healthy, and not disabling or modifying logs simply because they are filling a disk. Second, you should assume that your own actions on sensitive systems are being logged. That is not meant to intimidate you; it is there to protect everyone. When you follow procedure, the logs show you did the right thing. When someone misuses access, the logs can reveal that quickly.

All of these themes get much easier to handle in practice when an organization has a clear **data classification** scheme. Classification is simply a way of labeling information according to how sensitive it is and what protections it requires. Labels differ between organizations, but you will commonly see tiers like public, internal, confidential, and highly confidential. A public marketing brochure can be shared freely; an internal procedure manual should stay within the company; a list of customer Social Security numbers would be confidential or highly confidential and subject to strict controls. For a support professional, classification should influence how you behave whenever you handle data. If the screen you are troubleshooting contains information marked "confidential," you think twice before capturing a screenshot. If a log file you are about to email contains usernames and internal IP addresses, you verify that email is an approved, secure channel and that the recipient is authorized to see that information.

Ticketing systems are a common place where classification and compliance collide with everyday habits. When you are describing a problem, it is tempting to paste full error logs or include the exact text of a user's complaint, including whatever they wrote. A compliant approach is more selective. You include just enough technical detail to troubleshoot and to document what happened, but you avoid pasting in full account numbers, full credit card details, medical diagnoses, or anything else your policy treats as sensitive. If your organization has special secure fields for certain identifiers, you use those instead of free-text comments. The same logic applies to screenshots: either avoid capturing sensitive portions of the screen, or, if policy and tools allow, redact or blur them before they are stored or shared.

Underneath many of these practices are two core access principles that you have seen before in a security context, but which are equally important for compliance: **least privilege** and **need-to-know**. Least privilege says that each user account, including your own, should only have the minimum access needed to do its job. In a support environment, that often translates into using a normal user account for routine work and only elevating to an administrative account when a documented task requires it. You do not leave yourself permanently logged in as a domain admin because "it saves time," and you do not grant permanent local admin rights to users who only need them once. Need-to-know is more about behavior than permissions. It reminds you that just because you technically can see something does not mean you should. If you are troubleshooting a billing system, you may need to confirm that a user can open a customer record, but there is no need to scroll through dozens of accounts reading details unrelated to the ticket.

These principles intersect directly with **policies, consent, and user expectations**. Most organizations present users with an **Acceptable Use Policy** when they receive their accounts, often requiring them to acknowledge it. That policy defines what they can and cannot do with company systems: rules about personal use, installing software, accessing certain categories of websites, and handling company data. As a technician, you are expected to follow that same policy and to help enforce it. If a user calls and asks you to install an unapproved peer-to-peer application that obviously violates the AUP, your correct, compliant response is to decline and cite the policy, even if the user insists their manager "said it was fine." Managers do not have the authority to override compliance rules that protect the organization as a whole.

Similarly, organizations publish **privacy notices** to tell customers and employees what information is collected about them and how it will be used. Those statements often promise that data will not be used beyond specific purposes, or that it will not be shared outside certain boundaries. As someone who can see or touch that data, you are part of the organization's promise. For example, if a customer database is used to provide support, that does not mean you can export customer emails and use them to build your own mailing list, or pull real customer records into a slide deck for an internal lunch-and-learn. User consent also has limits: even if a user tells you, "You have my permission to email this company spreadsheet to my personal Gmail so I can finish it at home," your obligation is to follow company policy, which may prohibit sending sensitive files to personal email addresses entirely. On the exam, these scenarios often appear as subtle traps. The user's request sounds reasonable, but the compliant answer recognizes that user consent does not cancel organizational or regulatory obligations.

Remote support is one of the best places to see all of this come together in a realistic scenario. Imagine you are assisting someone in the finance department who cannot generate a report in the accounting system. You initiate a remote desktop session, and when their screen appears, you see a large spreadsheet listing hundreds of customers with names, account numbers, and partial card details. From a purely technical standpoint, the quickest way to get help from a more experienced colleague might be to take a full-screen screenshot and email it over with a note asking, "Have you seen this error before?" From a compliance and regulatory standpoint, that would be a serious problem. You would be capturing and spreading sensitive financial and personal data far beyond the original context, probably in violation of both internal policy and external standards.

A more compliant approach starts with recognizing what you are looking at: finance data, identifiable customer records, and partial payment card information. You know from your training that this kind of data is tightly regulated and should be accessed only on a need-to-know basis. In this case, the need is to fix a reporting issue, not to review customer details. So instead of taking that screenshot, you ask the user to minimize or close the spreadsheet and try to reproduce the issue using a test account or sanitized sample data. If your organization has an approved method for sharing screenshots that automatically redacts certain fields, you might use that, but you still aim to capture only the error message or user interface elements you truly need. On a Security+ exam question, several options might technically fix the problem, but the correct one will be the option that avoids exposing real customer data and explicitly mentions following policy or using test data.

Password resets create similar dilemmas. Suppose someone calls from an unknown mobile number, insists they are a manager, and demands an urgent password reset because they are about to join a critical meeting. They are impatient and push you to skip the normal identity verification questions, promising they will "change the password later." Technically, you could reset the password in a few seconds and be the hero in their story. But your documented procedure requires verifying identity using two factors, such as an employee ID and a code sent to a registered device. Those steps exist because unauthorized password resets are a common way attackers gain access to systems. From a compliance perspective, skipping verification is never acceptable, no matter how stressed the caller sounds or how important the meeting is.

In that situation, the compliant action is to stay calm and professional, but firm. You explain that for their security and the organization's protection, you must complete the verification steps and that you will move through them as quickly as possible. If the caller becomes hostile or refuses to cooperate, you do not improvise a shortcut; instead, you escalate the call according to your escalation procedure, perhaps involving a supervisor or security team. On exam questions, this balance between customer service and policy adherence is a common theme. The attractive but wrong answer is the one that "helps" the user by ignoring rules. The correct answer is the one that maintains courtesy while refusing to violate procedure.

All of these activities—remote sessions, password resets, log reviews, mailbox access—share one more compliance thread: **documentation and accountability**. Regulations and standards often require organizations to be able to show, after the fact, what actions were taken, by whom, and why. That is one reason why you are asked to document your troubleshooting steps in tickets and to record changes in change management systems. When done correctly, that documentation protects you as much as the organization. If a question arises about why a certain account was unlocked, your notes should show that you followed the password reset procedure, verified identity, and recorded the time and reason for the change. If you notice behavior that seems non-compliant—such as coworkers sharing passwords, or printed reports with sensitive data left in public areas—your responsibility is not to look the other way. It is to report the issue through the established process so that it can be addressed before it turns into a larger problem.

In practice, entry-level technicians are often the first people to see how policies and regulations play out in real workflows. You are the one who notices when users are constantly asking for the same unauthorized shortcut, or when a particular process makes it too easy to mishandle data. While you should not rewrite policy on your own, you can and should raise these observations to supervisors or security teams. That feedback loop is how organizations refine their policies so that they remain both compliant and workable, and it is how you start to grow from simply following rules to understanding and influencing the broader security program you are part of.

Knowledge Check

Question 1: A help desk technician is asked by a user to "just bypass the normal identity verification" because they are late for an important meeting and urgently need a password reset. Which factor should most strongly guide the technician's response in this situation?

A. The urgency of the user's business need
B. The organization's documented policies and procedures
C. The technician's personal judgment of the caller's trustworthiness
D. The user's job title and seniority

Question 2: A retailer processes credit card payments and is required by its payment processor to follow specific technical and procedural controls to protect cardholder data. These requirements are best described as:

A. Internal policies
B. Industry standards and frameworks
C. Optional best practices
D. Government laws and regulations

Question 3: While providing remote support to a finance user, a technician sees a spreadsheet with hundreds of customer names, account numbers, and partial card details. The user asks the technician to screenshot the full screen and email it to a colleague for help. Which action is the most compliant response?

A. Take the screenshot, then delete the email after the issue is resolved
B. Take the screenshot but store it only on an encrypted network drive
C. Crop the screenshot so only the error message and application window border are included
D. Ask the user to close or minimize the sensitive data and attempt to reproduce the issue with test or sanitized data instead

Question 4: A technician is unsure whether it is acceptable to copy a customer's full bank account number into a ticket comment field when documenting an issue. What is the FIRST step they should take to determine the correct action?

A. Review the organization's data handling and ticketing policies
B. Ask the customer for written consent to include the account number
C. Check with the customer's manager for informal approval
D. Proceed, as the information is needed to troubleshoot the issue

Question 5: A school IT support specialist prints a report showing student names and grades to diagnose a printing issue and then accidentally leaves it on a shared printer in a hallway. Which compliance principle has been most clearly violated?

A. Acceptable Use Policy (AUP)
B. Change management
C. Protection of children's or student data
D. Software licensing requirements

Question 6: A company classifies information as Public, Internal, Confidential, and Highly Confidential. A support technician is about to email a log file marked "Confidential" that contains usernames and internal IP addresses. What should most influence whether this email is appropriate?

A. The size of the log file and email attachment limits
B. Whether the recipient requested the file in writing
C. Whether the technician will delete the sent message after the issue is resolved
D. Confirm email is approved and recipient is authorized to access it

Question 7: A user asks a technician to install an unapproved peer-to-peer file sharing application, saying their manager has already "okayed it." The technician knows the Acceptable Use Policy explicitly forbids such software. What should the technician do?

A. Decline to install the software and cite the Acceptable Use Policy
B. Install the software because the user's manager approved it
C. Install the software but document the exception in the ticket
D. Temporarily install the software, then uninstall it after use

Question 8: A customer tells a technician, "You have my permission to email this sensitive company spreadsheet to my personal Gmail so I can work on it at home." Company policy prohibits sending sensitive files to personal email accounts. How should the technician respond?

A. Send the file because explicit user consent overrides internal policy
B. Password-protect the file and send it to the personal email account
C. Refuse to send the file to personal email and explain that company policy and regulatory obligations must be followed
D. Split the spreadsheet into multiple smaller files before sending to reduce sensitivity

ANSWERS

1: Correct Answer: B
Rationale: The technician must follow documented identity verification procedures. Policies and procedures govern authentication and cannot be bypassed due to user urgency, role, or perceived trustworthiness.

2: Correct Answer: B
Rationale: Controls required by a payment processor to protect cardholder data (such as PCI DSS) are industry standards/frameworks tied to contractual obligations, not internal-only policies or government statutes.

3: Correct Answer: D
Rationale: Compliance and data protection require minimizing exposure of real customer financial data. The technician should avoid capturing or transmitting sensitive data and instead work with closed/minimized data and test or sanitized information.

4: Correct Answer: A
Rationale: The first step is to consult the organization's data handling and ticketing policies, which implement legal and regulatory requirements. Customer consent or informal approval does not override these rules.

5: Correct Answer: C
Rationale: Student names and grades are protected student/children's data. Leaving such a report on a shared printer exposes this information and violates confidentiality requirements for student records.

6: Correct Answer: D
Rationale: Data classification dictates how information may be transmitted and who may receive it. The key concern is whether email is an approved secure channel for Confidential data and whether the recipient is authorized.

7: Correct Answer: A
Rationale: The technician must enforce the Acceptable Use Policy, which explicitly forbids the software. A manager's informal approval or temporary use does not override organizational policy or security requirements.

8: Correct Answer: C
Rationale: User permission does not supersede company policy or regulatory obligations. The technician must refuse to send sensitive data to personal email and adhere to established data handling rules.

6.5 Audits, Assessments & Testing

When you first learn how to secure systems, most of the focus is on "doing the right things": enabling encryption, applying patches, setting permissions, configuring firewalls. After a while, though, every organization runs into the same problem: how do we know people are actually doing those things, and that they are still in place months later? Systems drift, shortcuts get taken, and new vulnerabilities appear every week. That is where audits, assessments, and testing fit into the bigger security program. They are the mechanisms organizations use to check themselves and to prove to others—regulators, customers, and business partners—that controls are not just written down in policies, but working in reality.

As an IT support technician, you are often on the receiving end of these activities. You may not be designing the entire security program or choosing the audit framework, but you will be the person who gets the email saying, "We need screenshots of the local firewall configuration for all laptops you manage" or, "Please do not reboot these servers during the vulnerability scan window." Understanding what kind of activity is happening—an audit, an assessment, or a test—helps you respond appropriately, avoid interfering with the process, and protect both yourself and your organization.

Audits: Proving You Do What You Say

The word **audit** can sound intimidating, but at its core it simply means a structured, documented check to see whether reality matches expectations. Those expectations come from somewhere: internal policies, standards your organization decided to adopt, or external regulations and contracts. In other words, an audit is asking, "Are we doing what we said we would do, and can we prove it?" If the policy says, "All company laptops must use full-disk encryption," an audit will not just take your word for it. It will look for evidence that encryption is actually enabled.

You will encounter two broad flavors of audits: **internal** and **external**. An internal audit is performed by people within your organization, such as an internal audit department or the security team. Their job is to check compliance and help management understand where there are gaps. An external audit is performed by a third party—perhaps a consulting firm, a regulator, or a certification body verifying something like PCI DSS or ISO 27001 compliance. External auditors usually must be independent; they should not be the same people who built or operate the systems they are evaluating. For you as a technician, the main difference is that interactions with external auditors are often more tightly controlled. You might be asked to route all communication through a designated point of contact and avoid giving off-the-cuff answers or access without approval.

Auditors work with **evidence**. Evidence can be screenshots of configurations, log extracts, system-generated reports, tickets in a change-management system, or even emails showing that a process was followed. Suppose the backup policy requires daily backups with weekly restore tests. The auditor may ask you to produce backup job logs for a certain date range and documentation of the last restore test. If the security standard says "local administrator accounts must have complex passwords," you might be asked to show the password policy configured in Group Policy or in your endpoint management tool. In all these cases, your role often involves generating or exporting that evidence and making sure it accurately reflects the current state.

Within audits, you can also distinguish **security audits** from **compliance audits**, though they overlap in practice. A security audit focuses on whether specific technical and procedural security controls are in place and operating correctly: are firewalls enabled, antivirus up to date, multi-factor authentication enforced, logging configured, and so on. A compliance audit, in contrast, focuses on whether you are meeting defined requirements from laws, regulations, or internal standards. For example, a compliance auditor reviewing a privacy regulation might ask how long you retain user activity logs and whether you anonymize certain data. In the exam, you might see a scenario where someone is reviewing password minimum length settings and log retention periods against a written policy. That is classic audit behavior: comparing actual configurations to written requirements.

Historically, audits were periodic; a big external audit might happen once a year. Increasingly, organizations blend that with **continuous auditing** or automated compliance checking. Tools might run daily or weekly to compare system settings against a secure baseline and generate reports highlighting drift. From your perspective, that might show up as regular emails listing machines that are "noncompliant" with a particular control or as scheduled jobs that you are asked not to interrupt. Even though these checks are automated, they are still audits in the sense that they are systematically comparing what exists to what should exist.

It is worth emphasizing that auditors are not out to "catch you" personally. They are there to give an accurate picture of the organization's state. Your professional responsibility is to be honest, avoid altering logs or configurations just to "look good," and escalate if you are ever asked to do something questionable. For example, manually flipping a setting right before an auditor looks at it, and then flipping it back later, may sound tempting to someone under pressure, but it undermines the whole process and can have serious consequences if discovered.

Security Assessments and Vulnerability Scans: Where Are We Weak?

While audits revolve around compliance with expectations, **security assessments** are broader evaluations of your overall security posture. They are less about "Did we follow this policy line by line?" and more about "Where are we exposed, regardless of what the policies say?" Within assessments, one of the most common activities you will encounter is a **vulnerability assessment**.

A vulnerability assessment uses tools called **vulnerability scanners** to probe systems and networks for known weaknesses. These tools typically maintain a database of vulnerabilities—mapped to identifiers such as CVEs (Common Vulnerabilities and Exposures)—and compare what they see on your systems to that database. The scanner might identify a web server that is running an outdated version with a known remote code execution flaw, a workstation with missing critical patches, a service listening on a port that should not be exposed, or a weak configuration such as SMBv1 being enabled.

The output from a vulnerability scan usually lists hosts, detected vulnerabilities, severity ratings such as low, medium, high, or critical, and sometimes recommendations or links to vendor advisories. As a technician, you are rarely expected to dissect every detail, but you should be comfortable reading such a report at a basic level. If you see that ten workstations you manage are flagged as missing a critical operating system update, the next steps are fairly clear: confirm those systems are in your scope, schedule the update through proper change-control, apply it, and, if required, provide updated evidence showing that they are now compliant.

Your role around vulnerability assessments also includes making sure scanning can actually happen. That may involve ensuring that endpoints are powered on and connected during the scan window, that host-based firewalls are not blocking the authorized scanner IPs, and that you do not inadvertently shut down or isolate the scanner because you mistake it for an attack. Authorized scans are usually communicated in advance by the security team, including what IPs or hostnames to expect. When in doubt, you verify rather than assume. If your monitoring tools show a spike of port scans from an address you do not recognize, and you are not aware of any scheduled assessment, you treat that as a potential security incident and escalate.

It is helpful to anchor the distinction between audits and vulnerability assessments in their core questions. An audit asks, "Are we following our stated rules?" A vulnerability assessment asks, "What vulnerabilities exist in our environment?" You can have a perfectly written password policy and still have a vulnerability assessment reveal that a critical service is running with default credentials. Conversely, an audit might fault you for not having a documented process, even if, in practice, you are applying patches diligently. Both perspectives matter, and both show up in real organizations.

Penetration Testing: Authorized Attacks with Clear Boundaries

If a vulnerability assessment tells you what openings exist, **penetration testing** goes a step further and asks, "What could an attacker actually do with those openings?" A penetration test, or **pen test**, is an authorized attempt to exploit vulnerabilities in order to demonstrate real-world risk. Organizations often hire specialized third parties for this work precisely because of the skills and independence required.

A hallmark of legitimate penetration testing is formal **scope** and **rules of engagement**. The scope spells out which systems, networks, and applications may be targeted, and often when. For example, the scope might allow testing of a non-production web application but prohibit any disruptive attacks against the production environment. The rules of engagement further define boundaries: perhaps no denial-of-service attacks, no social engineering against certain departments, or testing only during specified windows to avoid impacting critical operations. These documents are not just legal protections; they are operational guidelines you must respect.

From your vantage point, penetration testing can look very similar to an attack. You may see aggressive port scanning, repeated failed logins, attempts to upload or execute strange files, or alerts from intrusion detection and antivirus systems. The difference is that these activities are coming from an authorized party at an agreed time. Even so, your default behavior should be to treat suspicious activity seriously, follow your organization's playbook for how to handle pen tests, and escalate through the proper channels. In some organizations, the security team will inform the help desk of test windows and provide instructions such as, "Continue logging tickets as normal, but route anything related to these IPs to the security team and do not block them unless told to."

One of the worst mistakes a well-intentioned technician can make during a pen test is to quietly "clean up" vulnerabilities or alter configurations in the middle of the test without coordination. This changes the environment mid-measurement and can invalidate results, making it harder for the organization to understand its true risk. It may also invalidate the contract with the testing firm if the agreed conditions are not maintained. Your professional stance should be: respond to issues through established processes, and if you think an immediate change is necessary for safety or stability, communicate that through the security team or test coordinator so they can adjust the test plan.

The exam may not ask you to perform exploitation techniques, but it does expect you to recognize scenarios describing penetration testing. When you read that an organization "hired a third party to attempt to gain unauthorized access to its systems and report on weaknesses," that is a pen test, not simply a vulnerability scan or an audit.

Other Testing Activities You Will See

Beyond vulnerability scanning and pen testing, you will encounter several other testing activities that aim to evaluate different aspects of security. One common category is **social engineering tests**, often in the form of phishing simulations. Here, the security team or an external provider sends crafted emails to employees to see who clicks suspicious links, enters credentials into fake login pages, or reports the message as suspicious. From a help desk perspective, this might show up as users calling in asking whether a strange message is legitimate. The correct reaction is to follow your usual verification and reporting process, not to dismiss concerns with, "It's probably just a test." The whole point is to reinforce good behavior, and your responses are part of that ecosystem.

Another routine activity is **password auditing** and **user access review**. A password audit might involve checking password hashes against lists of known weak or breached passwords, or confirming that accounts comply with complexity and change policies. Access reviews involve managers or system owners confirming that users still need the permissions they have. As a technician, you may be asked to disable stale accounts, remove group memberships that are no longer appropriate, or enforce password changes based on audit results. These are not random cleanups; they are reactions to testing that revealed security exposures like shared accounts or over-privileged users.

Configuration and patch **compliance checks** fit into this family as well. Many organizations maintain secure baselines for different device types: workstations should have certain services disabled, servers must have specific audit settings enabled, and so forth. Automated tools will regularly compare actual configurations and patch levels against these baselines. Noncompliant systems generate findings that land on your task list: update this software, enable that control, or document the exception if a system cannot meet the baseline for a valid reason. Understanding that these requests flow from ongoing testing helps you prioritize them appropriately rather than seeing them as arbitrary demands.

Attestation: Saying "Yes" with Accountability

Throughout audits and assessments, another concept appears that has special significance for you as a professional: **attestation**. To attest to something means to make a formal statement that it is true, often in writing, with your name or role attached. In a security context, attestation usually means asserting that a system, process, or set of devices complies with a policy or requirement.

Imagine you receive a form from the compliance team asking you to attest that "all laptops in the sales department have full-disk encryption enabled according to policy." Signing that form is not the same as casually telling a colleague, "Yeah, they should all be encrypted." It is a statement the organization might rely on in audits, in regulatory submissions, or even in legal proceedings if there is a breach. Your ethical obligation is to base that attestation on evidence, not on memory or assumptions. In practice, that means running a current report from your endpoint management tool, verifying the encryption status of each device, addressing any gaps you find, and only then signing. If you cannot verify all devices—for example, some are offline or unmanaged—you document that fact and involve your manager instead of putting your name on a blanket statement.

Attestations are not just for technicians. Managers attest that access reviews were completed, that training was delivered, or that specific processes were followed. Auditors often treat these attestations as pieces of evidence and may test a sample of items to see whether the attestation holds up. If they find discrepancies—say, you attested that all systems had a certain patch but find several that do not—it not only undermines the audit but also calls into question the reliability of future attestations. For your career, maintaining a reputation for accurate, honest attestation is far more valuable than making a problem temporarily disappear on paper.

Responding to Findings and Respecting the Chain of Command

All of these activities—audits, assessments, penetration tests, phishing simulations, compliance checks—produce **findings**. A finding might be as simple as "ten systems are missing a critical patch" or as complex as "an attacker could pivot from a compromised user workstation to a database server and exfiltrate customer data." Your day-to-day involvement is often dealing with the more concrete items on that list. When a report lands in your inbox, your first step is to understand which systems or responsibilities it touches. If a vulnerability report lists servers managed by a different team, you route it appropriately rather than trying to "fix" them yourself.

Once you determine the items that are within your scope, you balance urgency with process. A critical vulnerability on public-facing systems may require rapid response, but even then, you generally follow change-management procedures: create or update a ticket, schedule maintenance if required, document the change, and verify the result. For lower-severity issues, you may batch the remediation work into normal maintenance cycles. The exam often tests this judgment indirectly by presenting a scenario and asking what you should do next. Answers that ignore process entirely in favor of immediate action, or that ignore significant issues because "no one complained," are usually not the best choices.

Finally, all of this operates within a **chain of command**. If an auditor or penetration tester asks you for access, changes, or information that seems outside your authority, you do not improvise. You check your organization's policy, consult your supervisor or the security team, and make sure you are acting within your role. You also protect sensitive information from being shared more widely than necessary. Audit and test reports often contain details that would be valuable to attackers; they are not casual reading material to be forwarded around for curiosity.

When you look at audits, assessments, and testing through this lens, they are less about catching people out and more about keeping the organization honest, secure, and continuously improving. Your understanding of what is happening, and your disciplined, ethical behavior when these activities occur, are foundational parts of being trusted in any security-conscious environment.

Knowledge Check

Question 1: A security team is reviewing actual password settings and log retention periods on servers and comparing them directly to the written security policy. Which type of activity is this primarily describing?

- **A.** Audit
- **B.** Penetration test
- **C.** Business impact analysis
- **D.** Backup and restore test

Question 2: A company hires an external firm to attempt to exploit vulnerabilities in its environment and demonstrate what data an attacker could access, using a defined scope and rules of engagement. Which activity is being performed?

- **A.** Internal audit
- **B.** Vulnerability assessment
- **C.** Configuration compliance check
- **D.** Penetration test

Question 3: A vulnerability scanner report lists several servers with missing critical patches, rated as "high" severity, along with references to CVE identifiers. What is the technician's most appropriate next step for the systems they manage?

- **A.** Immediately remove the systems from the network without change control
- **B.** Patch according to change management procedures
- **C.** Ignore the findings until users report issues
- **D.** Disable logging on the affected systems to reduce alerts

Question 4: Which statement best differentiates a security audit from a security assessment?

- **A.** An audit checks whether controls match documented requirements, while an assessment focuses on the overall security posture and exposures
- **B.** An audit is always external, while an assessment is always internal
- **C.** An audit only examines technical controls, while an assessment only examines administrative controls
- **D.** An audit identifies new vulnerabilities, while an assessment only verifies existing ones

Question 5: A technician receives a form asking them to confirm that all laptops they manage have full-disk encryption enabled according to company policy. According to best practice, how should they respond?

- **A.** Sign the form immediately based on their recollection of past deployments
- **B.** Refuse to sign any documents related to security due to personal liability
- **C.** Verify current encryption status using management tools, remediate gaps, then attest based on evidence
- **D.** Ask a coworker to sign on their behalf so they are not personally responsible

Question 6: During an authorized vulnerability scan, the help desk notices a spike in port-scanning activity from a known scanner IP. What is the most appropriate behavior for the technician?

- **A.** Block the scanner IP at the firewall to prevent further scanning
- **B.** Follow the organization's and avoid interfering unless directed
- **C.** Reboot all systems being scanned to reduce performance impact
- **D.** Shut down the vulnerability scanner server to stop what appears to be an attack

Question 7: An internal control tool runs daily to compare server configurations and patch levels against a secure baseline, then emails a list of "noncompliant" systems to administrators. What is this activity best described as?

- **A.** Penetration testing
- **B.** Business continuity planning
- **C.** Continuous auditing or automated compliance checking
- **D.** Digital forensics and incident response

Question 8: A security team sends simulated phishing emails to employees to see who clicks the links and who reports the messages as suspicious. From a help desk technician's perspective, how should they handle calls from users about these emails?

- **A.** Tell users it is just a test and they can safely ignore future suspicious emails
- **B.** Follow normal verification and reporting procedures, treating the messages as potentially malicious
- **C.** Instruct users to click the links so the test data is more complete
- **D.** Delete the emails from users' mailboxes without documenting any actions

ANSWERS

1: Correct Answer: A
Rationale: An audit compares actual configurations and practices to documented policies and standards to verify compliance, which matches reviewing password and log settings against policy.

2: Correct Answer: D
Rationale: A penetration test is an authorized attempt to exploit vulnerabilities within a defined scope and rules of engagement to show what an attacker could access.

3: Correct Answer: B
Rationale: After identifying missing critical patches, the technician should use formal change-management to plan, approve, apply, and verify the patches, not act ad hoc or ignore the issues.

4: Correct Answer: A
Rationale: Audits focus on whether controls align with documented requirements, while assessments look more broadly at security posture and risk exposure, regardless of existing documentation.

5: Correct Answer: C
Rationale: Security attestations should be evidence-based. The technician should confirm encryption status with tools, fix noncompliance, and then sign based on verified data.

6: Correct Answer: B
Rationale: When scans are authorized, staff should follow established procedures and not interfere unless instructed, even if the traffic resembles hostile activity.

7: Correct Answer: C
Rationale: Automatically comparing systems to a baseline and flagging deviations on a recurring basis is continuous auditing or automated compliance checking, not testing, BCP, or forensics.

8: Correct Answer: B
Rationale: Phishing simulations are training tools; the help desk should reinforce correct behavior by treating them like real suspicious emails and following standard verification and reporting steps.

6.6 Security Awareness & Training

If you talk to experienced security professionals about where most breaches start, you'll hear the same thing over and over: someone clicked something. Not a zero-day exploit, not an elite nation-state attack, but an ordinary user under pressure, tired, or just trying to be helpful. That's why organizations sometimes call users the "weakest link," but a better way to think about it—and the way modern security programs are designed—is that every user can become an additional security control. Firewalls, antivirus, and access controls are still critical, but they are only part of the picture. Security awareness and training are what turn written policies into real, everyday behavior, and as an entry-level technician or junior administrator, you sit right in the middle of that translation.

From the help desk, you see people at the exact moment when security decisions are being made: when they open an email they're not sure about, when their browser suddenly pops up a strange warning, or when they find a USB drive in the parking lot. You are often the first person they ask, "Is this okay?" The way you answer, the questions you ask back, and the guidance you provide all either reinforce the organization's security culture or quietly undermine it. This chapter is about building the mindset and vocabulary to recognize risky behavior, explain it in plain language, and route potential incidents through the right channels.

Social Engineering and the Art of Manipulation

Most modern attacks on organizations don't begin with a technical exploit; they begin with **social engineering**, which is simply manipulating people into doing something that helps the attacker. Instead of trying to crack encryption, the attacker tries to crack trust. Social engineering succeeds when it can either bypass normal procedures ("Just this once, can you rush this payment?") or harvest information and credentials that make later attacks easier ("Can you confirm your username and password so I can reset your VPN?"). As a technician, you don't just need to know the definitions of these attacks for the exam—you need to be able to recognize how they show up in real-world tickets and conversations.

The most common form you'll see described on the exam is **phishing**: generic, malicious messages sent to many potential victims, usually by email. A typical phishing email might claim that your mailbox is full, your bank account is locked, or a shipping delivery failed. It almost always tries to push the user into action, fast, before they stop to think. That's why you see urgent language, deadlines, threats, or tempting offers. The sender's address often looks close but not quite right, and links might lead to fake login pages that capture credentials. These details become clues in exam scenarios, where you'll be asked to identify the type of attack and the safest next step.

When that same style of attack is customized to a specific person or small group, you're looking at **spear phishing**. Instead of "Dear Customer," the message might use the victim's name, reference their department, or mention a real ongoing project scraped from LinkedIn or social media. The goal is to lower suspicion by sounding familiar and relevant. If the target is an executive or someone with high-value access, such as a CFO or CEO, the exam may describe this as **whaling**. The content might focus on wire transfers, confidential strategy documents, or legal issues—things senior leaders legitimately deal with. In a typical scenario, a finance employee might receive a rushed request "from the CEO" to process a confidential payment. Your job is to see past the story, notice the slightly wrong email address or unusual channel, and recognize it as a whaling attempt, then choose the response that involves verifying and reporting, not just clicking or complying.

Email is not the only path. Attackers also use the phone and SMS because people often drop their guard there. **Vishing**—voice phishing—shows up as phone calls from "IT support," "the bank," "the IRS," or "technical support from your vendor," asking for one-time codes, passwords, or remote access. The caller may use a spoofed phone number to look legitimate. Similarly, **smishing** uses SMS or other messaging platforms to send malicious links or urgent instructions, such as package delivery texts asking for payment details or "security alerts" about your account. On the exam, when you see a scenario involving a user who received a text with a suspicious link, or a call claiming to be from the help desk asking for an MFA code, recognize that as social engineering and think in terms of stopping, verifying through a trusted channel, and reporting.

Underneath all these variations are some consistent red flags: messages or calls that are out of context, unusually urgent, request sensitive information, or ask users to bypass normal procedures. Security awareness training teaches users to pause when they see those signs. Your role is not to turn users into security experts but to help them notice those cues and feel comfortable asking, "Does this look right?" instead of acting automatically.

Turning Awareness into Everyday Behavior

Knowing that phishing and social engineering exist is only the starting point. Awareness becomes useful when it translates into specific user behaviors, especially around email and web use. When a user forwards you a suspicious email and asks what to do, you are not being asked to run deep forensics; you are being asked to model safe behavior. The safest response is almost always to avoid interacting with the message at all: don't open attachments, don't click links, don't reply to "unsubscribe." Instead, you direct the user to follow your organization's reporting procedures—maybe that's a phishing-report button, a security mailbox, or opening a ticket and attaching the email as evidence.

At the same time, that interaction is a teaching opportunity. Instead of simply saying, "Yes, it's phishing," you can briefly highlight what made it suspicious in user-friendly language: the mismatched sender domain, the urgent tone, the unexpected attachment. That kind of quick explanation helps the user feel smarter rather than scolded, and it reinforces the idea that they did the right thing by asking first. Many exam questions will implicitly test this communication style by asking which technician response is most appropriate. Answers that combine correct technical advice with clear, respectful education tend to be the best choice.

Safe browsing habits are another core theme. Awareness training typically warns users away from downloading software from unknown sites, clicking on "free" toolbars or pirated content, or entering credentials into login pages that don't look like the company's normal single sign-on screen. When you clean up a malware infection caused by a user installing a "free video converter" they found via search, the technical fix might be straightforward. The exam, however, expects you to also recognize that part of your job is to explain what happened and suggest safer alternatives, such as using approved software from the internal app catalog. Your explanation should be simple: where they clicked, why that was risky, and how to avoid similar traps.

Removable media is another area where awareness matters more than technology. Many organizations run antivirus on USB drives, but that doesn't make unknown devices safe to plug in. Attackers have been known to seed parking lots or common areas with USB drives labeled in ways that tempt curiosity, hoping someone plugs one into a corporate machine. If an employee brings a found USB to the help desk and asks you to "plug it in and see whose it is," that's exactly the moment where awareness training collides with real behavior. The correct, exam-aligned action is to refuse to connect it to any workstation, treat it as potentially malicious, and follow your organization's process for handling lost hardware or suspicious media. Again, this is a chance to explain why: malware can auto-run, and simply "checking what's on it" could compromise systems.

Authentication, Passwords, and Everyday Access

Security awareness training also spends a lot of energy on **password hygiene** and authentication because attackers know that stolen or reused credentials are often the easiest way in. Users are expected to create strong, unique passwords, not share them—even with people claiming to be IT—and avoid writing them on sticky notes under keyboards or on monitors. Modern organizations increasingly pair passwords with multifactor authentication (MFA), which adds its own training needs. Users must learn what legitimate MFA prompts look like and, equally important, when to deny them.

A subtle but common attack involves bombarding a user with MFA push notifications, hoping that in frustration or distraction they will approve one they didn't initiate. When a user calls the help desk complaining about constant MFA prompts, your job is to recognize that this is not just an annoyance but potentially an indicator that someone has their password and is trying to log in. The right response is to treat it as a security event: advise the user not to approve any unexpected requests, assist with changing their password, and escalate according to incident response procedures. In explaining it, you reinforce the message that MFA prompts should only be approved when the user themselves has just tried to log in.

Technicians also help users adopt safer behaviors by supporting tools like password managers. While design and policy decisions about these tools are made elsewhere, you are often the one sitting with the user, helping them set it up and answering questions. That is another moment for subtle awareness training: clarifying that the password manager is the right place to store passwords, that they still should not share those, and that anyone—caller, email sender, or even someone physically nearby—asking for their master password is a red flag.

Physical Security and the Human Perimeter

Security awareness is not just about screens and keyboards. Physical behavior in the workplace can be as critical as any firewall rule, especially in environments with restricted areas or sensitive information visible on desks. Concepts like **tailgating** and **piggybacking** come up frequently in training and on the exam. Tailgating usually means slipping in behind someone through a secure door without authenticating; piggybacking often describes the authorized person actively holding the door for someone not properly badged. Both feel like normal politeness in everyday life, which makes them effective attack techniques.

Awareness training tries to reframe that politeness. Users are encouraged not to hold doors for people they don't recognize in secure areas, to ensure every person badging in uses their own credentials, and to report unfamiliar individuals without visible badges. As IT staff, you model this yourself: you badge in even if someone is ahead of you, you don't complain about having to escort visitors, and you spread the message that "it's okay to be politely suspicious" in sensitive areas. Exam scenarios may describe a user letting someone in "because they were carrying a lot of boxes" and ask you to identify the problem; recognizing that as a physical social engineering issue is the first step to choosing the right response.

A related concept is the **clean desk** approach. Users handling confidential information are expected to lock their screens when stepping away, secure printed documents when not in use, and avoid leaving whiteboards or open files visible to unauthorized visitors. If you walk by a workstation and see an unlocked session with sensitive data on screen, even though that's not a "ticketed" issue, it is a moment to gently remind the user of policy and potentially open a documentation entry if your organization tracks recurring violations. You are both a technical resource and a visible example of how seriously (or not) the company takes its own rules.

Reporting, Escalation, and Culture

All of this awareness would be useless without clear reporting and escalation paths. Users need to know what to report, how to report it, and how quickly. In practice, that includes suspicious emails, strange system behavior, unexpected pop-ups, lost or stolen devices, misdirected emails containing sensitive information, and observed policy violations such as someone accessing data they shouldn't. For you, the key exam skill is recognizing that "what should you do next?" often means "follow incident reporting procedures," not "quietly fix the symptom and move on."

When a user reports that they clicked on a link in a suspicious email and entered their password, you might feel an urge to immediately reset the password, run malware scans, and tell them to delete the email. Those steps may eventually be required, but the first move—according to good practice and what the exam expects—is to preserve evidence and escalate. That usually means capturing details about the email, collecting logs if appropriate, and notifying the security or incident response team, all while reassuring the user that reporting quickly was the right thing to do. Deleting the email without documentation destroys potentially important evidence about the attack, which is a common exam trap.

Your tone during these moments matters as much as your technical accuracy. Blaming language—"You shouldn't have done that"—discourages users from reporting the next time. Awareness programs increasingly emphasize creating a supportive culture where users feel safe admitting mistakes. As the person they most often talk to, you embody that culture. When you thank a user for checking before acting, or for promptly reporting that they may have made an error, you strengthen the organization's defenses more than any single malware scan.

Finally, it is important to connect all these day-to-day actions back to the policies you saw earlier in this chapter: acceptable use, password policy, data classification, incident response. Awareness and training are how those documents become real. When an exam scenario describes a user installing unapproved software from the internet or syncing work files to a personal cloud account, the best technician response will typically involve more than just removing the software or disabling the sync. It will also reference policy, explain why the behavior is risky, and document or escalate if required. That combination—technical fix, policy reinforcement, and proper reporting—is exactly the pattern you want to internalize, because it's the pattern both the exam and real organizations rely on to keep human behavior aligned with security goals.

Knowledge Check

Question 1: A finance employee receives an email claiming to be from their bank stating, "Your account will be closed in 24 hours unless you verify your identity," with a link to a login page. The message is generic and sent to many recipients. Which type of attack is this most likely describing?

- **A.** Whaling
- **B.** Phishing
- **C.** Vishing
- **D.** Smishing

Question 2: A help desk technician receives a call from a user who reports getting multiple SMS messages claiming to be from a shipping company, each with a link to "pay outstanding customs fees." The user is unsure if they should click the link. What is the BEST guidance the technician should provide first?

- **A.** Click the link only if it comes from a known phone number.
- **B.** Reply STOP to unsubscribe and then delete the messages.
- **C.** Forward the messages to coworkers to see if they also received them.
- **D.** Do not click the link, delete the messages, and report them per the organization's procedures.

Question 3: A user reports that someone called them claiming to be from the IT help desk, asking for their MFA code to "complete a system upgrade." The caller ID showed the company's main number. Which type of attack does this MOST likely represent?

- **A.** Smishing
- **B.** Spear phishing
- **C.** Vishing
- **D.** Tailgating

Question 4: An employee receives an email that appears to be from the CEO asking them to urgently process a confidential wire transfer. The sender address is slightly misspelled and the request bypasses the normal approval process. What is the MOST appropriate action for the employee to take?

A. Complete the transfer quickly to avoid delays, then notify IT.
B. Verify the request using a known, trusted channel and report the email as suspicious.
C. Reply to the email asking for more details about the transfer.
D. Mark the email as read and ignore it to avoid making a mistake.

Question 5: A user finds a USB drive labeled "Quarterly Bonuses" in the company parking lot and brings it to the help desk, asking the technician to plug it into a workstation to see who it belongs to. What is the BEST response from the technician?

A. Avoid plugging in; follow the organization's process for suspicious media.
B. Plug it into an isolated workstation, browse the files, and identify the owner.
C. Allow the user to take it and plug it into their own workstation at their own risk.
D. Format the drive immediately and return it to the user for personal use.

Question 6: A user reports that they are receiving repeated MFA push notifications on their phone even though they are not trying to log in. What should the help desk technician do FIRST?

A. Instruct the user not to approve any prompts, assist them in changing their password, and escalate as a potential security incident.
B. Disable MFA for the user's account so the prompts stop.
C. Tell the user to approve one prompt so the notifications will clear.
D. Advise the user to power off their phone and ignore the issue.

Question 7: While walking through a restricted area, an IT technician notices an unlocked workstation displaying sensitive customer information, but no user is present. Which action BEST aligns with security awareness training principles?

A. Ignore it because it is not related to an open support ticket.
B. Take a photo of the screen as evidence and post it in an internal chat as a warning.
C. Lock the workstation and remind the user about the clean desk/screen lock policy.
D. Power off the workstation immediately to protect the data.

Question 8: A user contacts the help desk and admits they clicked a link in a suspicious email and entered their credentials on a website. What should the technician do NEXT according to best practices?

A. Tell the user to delete the email and not worry since they already reported it.
B. Ask the user to run a local antivirus scan and then close the ticket if nothing is found.
C. Immediately reset the user's password and delete the email from their mailbox without documentation.
D. Preserve the email as evidence, collect relevant details, escalate to the security team, and then assist with remediation.

ANSWERS

1: Correct Answer: B
Rationale: The email is generic, urgent, and sent broadly, which matches phishing. Whaling targets executives, vishing uses voice calls, and smishing uses SMS messages.

2: Correct Answer: D
Rationale: Suspicious SMS messages with links are smishing; users should not interact with them and should delete and report them per policy, not click, reply, or forward them.

3: Correct Answer: C
Rationale: A fraudulent phone call requesting MFA codes is vishing (voice phishing). Smishing uses texts, spear phishing uses targeted emails, and tailgating involves physical entry.

4: Correct Answer: B
Rationale: This is a CEO fraud/whaling-style email. The user should verify via a trusted channel and report it, not comply, reply to the suspicious email, or ignore a potential incident.

5: Correct Answer: A
Rationale: Unknown removable media may contain malware. It should not be connected to any system and must be handled according to the organization's suspicious media procedures.

6: Correct Answer: A
Rationale: Repeated unsolicited MFA prompts suggest an attacker has the password. The technician should prevent approvals, help change the password, and escalate as a security incident.

7: Correct Answer: C
Rationale: Locking the workstation protects data and later reminding the user reinforces screen lock and clean desk policies without exposing or mishandling sensitive information.

8: Correct Answer: D
Rationale: Entering credentials on a phishing site is a security incident. The technician should preserve evidence, gather details, escalate through incident response, then assist with actions like password resets.

ACCESS YOUR EXTRA STUDY MATERIALS

We hope this guide has helped you build a solid understanding of the CompTIA Security+ (SY0-701) exam objectives and feel more confident in your exam preparation. While this book provides a strong foundation, effective exam preparation is often reinforced through active practice and structured review. To support your continued progress, additional study tools are available to complement the material covered in this guide.

Here's what's waiting for you:

- **CompTIA Security+ Exam Simulator (SY0-701)**
  Generate unlimited custom practice exams with a realistic test simulator that mirrors actual exam conditions and helps you build confidence, speed, and accuracy before test day.
- **600+ Digital Flashcards**
  Reinforce your understanding of key cybersecurity concepts, acronyms, and security principles with dynamic flashcards that make even short study sessions productive and efficient.
- **Question Bank Download Center**
  Access over 3,600 downloadable, exam-style questions spanning all CompTIA Security+ domains. Test your knowledge on paper and strengthen your exam readiness.
- **The SYSTEM-14 Course**
  Master critical exam content in just 14 days with guided flashcard strategies and effective memory techniques.
- **Mindshift Video Program**
  Get insider tips on test-taking strategies, managing exam stress, and staying sharp under pressure—so you walk into the testing center with confidence and a clear plan.

These study tools are available for ongoing use.

To access them, visit the link below and enter the access code when prompted.

tinyurl.com/he-securityplus

Your secret code is: **security8787**